story DAVID HINE

chapter 1 art ERNESTO CHAPARRO

chapter 2-6 art TOMAS AIRA

chapter 2-6 inks EMILIANO URDINOLA

letters JAYMES REED

color DIGIKORE STUDIOS

cover JACEN BURROWS

chapter breaks & cover gallery
art MATT MARTIN, RAULO CACERES,
MATT BUSH, JACEN BURROWS,
GERMAN ERRAMOUSPE

avatar press

editor in chief WILLIAM CHRISTENSEN

creative director MARK SEIFERT

managing editor JIM KUHORIC

director of events DAVID MARKS

production assistant ARIANA OSBORNE

NIGHT OF THE LIVING DEAD AFTERMATH VOLUME 2. March 2014. Published by Avatar Press, Inc., 515 N.
Century Blvd. Rantoul, IL 61866. ©2014 Avatar Press, Inc. Night of the Living Dead and all related
properties TM & ©2013 Image Ten. All characters as depicted in this story are over the age of 18. The
stories, characters, and institutions mentioned in this magazine are entirely fictional. Printed in Canada.

HUNGRY FOR THE FLESH OF THE LIVING

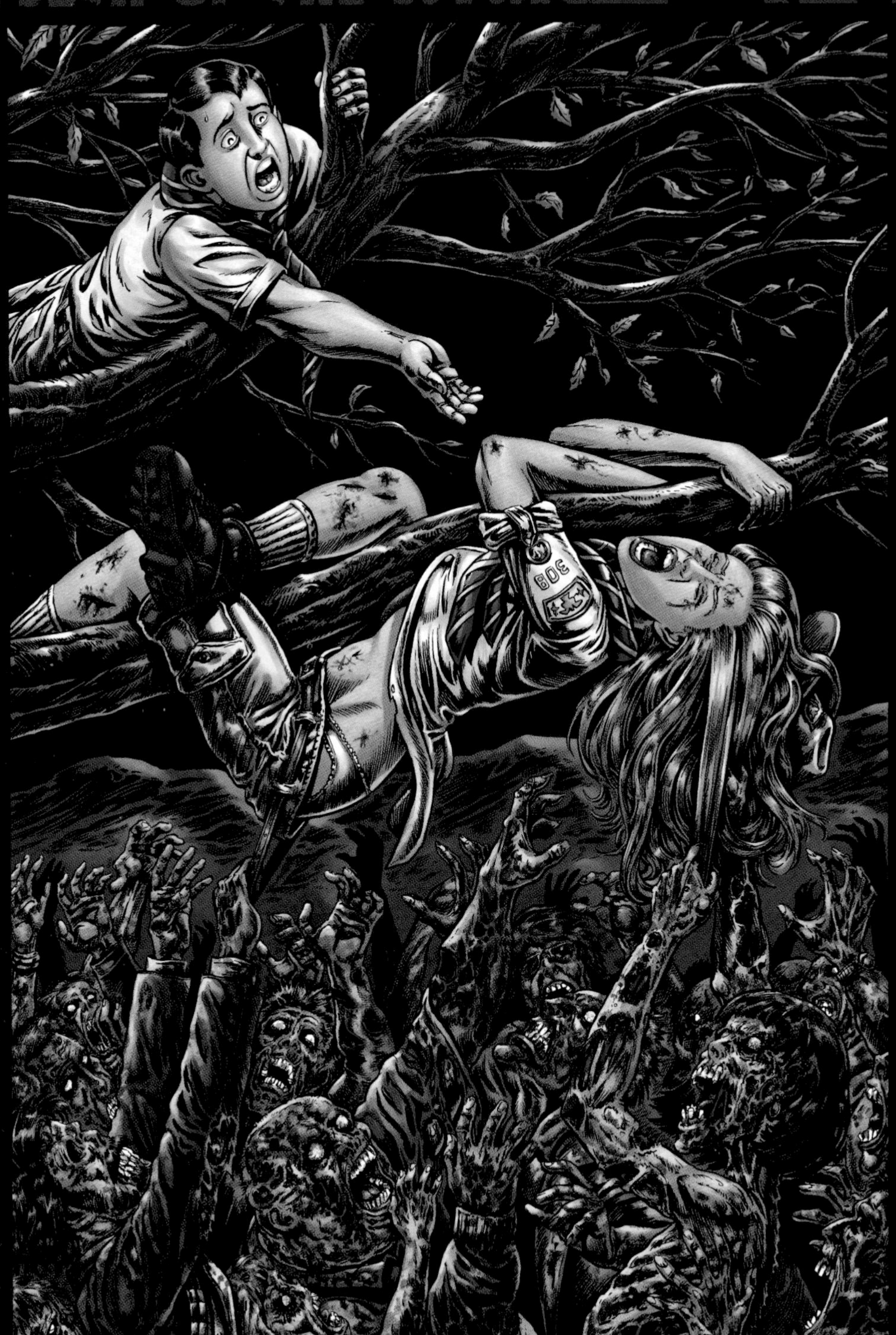

CHAPTER 1

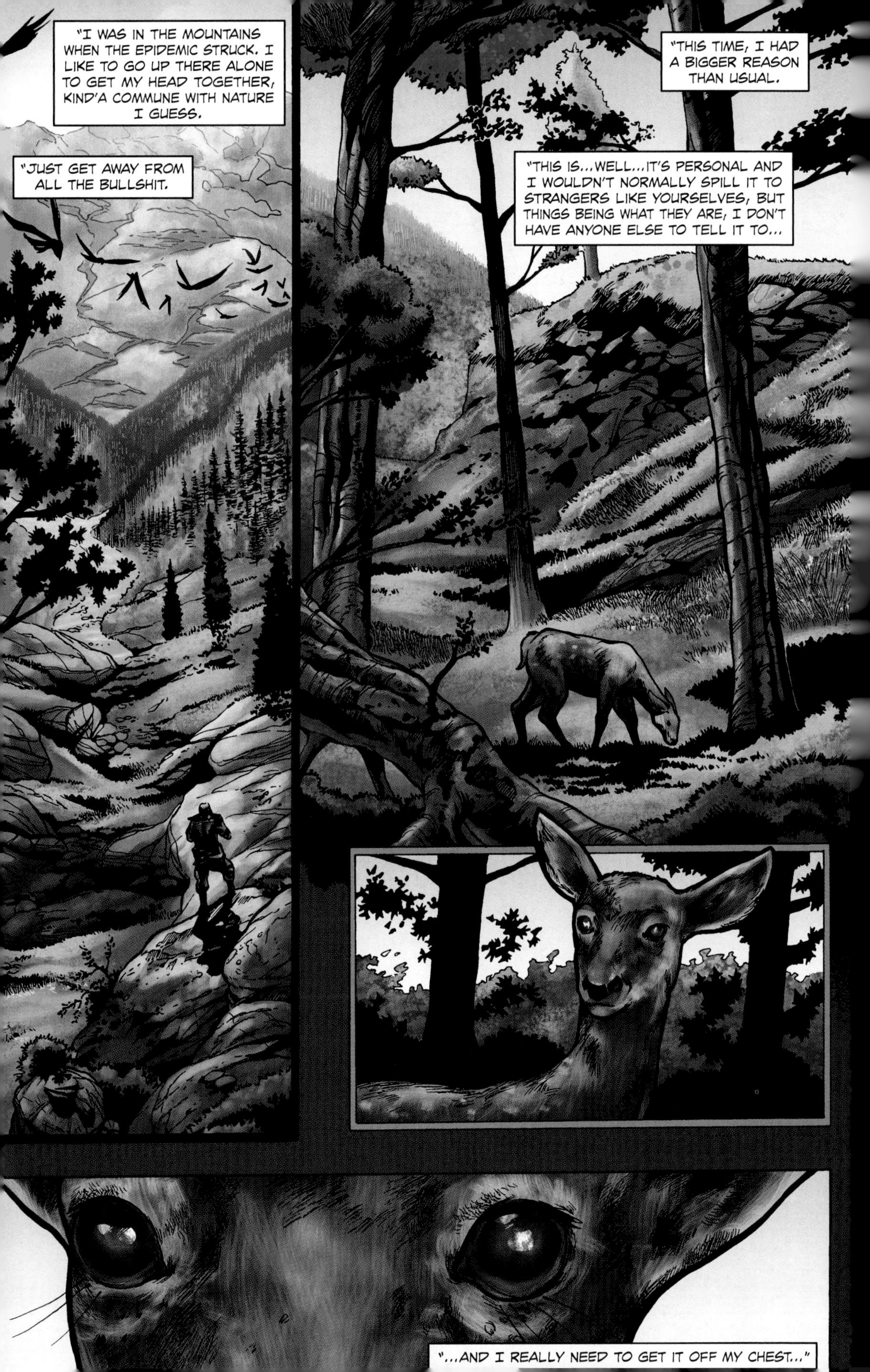
"I WAS IN THE MOUNTAINS WHEN THE EPIDEMIC STRUCK. I LIKE TO GO UP THERE ALONE TO GET MY HEAD TOGETHER, KIND'A COMMUNE WITH NATURE I GUESS.
"JUST GET AWAY FROM ALL THE BULLSHIT.
"THIS TIME, I HAD A BIGGER REASON THAN USUAL.
"THIS IS...WELL...IT'S PERSONAL AND I WOULDN'T NORMALLY SPILL IT TO STRANGERS LIKE YOURSELVES, BUT THINGS BEING WHAT THEY ARE, I DON'T HAVE ANYONE ELSE TO TELL IT TO...
"...AND I REALLY NEED TO GET IT OFF MY CHEST..."

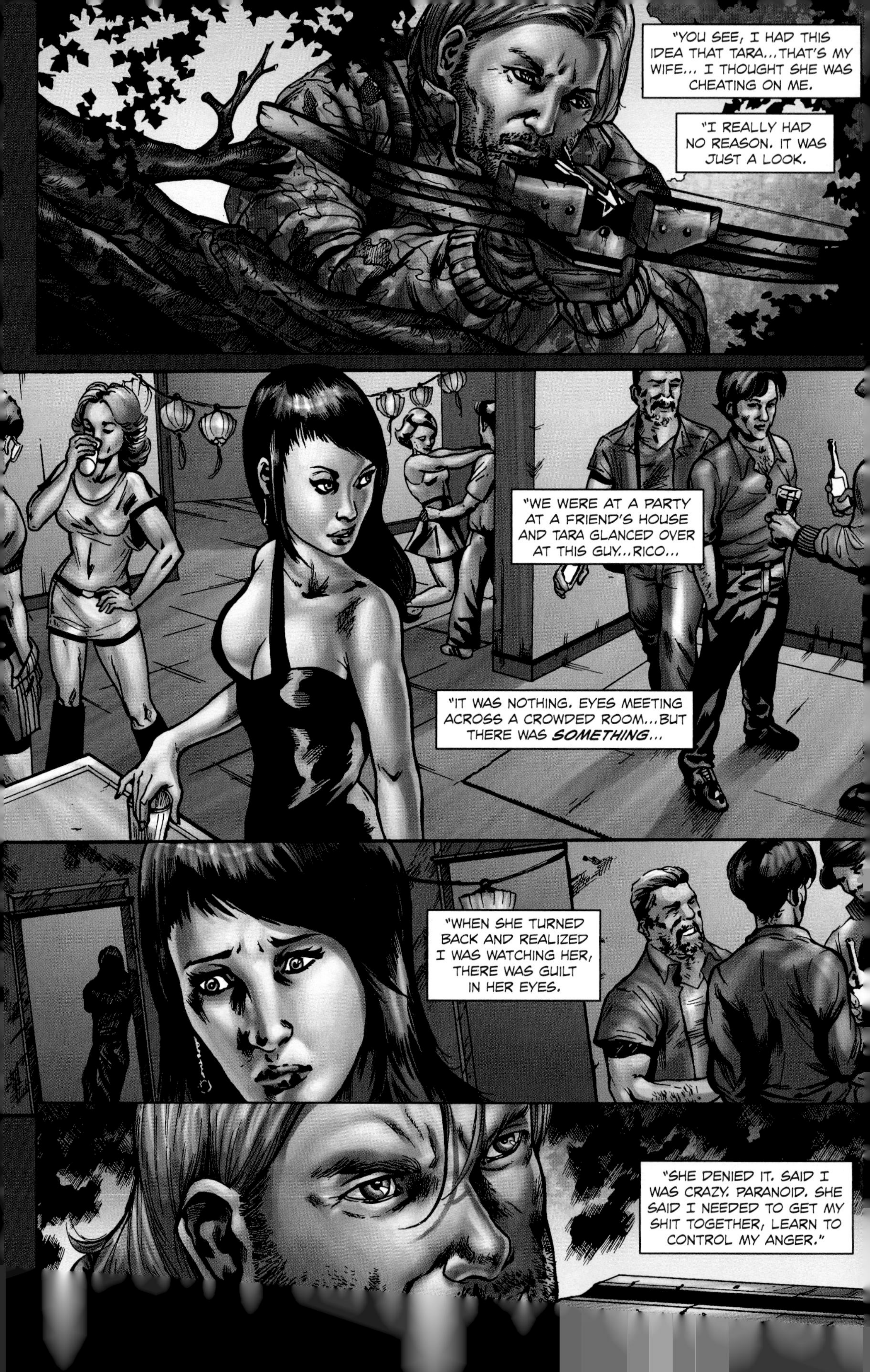
"YOU SEE, I HAD THIS IDEA THAT TARA...THAT'S MY WIFE... I THOUGHT SHE WAS CHEATING ON ME.
"I REALLY HAD NO REASON. IT WAS JUST A LOOK.
"WE WERE AT A PARTY AT A FRIEND'S HOUSE AND TARA GLANCED OVER AT THIS GUY...RICO...
"IT WAS NOTHING. EYES MEETING ACROSS A CROWDED ROOM...BUT THERE WAS ***SOMETHING***...
"WHEN SHE TURNED BACK AND REALIZED I WAS WATCHING HER, THERE WAS GUILT IN HER EYES.
"SHE DENIED IT. SAID I WAS CRAZY. PARANOID. SHE SAID I NEEDED TO GET MY SHIT TOGETHER, LEARN TO CONTROL MY ANGER."

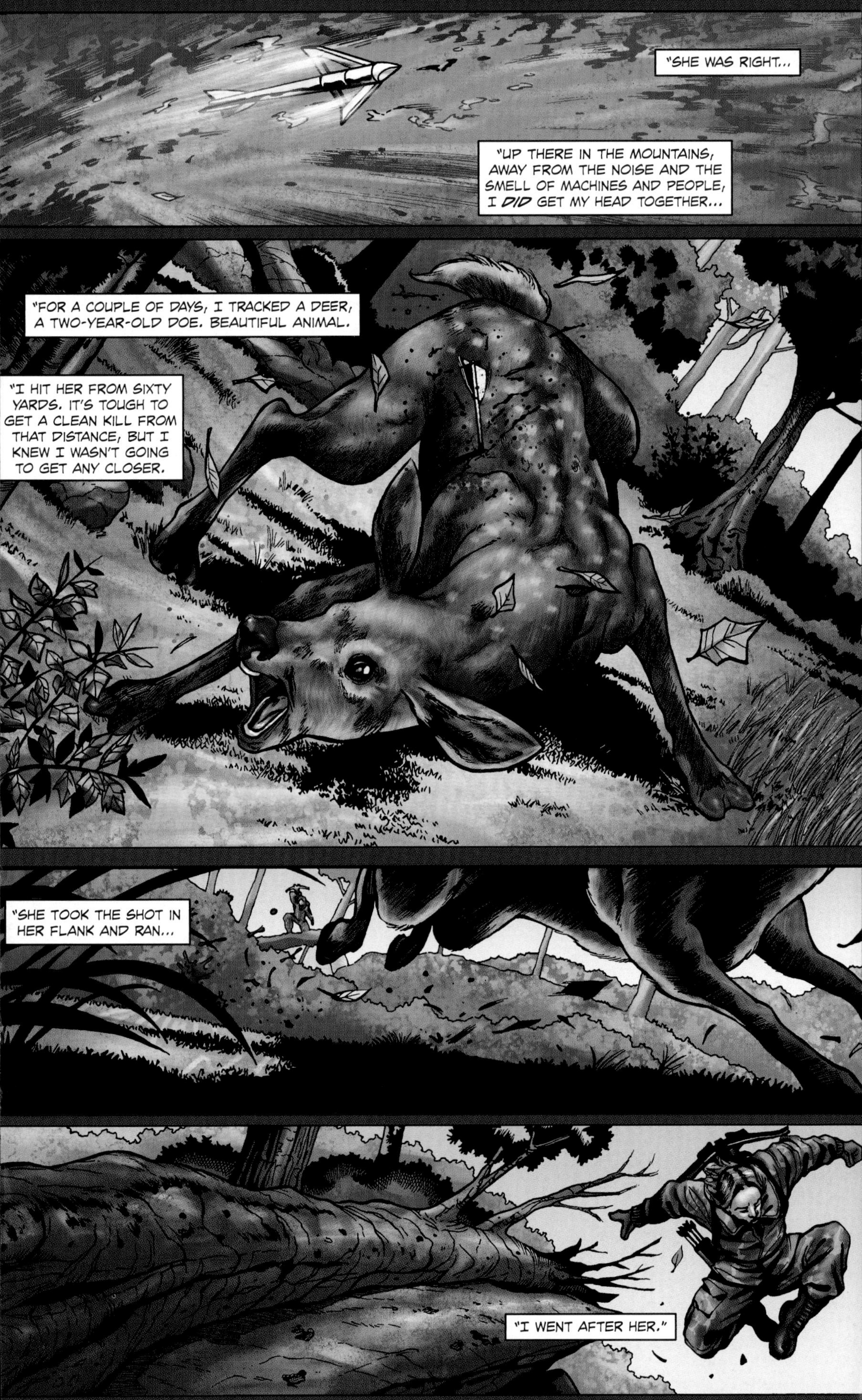

"SHE WAS RIGHT...
"UP THERE IN THE MOUNTAINS, AWAY FROM THE NOISE AND THE SMELL OF MACHINES AND PEOPLE, I *DID* GET MY HEAD TOGETHER...
"FOR A COUPLE OF DAYS, I TRACKED A DEER, A TWO-YEAR-OLD DOE. BEAUTIFUL ANIMAL.
"I HIT HER FROM SIXTY YARDS. IT'S TOUGH TO GET A CLEAN KILL FROM THAT DISTANCE, BUT I KNEW I WASN'T GOING TO GET ANY CLOSER.
"SHE TOOK THE SHOT IN HER FLANK AND RAN...
"I WENT AFTER HER."

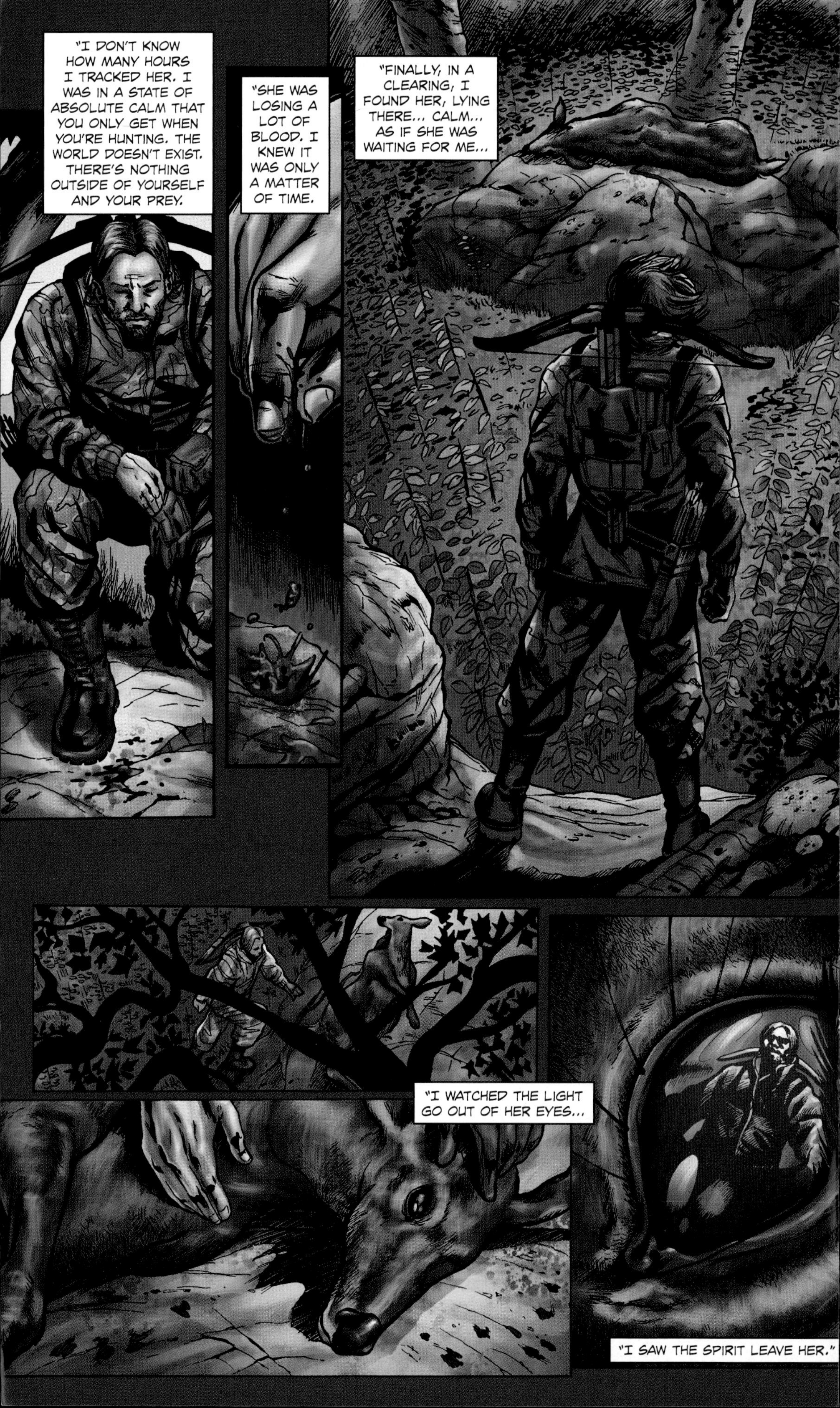
"I DON'T KNOW HOW MANY HOURS I TRACKED HER. I WAS IN A STATE OF ABSOLUTE CALM THAT YOU ONLY GET WHEN YOU'RE HUNTING. THE WORLD DOESN'T EXIST. THERE'S NOTHING OUTSIDE OF YOURSELF AND YOUR PREY.
"SHE WAS LOSING A LOT OF BLOOD. I KNEW IT WAS ONLY A MATTER OF TIME.
"FINALLY, IN A CLEARING, I FOUND HER, LYING THERE... CALM... AS IF SHE WAS WAITING FOR ME...
"I WATCHED THE LIGHT GO OUT OF HER EYES...
"I SAW THE SPIRIT LEAVE HER."

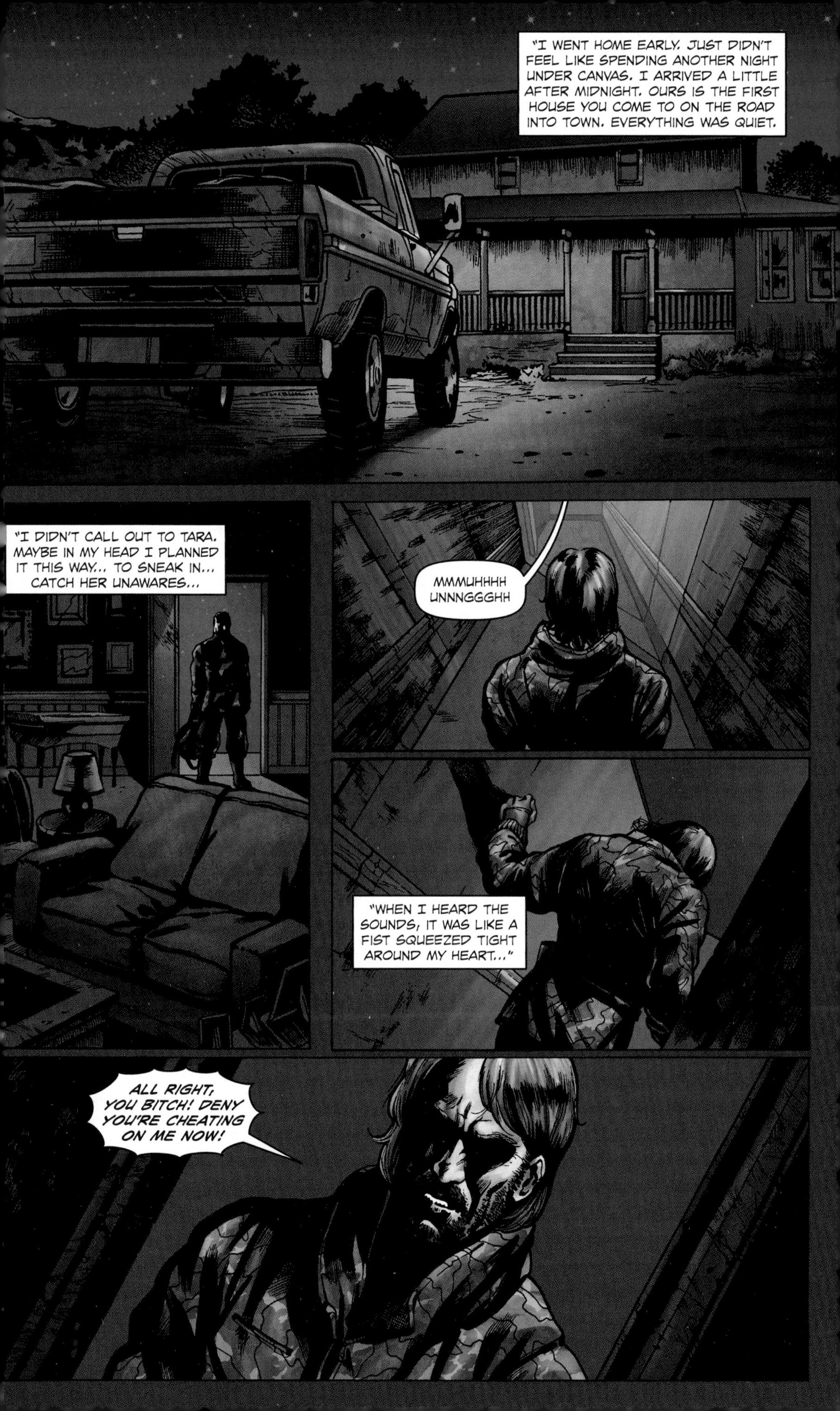
"I WENT HOME EARLY. JUST DIDN'T FEEL LIKE SPENDING ANOTHER NIGHT UNDER CANVAS. I ARRIVED A LITTLE AFTER MIDNIGHT. OURS IS THE FIRST HOUSE YOU COME TO ON THE ROAD INTO TOWN. EVERYTHING WAS QUIET.
"I DIDN'T CALL OUT TO TARA. MAYBE IN MY HEAD I PLANNED IT THIS WAY... TO SNEAK IN... CATCH HER UNAWARES...
MMMUHHHH UNNNGGGHH
"WHEN I HEARD THE SOUNDS, IT WAS LIKE A FIST SQUEEZED TIGHT AROUND MY HEART..."
ALL RIGHT, YOU BITCH! DENY YOU'RE CHEATING ON ME NOW!

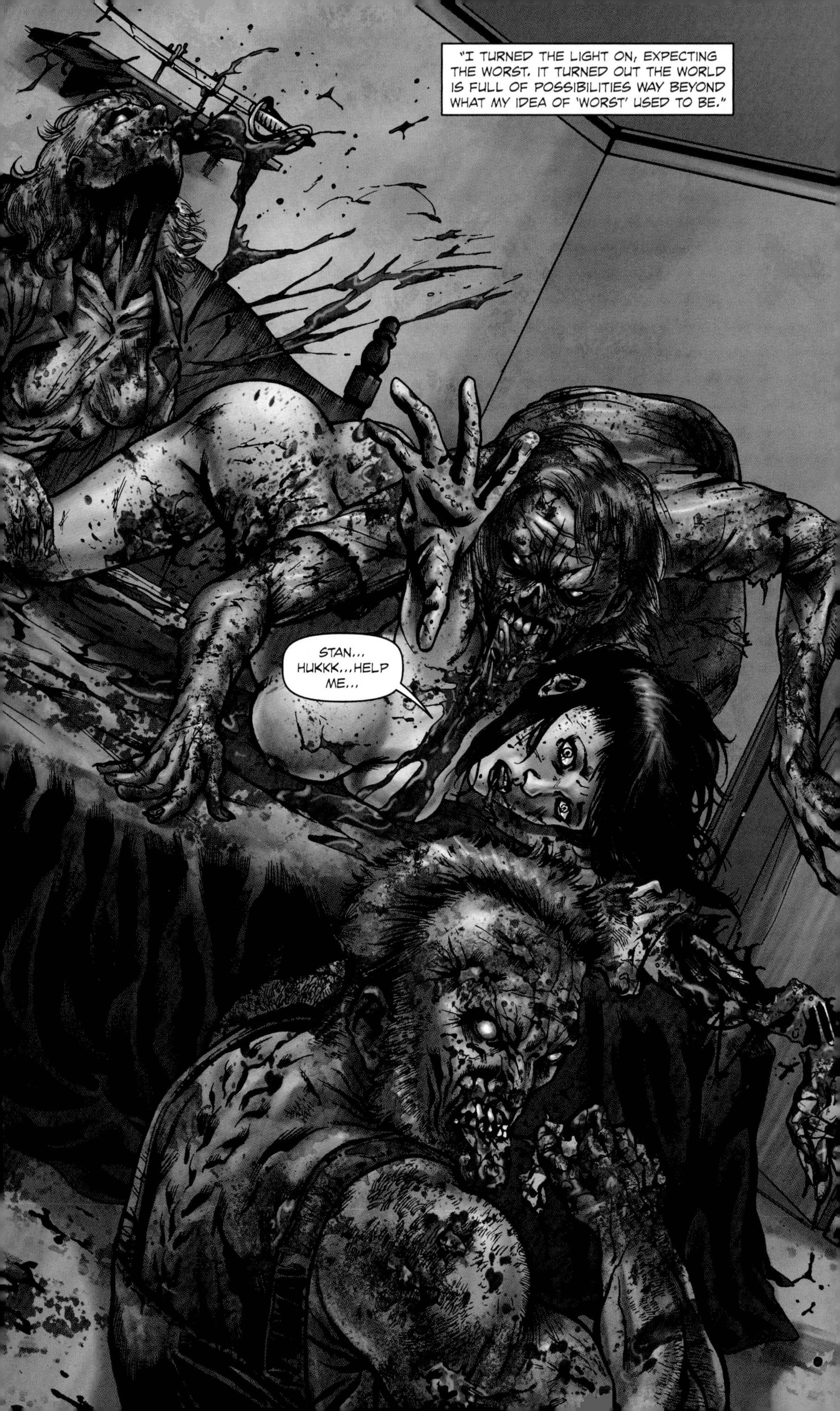
"I TURNED THE LIGHT ON, EXPECTING THE WORST. IT TURNED OUT THE WORLD IS FULL OF POSSIBILITIES WAY BEYOND WHAT MY IDEA OF 'WORST' USED TO BE."
STAN... HUKKK...HELP ME...

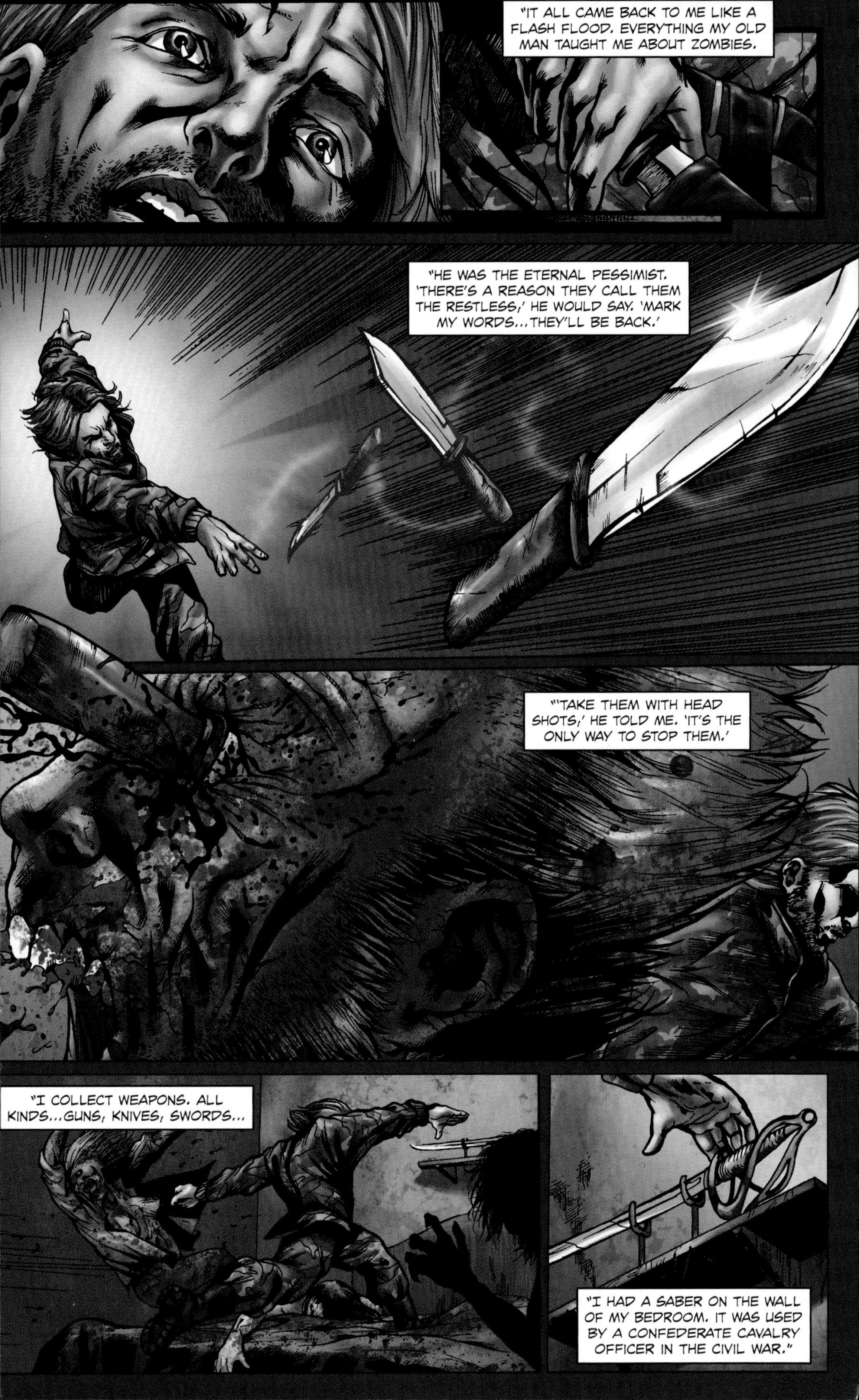
"IT ALL CAME BACK TO ME LIKE A FLASH FLOOD. EVERYTHING MY OLD MAN TAUGHT ME ABOUT ZOMBIES.
"HE WAS THE ETERNAL PESSIMIST. 'THERE'S A REASON THEY CALL THEM THE RESTLESS,' HE WOULD SAY. 'MARK MY WORDS...THEY'LL BE BACK.'
"'TAKE THEM WITH HEAD SHOTS,' HE TOLD ME. 'IT'S THE ONLY WAY TO STOP THEM.'
"I COLLECT WEAPONS. ALL KINDS...GUNS, KNIVES, SWORDS...
"I HAD A SABER ON THE WALL OF MY BEDROOM. IT WAS USED BY A CONFEDERATE CAVALRY OFFICER IN THE CIVIL WAR."

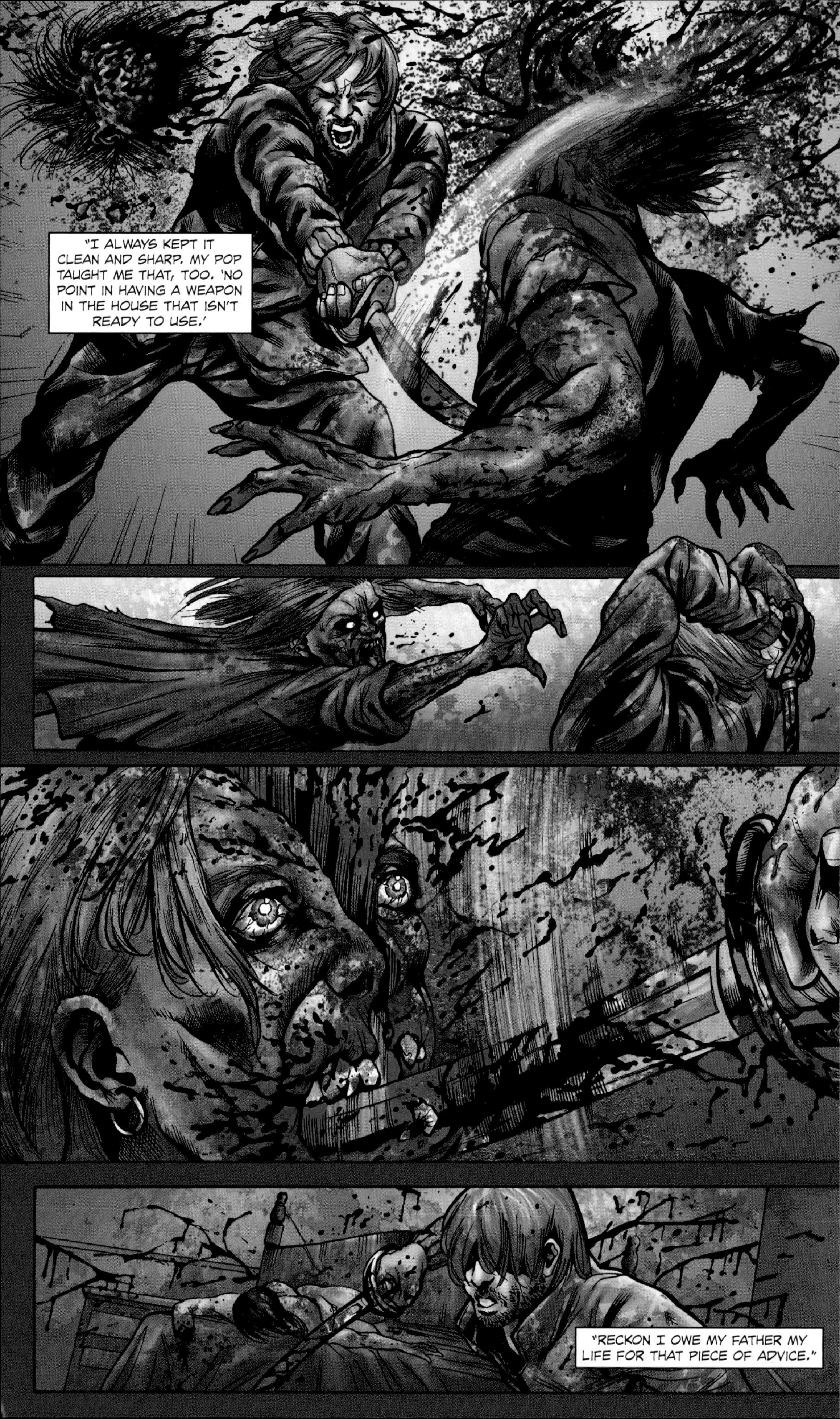
"I ALWAYS KEPT IT CLEAN AND SHARP. MY POP TAUGHT ME THAT, TOO. 'NO POINT IN HAVING A WEAPON IN THE HOUSE THAT ISN'T READY TO USE.'
"RECKON I OWE MY FATHER MY LIFE FOR THAT PIECE OF ADVICE."

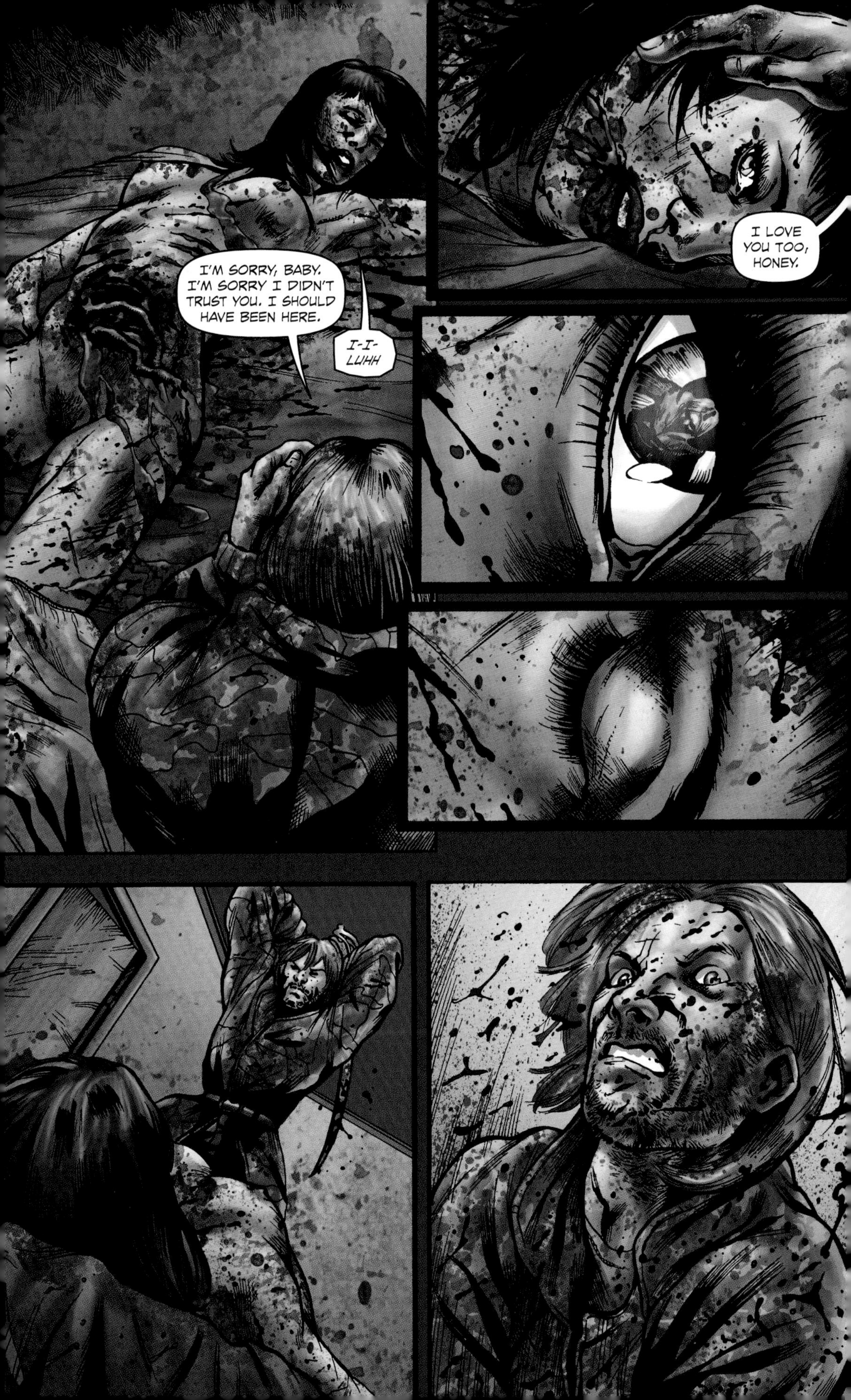
I'M SORRY, BABY. I'M SORRY I DIDN'T TRUST YOU. I SHOULD HAVE BEEN HERE.
I-I-LUHH
I LOVE YOU TOO, HONEY.

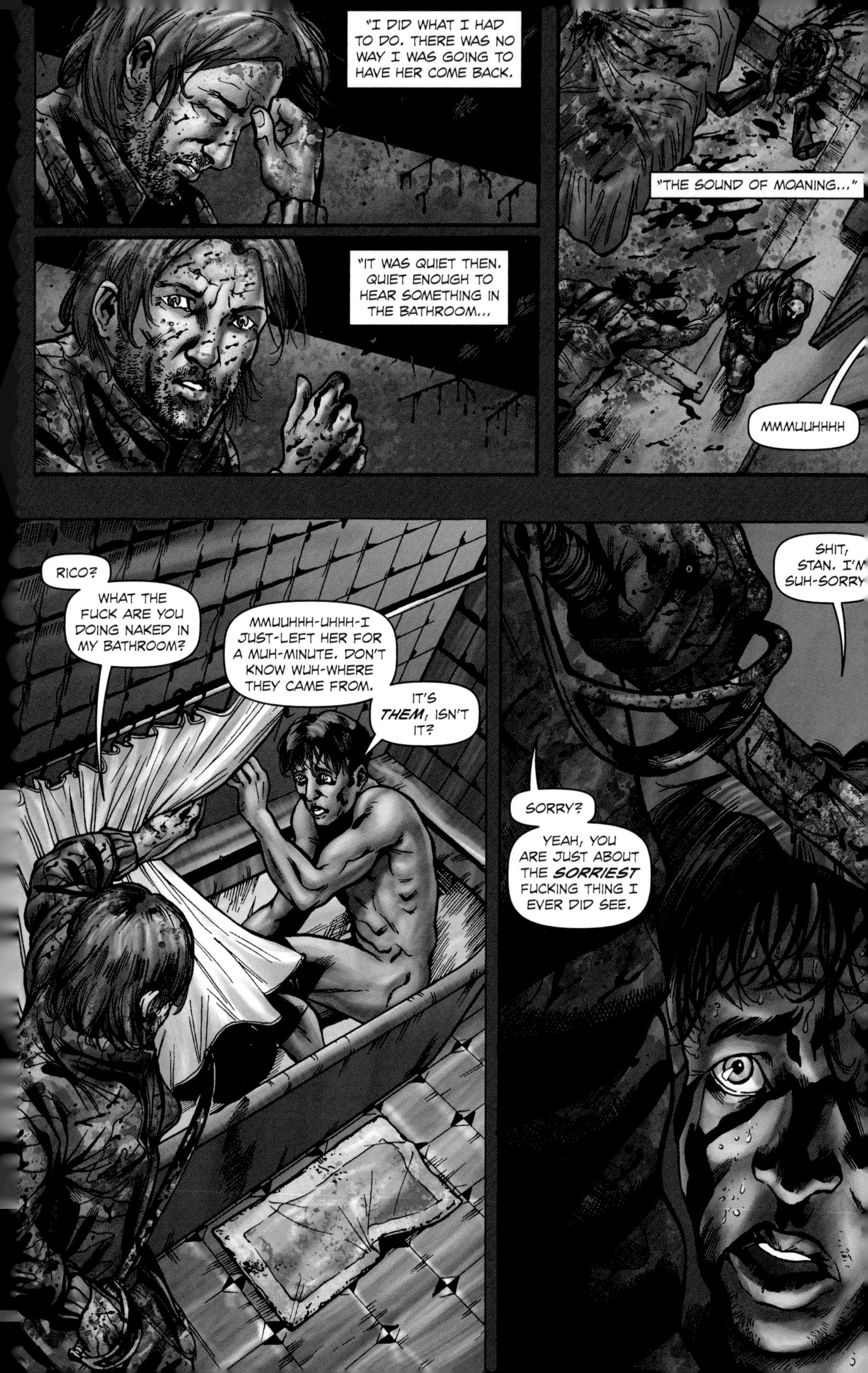
"I DID WHAT I HAD TO DO. THERE WAS NO WAY I WAS GOING TO HAVE HER COME BACK.
"IT WAS QUIET THEN. QUIET ENOUGH TO HEAR SOMETHING IN THE BATHROOM...
"THE SOUND OF MOANING..."
MMMUUHHHH
RICO?
WHAT THE FUCK ARE YOU DOING NAKED IN MY BATHROOM?
MMUUHHH-UHHH-I JUST-LEFT HER FOR A MUH-MINUTE. DON'T KNOW WUH-WHERE THEY CAME FROM.
IT'S *THEM*, ISN'T IT?
SHIT, STAN. I'M SUH-SORRY
SORRY?
YEAH, YOU ARE JUST ABOUT THE ***SORRIEST*** FUCKING THING I EVER DID SEE.

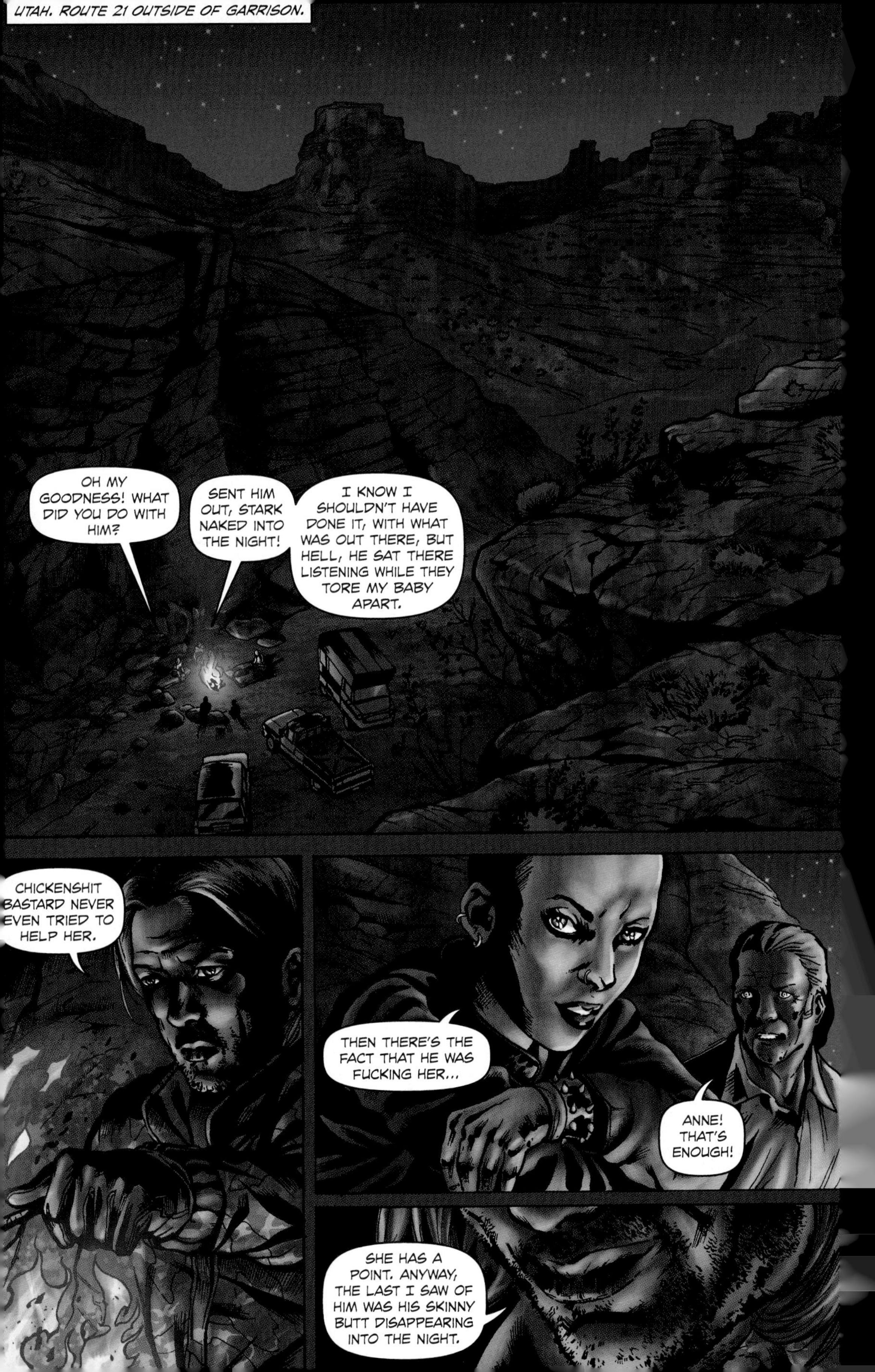
UTAH. ROUTE 21 OUTSIDE OF GARRISON.
OH MY GOODNESS! WHAT DID YOU DO WITH HIM?
SENT HIM OUT, STARK NAKED INTO THE NIGHT!
I KNOW I SHOULDN'T HAVE DONE IT, WITH WHAT WAS OUT THERE, BUT HELL, HE SAT THERE LISTENING WHILE THEY TORE MY BABY APART.
CHICKENSHIT BASTARD NEVER EVEN TRIED TO HELP HER.
THEN THERE'S THE FACT THAT HE WAS FUCKING HER...
ANNE! THAT'S ENOUGH!
SHE HAS A POINT. ANYWAY, THE LAST I SAW OF HIM WAS HIS SKINNY BUTT DISAPPEARING INTO THE NIGHT.

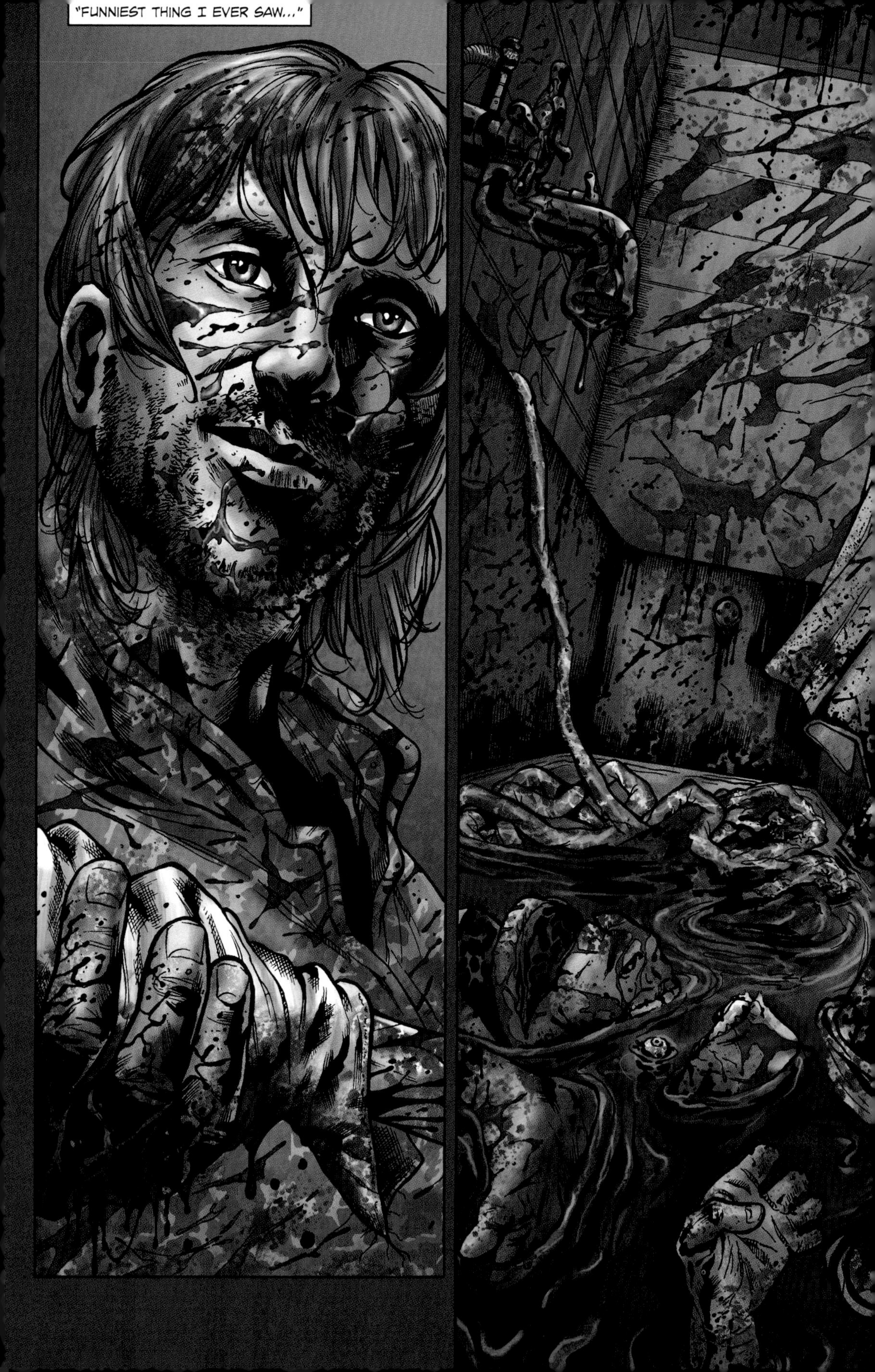
"FUNNIEST THING I EVER SAW..."

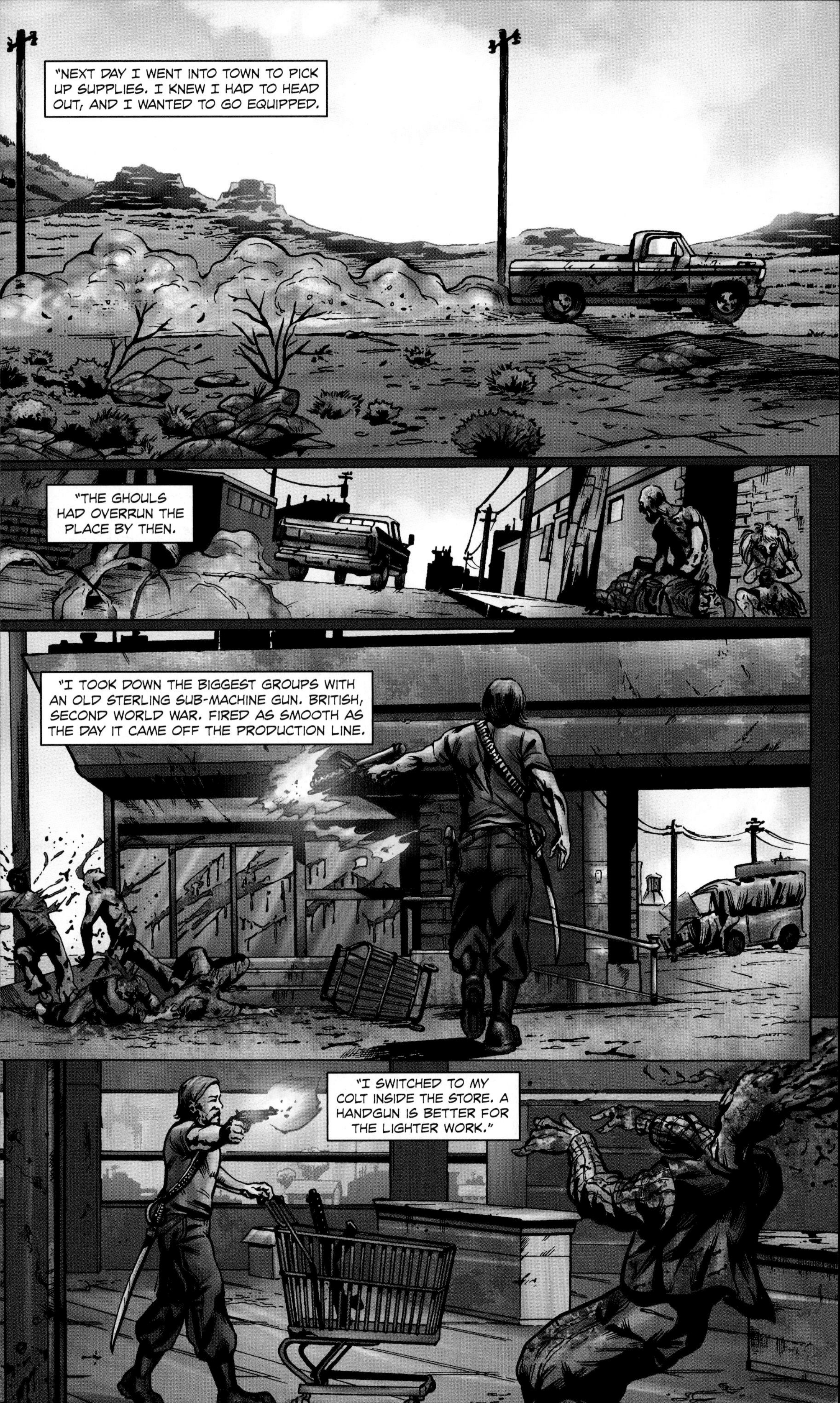
"NEXT DAY I WENT INTO TOWN TO PICK UP SUPPLIES. I KNEW I HAD TO HEAD OUT, AND I WANTED TO GO EQUIPPED.
"THE GHOULS HAD OVERRUN THE PLACE BY THEN.
"I TOOK DOWN THE BIGGEST GROUPS WITH AN OLD STERLING SUB-MACHINE GUN. BRITISH, SECOND WORLD WAR. FIRED AS SMOOTH AS THE DAY IT CAME OFF THE PRODUCTION LINE.
"I SWITCHED TO MY COLT INSIDE THE STORE. A HANDGUN IS BETTER FOR THE LIGHTER WORK."

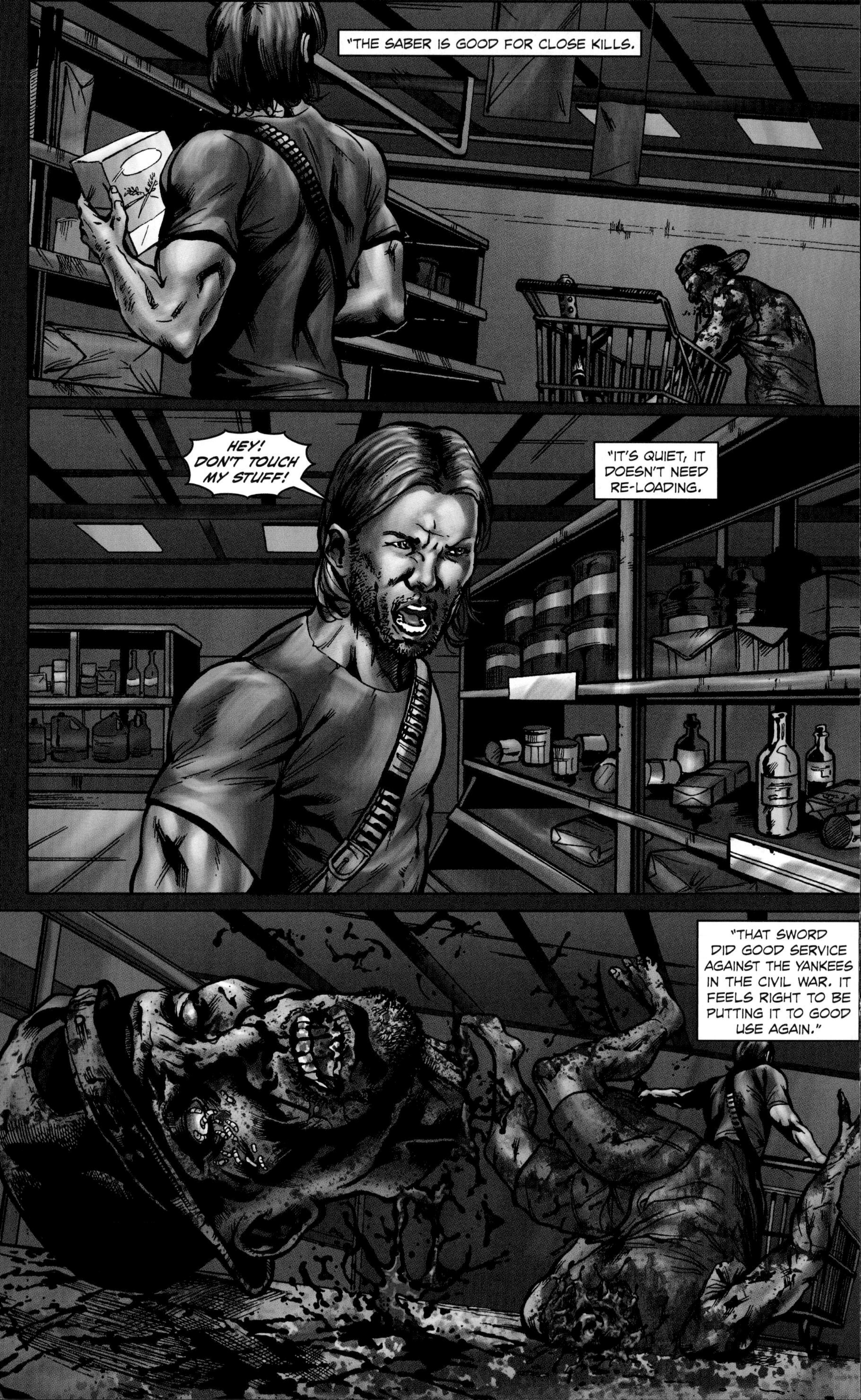
"THE SABER IS GOOD FOR CLOSE KILLS.
HEY! DON'T TOUCH MY STUFF!
"IT'S QUIET, IT DOESN'T NEED RE-LOADING.
"THAT SWORD DID GOOD SERVICE AGAINST THE YANKEES IN THE CIVIL WAR. IT FEELS RIGHT TO BE PUTTING IT TO GOOD USE AGAIN."

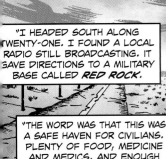

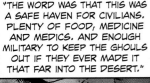

"I HEADED SOUTH ALONG TWENTY-ONE. I FOUND A LOCAL RADIO STILL BROADCASTING. IT GAVE DIRECTIONS TO A MILITARY BASE CALLED *RED ROCK*.
"THE WORD WAS THAT THIS WAS A SAFE HAVEN FOR CIVILIANS. PLENTY OF FOOD, MEDICINE AND MEDICS. AND ENOUGH MILITARY TO KEEP THE GHOULS OUT IF THEY EVER MADE IT THAT FAR INTO THE DESERT."
AND THEN I MET YOU GUYS.
YOU REALLY THINK THIS ARMY BASE IS LEGITIMATE?
SURE. EVERYONE KNOWS THE ARMY IS UP AT RED ROCK. THEY MUST BE SET UP TO SURVIVE FOR YEARS. IT MAKES SENSE TO GO THERE.
WE'RE HEADING EAST.
FOR THE NEW BORDER?
DO YOU KNOW HOW FAR IT IS TO THE MISSISSIPPI FROM HERE?
EVEN KEEPING TO THE SMALLER ROUTES, YOU'LL HAVE TO PASS THROUGH A HUNDRED COMMUNITIES, ALL OVER-RUN WITH THE RESURRECTED.
HE'S RIGHT. WE SHOULD HEAD FOR THIS BASE AND SIT IT OUT UNTIL THE EPIDEMIC DIES DOWN.
I AGREE WITH THE SENATOR.
ME TOO.
SENATOR?

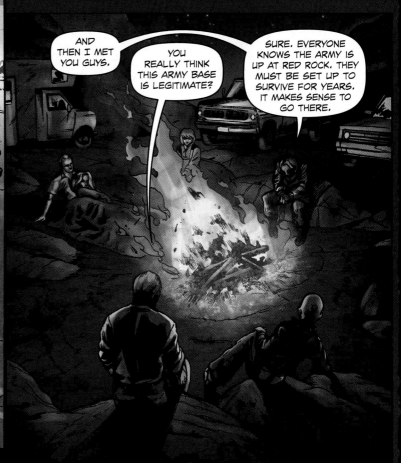

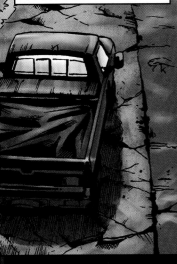

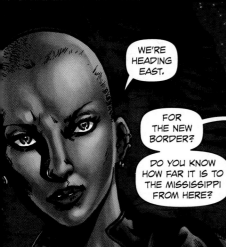

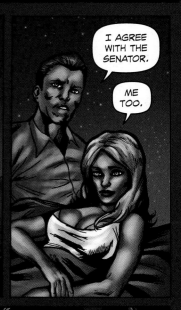

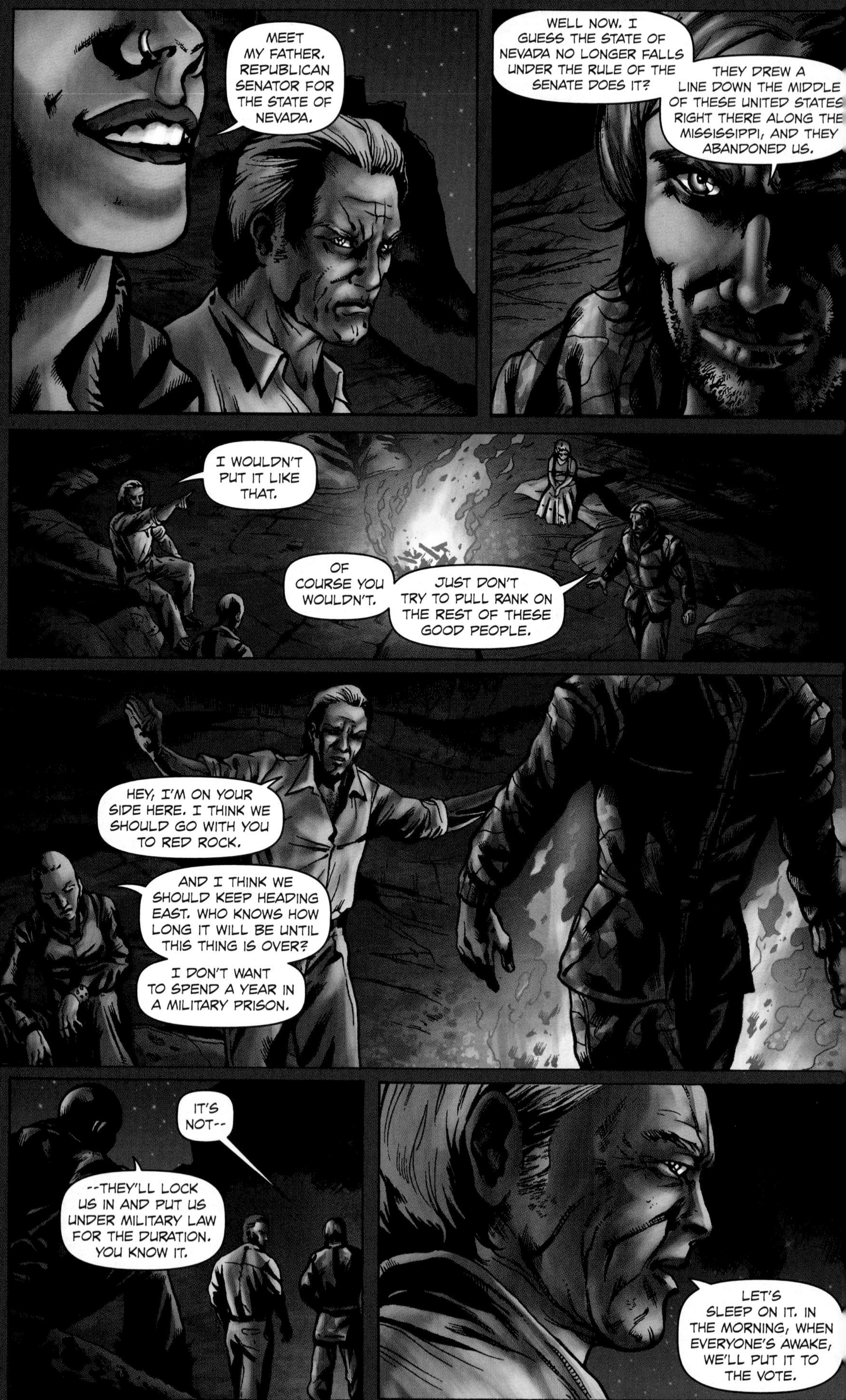
MEET MY FATHER. REPUBLICAN SENATOR FOR THE STATE OF NEVADA.
WELL NOW. I GUESS THE STATE OF NEVADA NO LONGER FALLS UNDER THE RULE OF THE SENATE DOES IT?
THEY DREW A LINE DOWN THE MIDDLE OF THESE UNITED STATES RIGHT THERE ALONG THE MISSISSIPPI, AND THEY ABANDONED US.
I WOULDN'T PUT IT LIKE THAT.
OF COURSE YOU WOULDN'T.
JUST DON'T TRY TO PULL RANK ON THE REST OF THESE GOOD PEOPLE.
HEY, I'M ON YOUR SIDE HERE. I THINK WE SHOULD GO WITH YOU TO RED ROCK.
AND I THINK WE SHOULD KEEP HEADING EAST. WHO KNOWS HOW LONG IT WILL BE UNTIL THIS THING IS OVER?
I DON'T WANT TO SPEND A YEAR IN A MILITARY PRISON.
IT'S NOT--
--THEY'LL LOCK US IN AND PUT US UNDER MILITARY LAW FOR THE DURATION. YOU KNOW IT.
LET'S SLEEP ON IT. IN THE MORNING, WHEN EVERYONE'S AWAKE, WE'LL PUT IT TO THE VOTE.

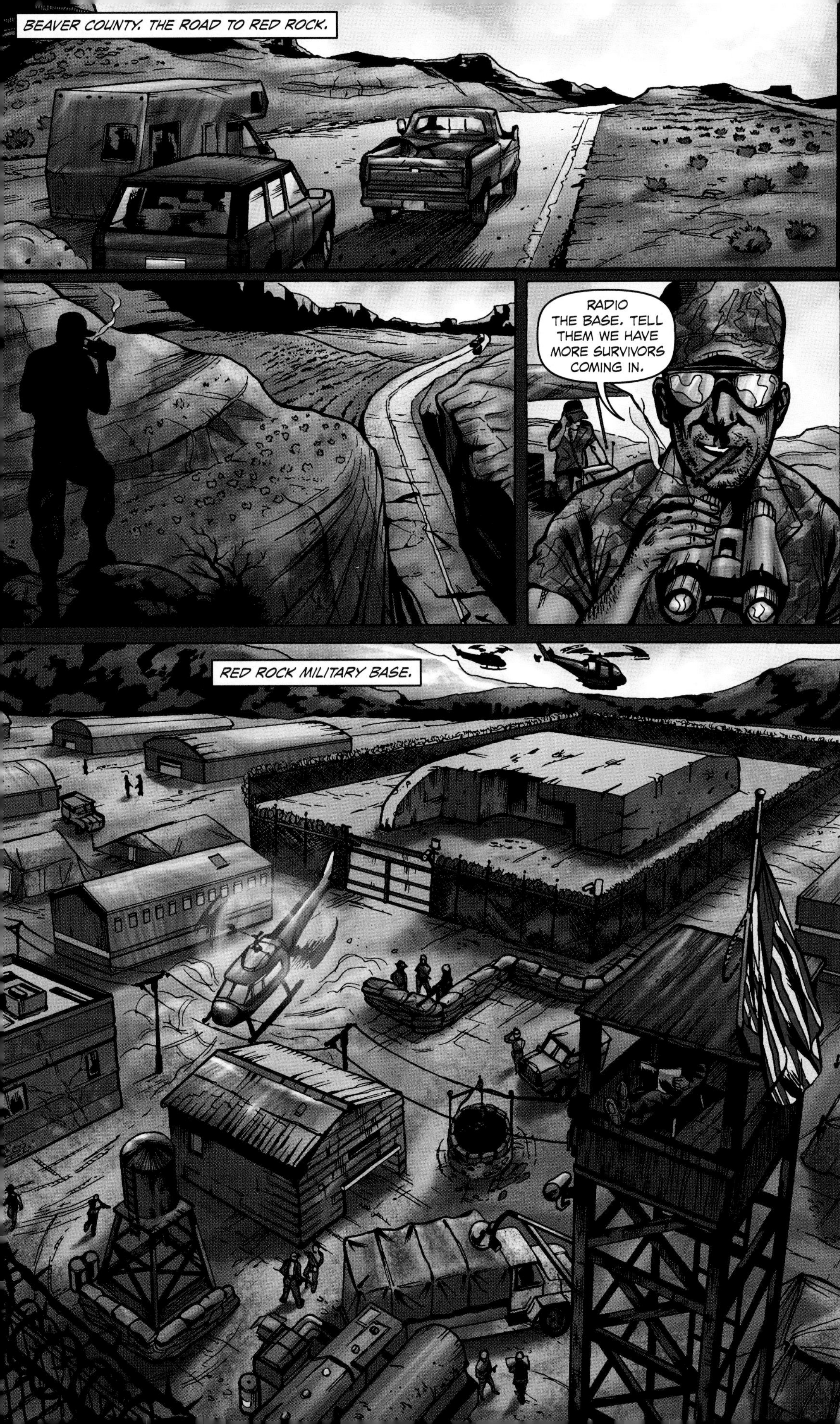
BEAVER COUNTY. THE ROAD TO RED ROCK.
RADIO THE BASE. TELL THEM WE HAVE MORE SURVIVORS COMING IN.
RED ROCK MILITARY BASE.

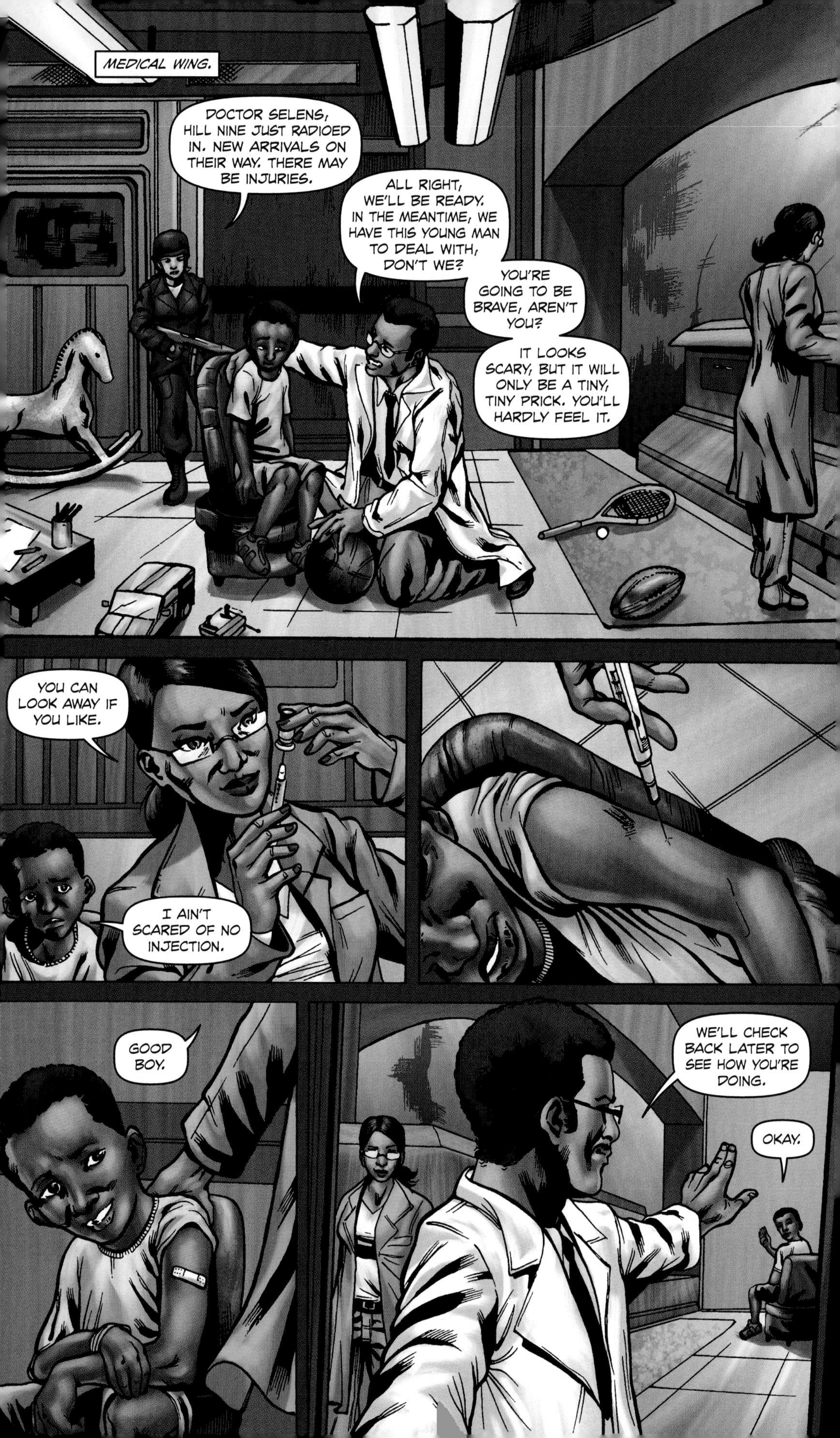
MEDICAL WING.
DOCTOR SELENS, HILL NINE JUST RADIOED IN. NEW ARRIVALS ON THEIR WAY. THERE MAY BE INJURIES.
ALL RIGHT, WE'LL BE READY. IN THE MEANTIME, WE HAVE THIS YOUNG MAN TO DEAL WITH, DON'T WE?
YOU'RE GOING TO BE BRAVE, AREN'T YOU?
IT LOOKS SCARY, BUT IT WILL ONLY BE A TINY, TINY PRICK. YOU'LL HARDLY FEEL IT.
YOU CAN LOOK AWAY IF YOU LIKE.
I AIN'T SCARED OF NO INJECTION.
GOOD BOY.
WE'LL CHECK BACK LATER TO SEE HOW YOU'RE DOING.
OKAY.

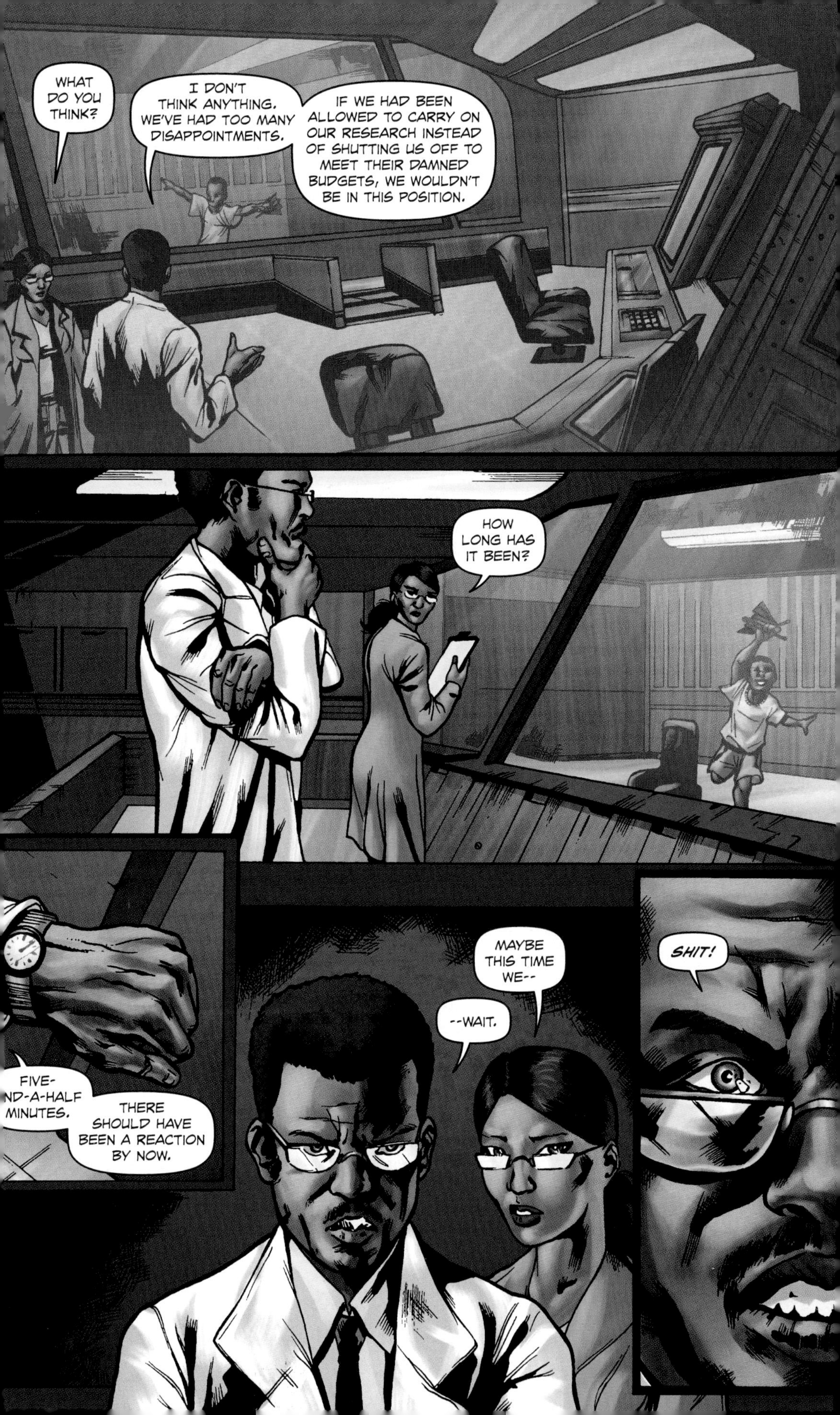
WHAT DO YOU THINK?
I DON'T THINK ANYTHING. WE'VE HAD TOO MANY DISAPPOINTMENTS.
IF WE HAD BEEN ALLOWED TO CARRY ON OUR RESEARCH INSTEAD OF SHUTTING US OFF TO MEET THEIR DAMNED BUDGETS, WE WOULDN'T BE IN THIS POSITION.
HOW LONG HAS IT BEEN?
FIVE-ND-A-HALF MINUTES.
THERE SHOULD HAVE BEEN A REACTION BY NOW.
MAYBE THIS TIME WE--
--WAIT.
SHIT!

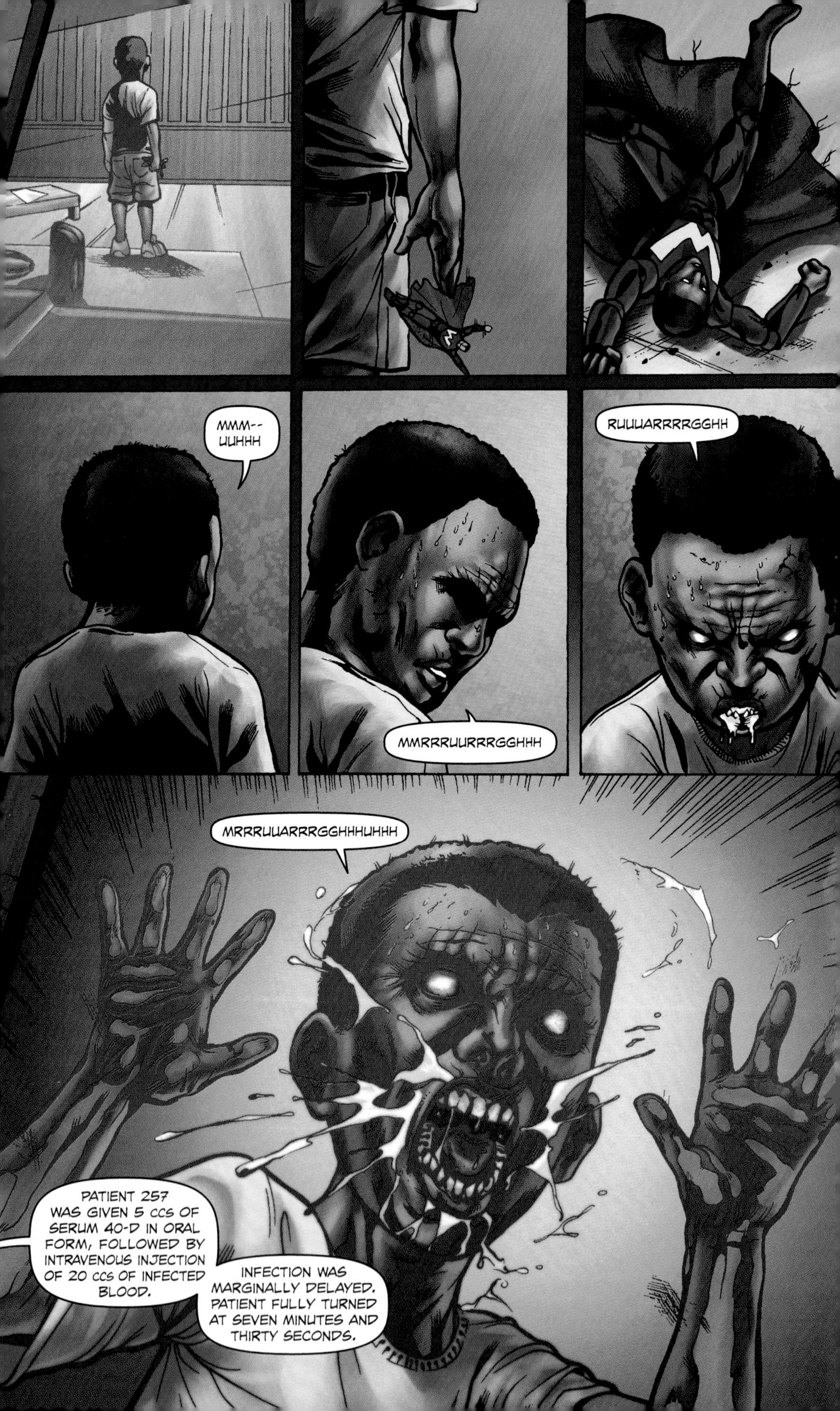
MMM--
UUHHH
MMRRRUURRRGGHHH
RUUUARRRRGGHH
MRRRUUARRRGGHHHUHHH
PATIENT 257 WAS GIVEN 5 CCS OF SERUM 40-D IN ORAL FORM, FOLLOWED BY INTRAVENOUS INJECTION OF 20 CCS OF INFECTED BLOOD.
INFECTION WAS MARGINALLY DELAYED. PATIENT FULLY TURNED AT SEVEN MINUTES AND THIRTY SECONDS.

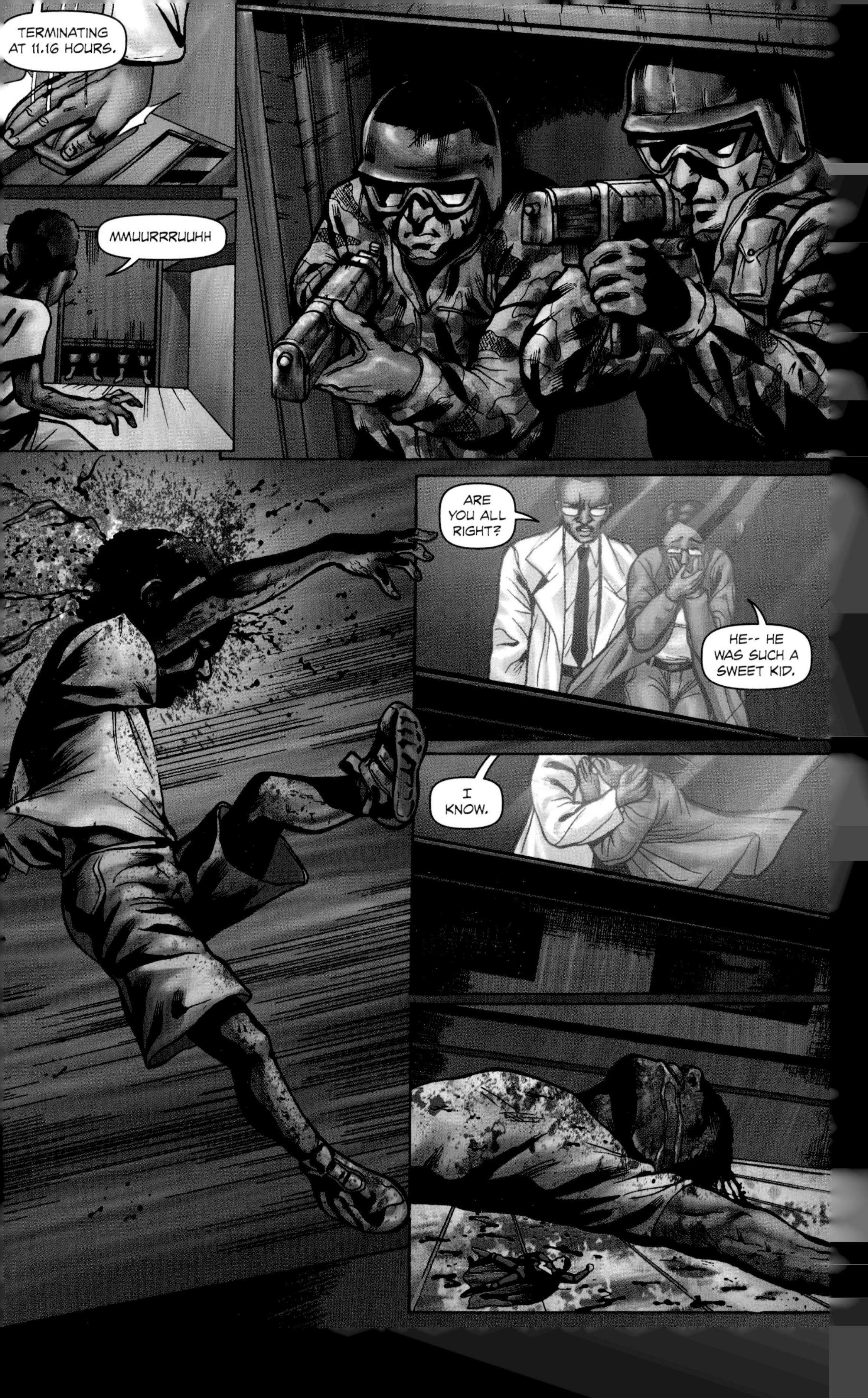
TERMINATING AT 11.16 HOURS.
MMUURRRUUHH
ARE YOU ALL RIGHT?
HE-- HE WAS SUCH A SWEET KID.
I KNOW.

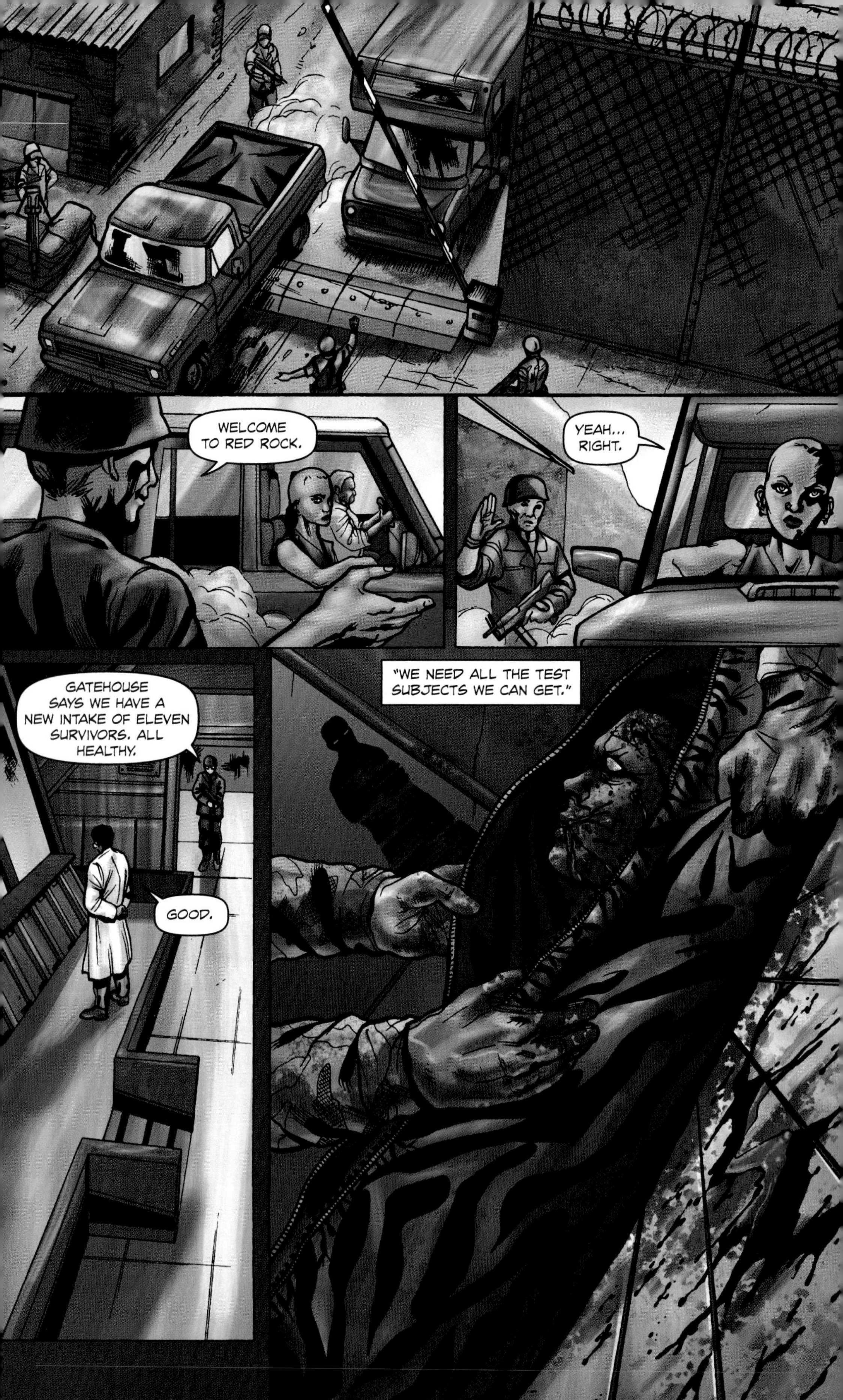

WELCOME TO RED ROCK.
YEAH... RIGHT.
GATEHOUSE SAYS WE HAVE A NEW INTAKE OF ELEVEN SURVIVORS. ALL HEALTHY.
GOOD.
"WE NEED ALL THE TEST SUBJECTS WE CAN GET."

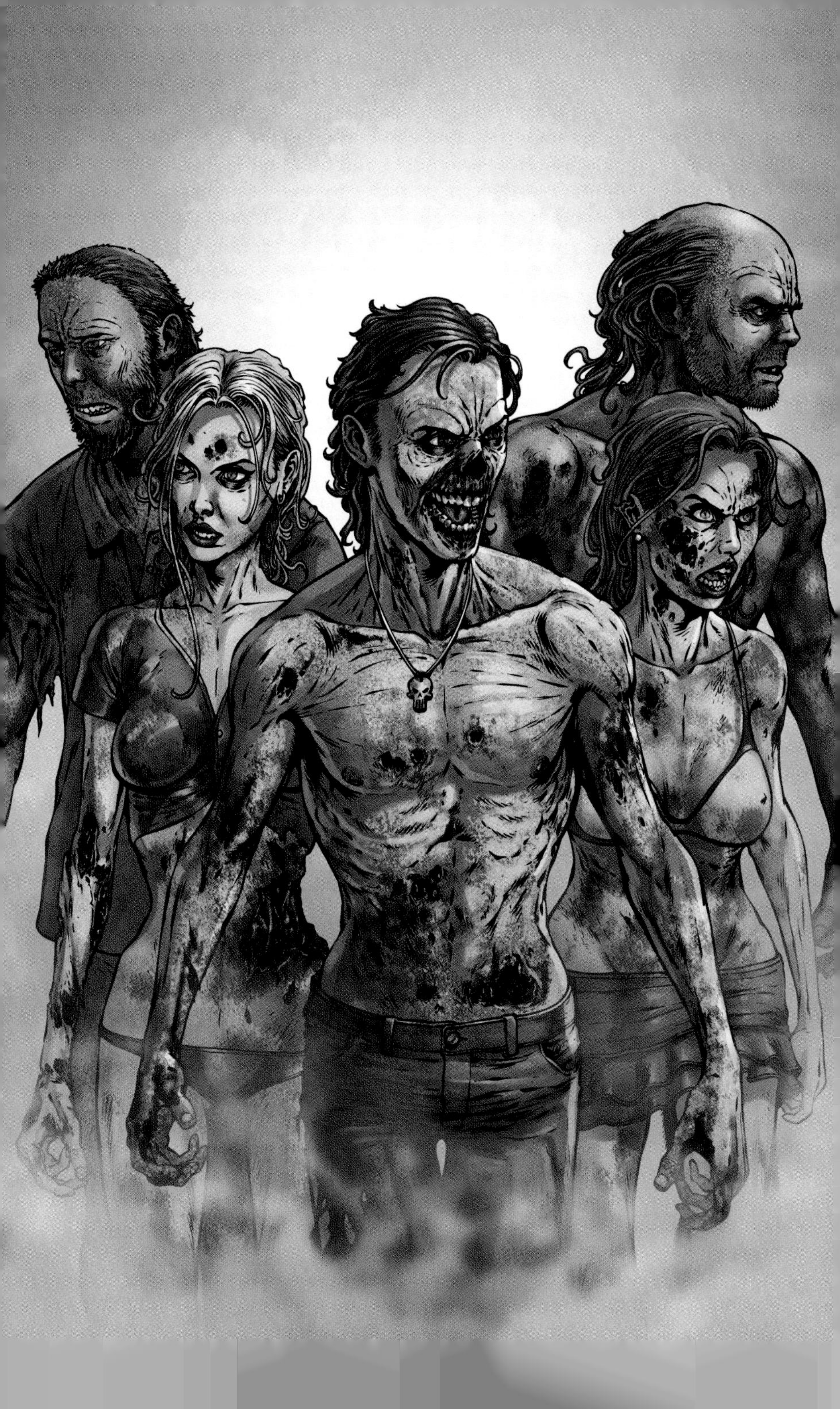

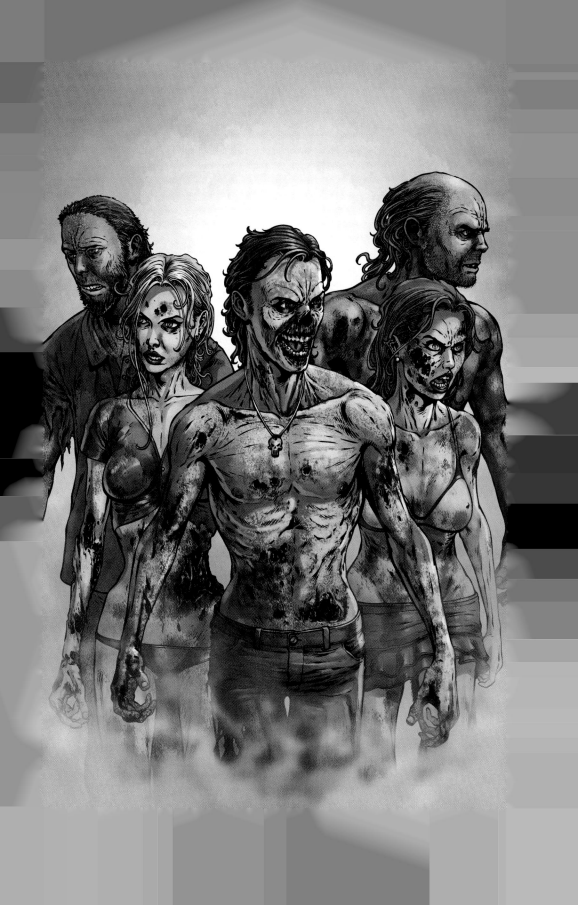

HUNGRY FOR THE FLESH OF THE LIVIN

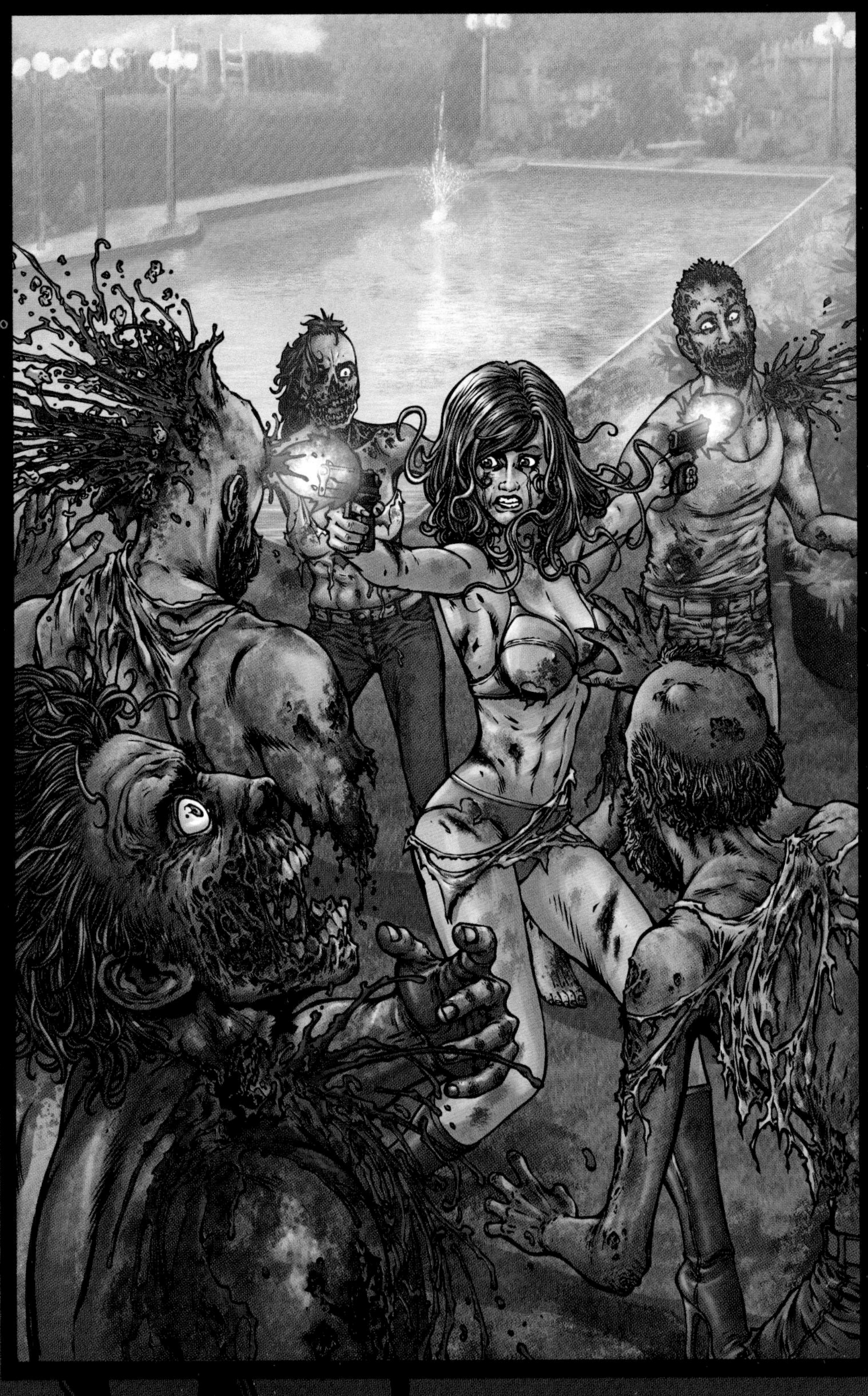

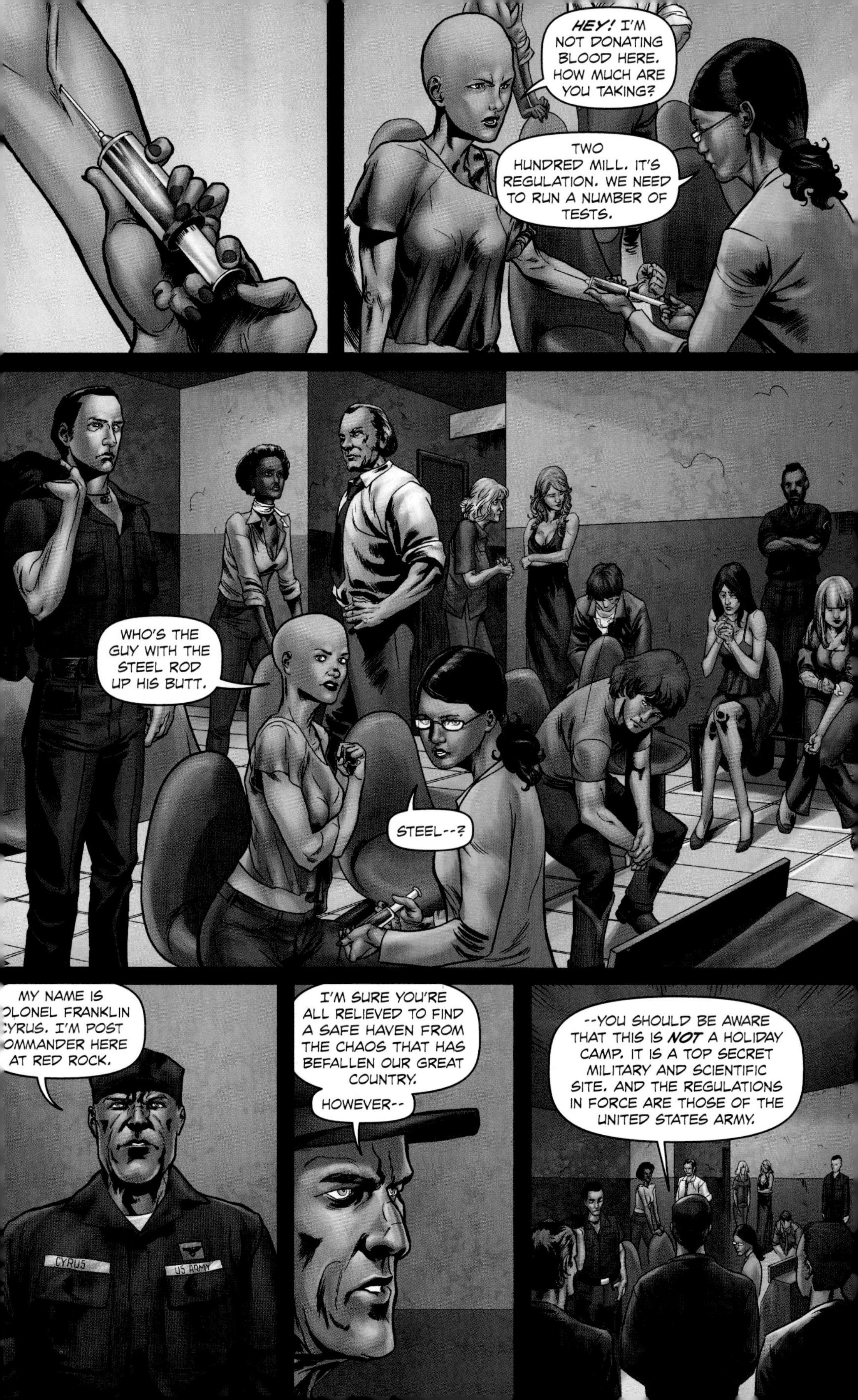
HEY! I'M NOT DONATING BLOOD HERE. HOW MUCH ARE YOU TAKING?
TWO HUNDRED MILL. IT'S REGULATION. WE NEED TO RUN A NUMBER OF TESTS.
WHO'S THE GUY WITH THE STEEL ROD UP HIS BUTT.
STEEL--?
MY NAME IS OLONEL FRANKLIN CYRUS. I'M POST OMMANDER HERE AT RED ROCK.
CYRUS
US ARMY
I'M SURE YOU'RE ALL RELIEVED TO FIND A SAFE HAVEN FROM THE CHAOS THAT HAS BEFALLEN OUR GREAT COUNTRY.
HOWEVER--
--YOU SHOULD BE AWARE THAT THIS IS NOT A HOLIDAY CAMP. IT IS A TOP SECRET MILITARY AND SCIENTIFIC SITE. AND THE REGULATIONS IN FORCE ARE THOSE OF THE UNITED STATES ARMY.

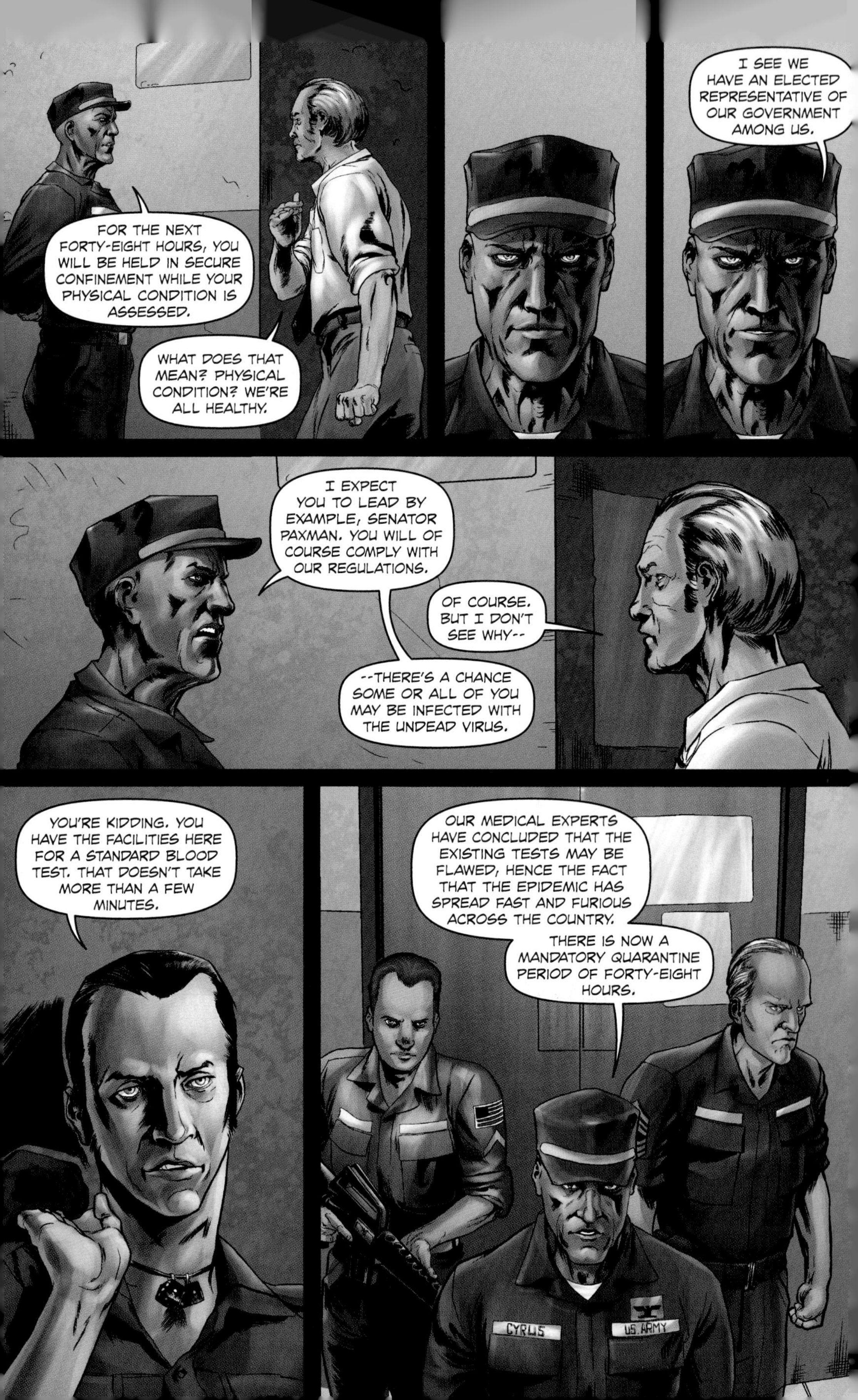

FOR THE NEXT FORTY-EIGHT HOURS, YOU WILL BE HELD IN SECURE CONFINEMENT WHILE YOUR PHYSICAL CONDITION IS ASSESSED.
WHAT DOES THAT MEAN? PHYSICAL CONDITION? WE'RE ALL HEALTHY.
I SEE WE HAVE AN ELECTED REPRESENTATIVE OF OUR GOVERNMENT AMONG US.
I EXPECT YOU TO LEAD BY EXAMPLE, SENATOR PAXMAN. YOU WILL OF COURSE COMPLY WITH OUR REGULATIONS.
OF COURSE. BUT I DON'T SEE WHY--
--THERE'S A CHANCE SOME OR ALL OF YOU MAY BE INFECTED WITH THE UNDEAD VIRUS.
YOU'RE KIDDING. YOU HAVE THE FACILITIES HERE FOR A STANDARD BLOOD TEST. THAT DOESN'T TAKE MORE THAN A FEW MINUTES.
OUR MEDICAL EXPERTS HAVE CONCLUDED THAT THE EXISTING TESTS MAY BE FLAWED, HENCE THE FACT THAT THE EPIDEMIC HAS SPREAD FAST AND FURIOUS ACROSS THE COUNTRY.
THERE IS NOW A MANDATORY QUARANTINE PERIOD OF FORTY-EIGHT HOURS.
CYRUS
U.S. ARMY

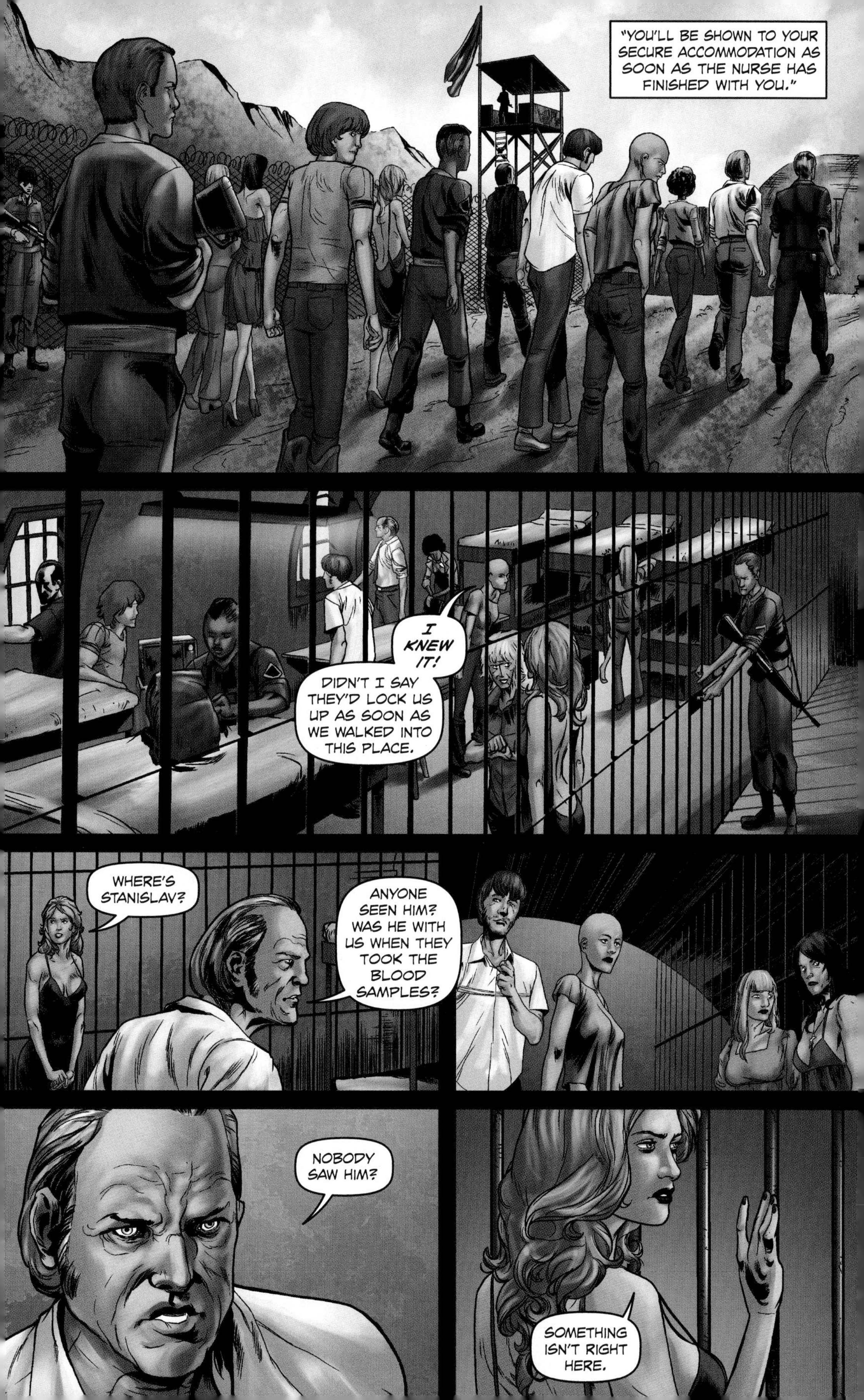
"YOU'LL BE SHOWN TO YOUR SECURE ACCOMMODATION AS SOON AS THE NURSE HAS FINISHED WITH YOU."
I KNEW IT!
DIDN'T I SAY THEY'D LOCK US UP AS SOON AS WE WALKED INTO THIS PLACE.
WHERE'S STANISLAV?
ANYONE SEEN HIM? WAS HE WITH US WHEN THEY TOOK THE BLOOD SAMPLES?
NOBODY SAW HIM?
SOMETHING ISN'T RIGHT HERE.

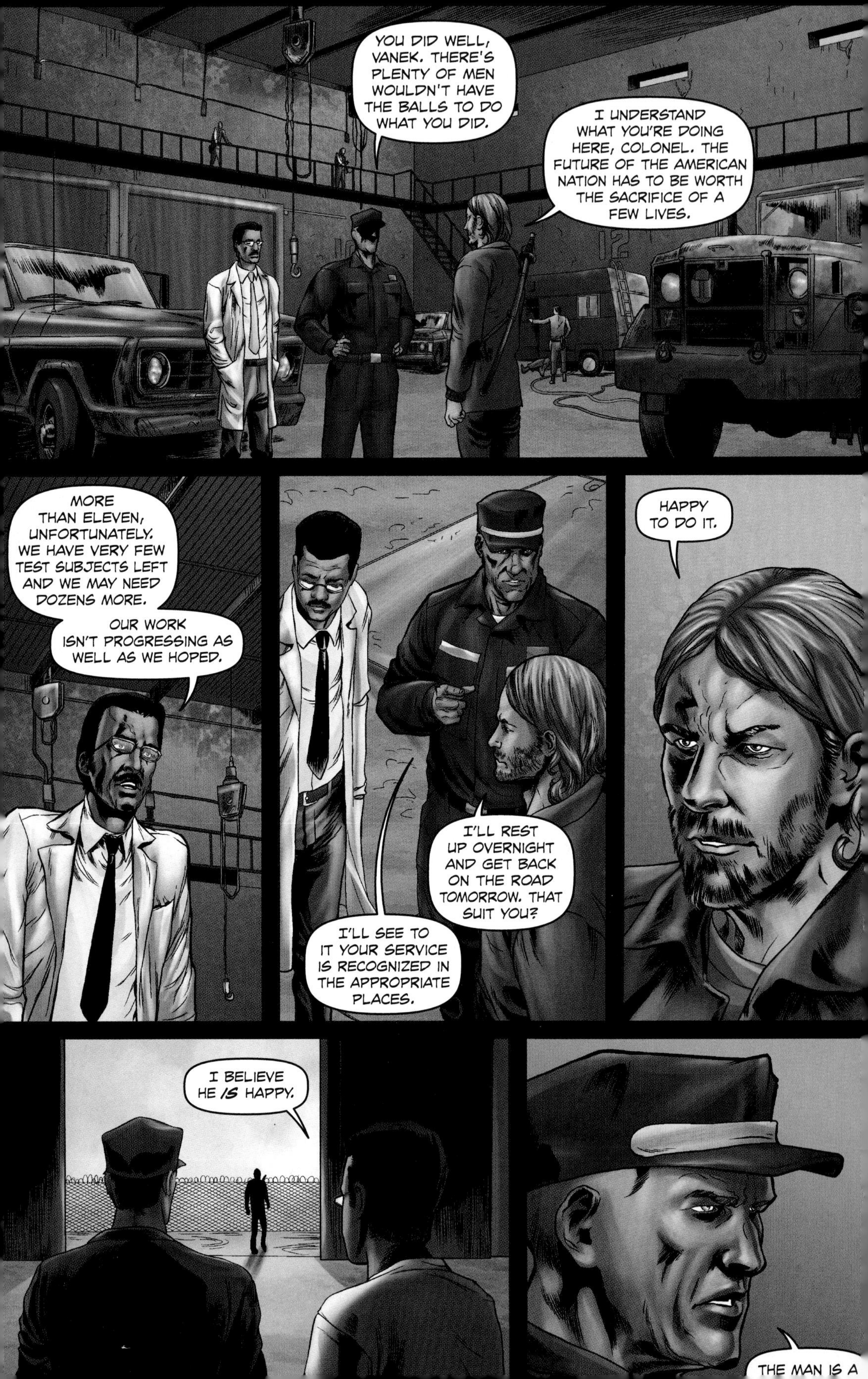
YOU DID WELL, VANEK. THERE'S PLENTY OF MEN WOULDN'T HAVE THE BALLS TO DO WHAT YOU DID.
I UNDERSTAND WHAT YOU'RE DOING HERE, COLONEL. THE FUTURE OF THE AMERICAN NATION HAS TO BE WORTH THE SACRIFICE OF A FEW LIVES.
MORE THAN ELEVEN, UNFORTUNATELY. WE HAVE VERY FEW TEST SUBJECTS LEFT AND WE MAY NEED DOZENS MORE.
OUR WORK ISN'T PROGRESSING AS WELL AS WE HOPED.
I'LL SEE TO IT YOUR SERVICE IS RECOGNIZED IN THE APPROPRIATE PLACES.
I'LL REST UP OVERNIGHT AND GET BACK ON THE ROAD TOMORROW. THAT SUIT YOU?
HAPPY TO DO IT.
I BELIEVE HE *IS* HAPPY.
THE MAN IS A

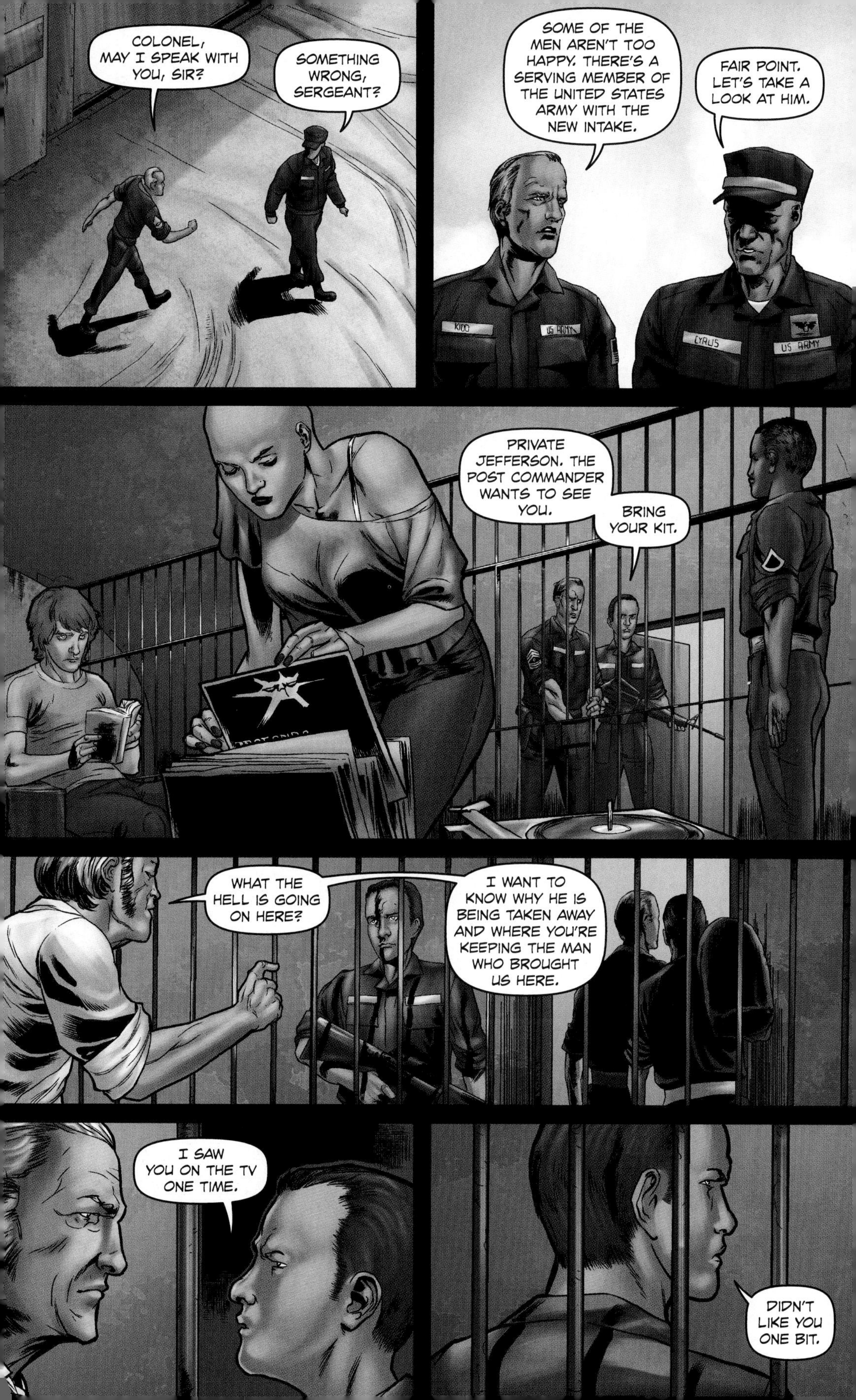
COLONEL, MAY I SPEAK WITH YOU, SIR?
SOMETHING WRONG, SERGEANT?
SOME OF THE MEN AREN'T TOO HAPPY. THERE'S A SERVING MEMBER OF THE UNITED STATES ARMY WITH THE NEW INTAKE.
FAIR POINT. LET'S TAKE A LOOK AT HIM.
KIDD
US ARMY
CYRUS
US ARMY
PRIVATE JEFFERSON. THE POST COMMANDER WANTS TO SEE YOU.
BRING YOUR KIT.
WHAT THE HELL IS GOING ON HERE?
I WANT TO KNOW WHY HE IS BEING TAKEN AWAY AND WHERE YOU'RE KEEPING THE MAN WHO BROUGHT US HERE.
I SAW YOU ON THE TV ONE TIME.
DIDN'T LIKE YOU ONE BIT.

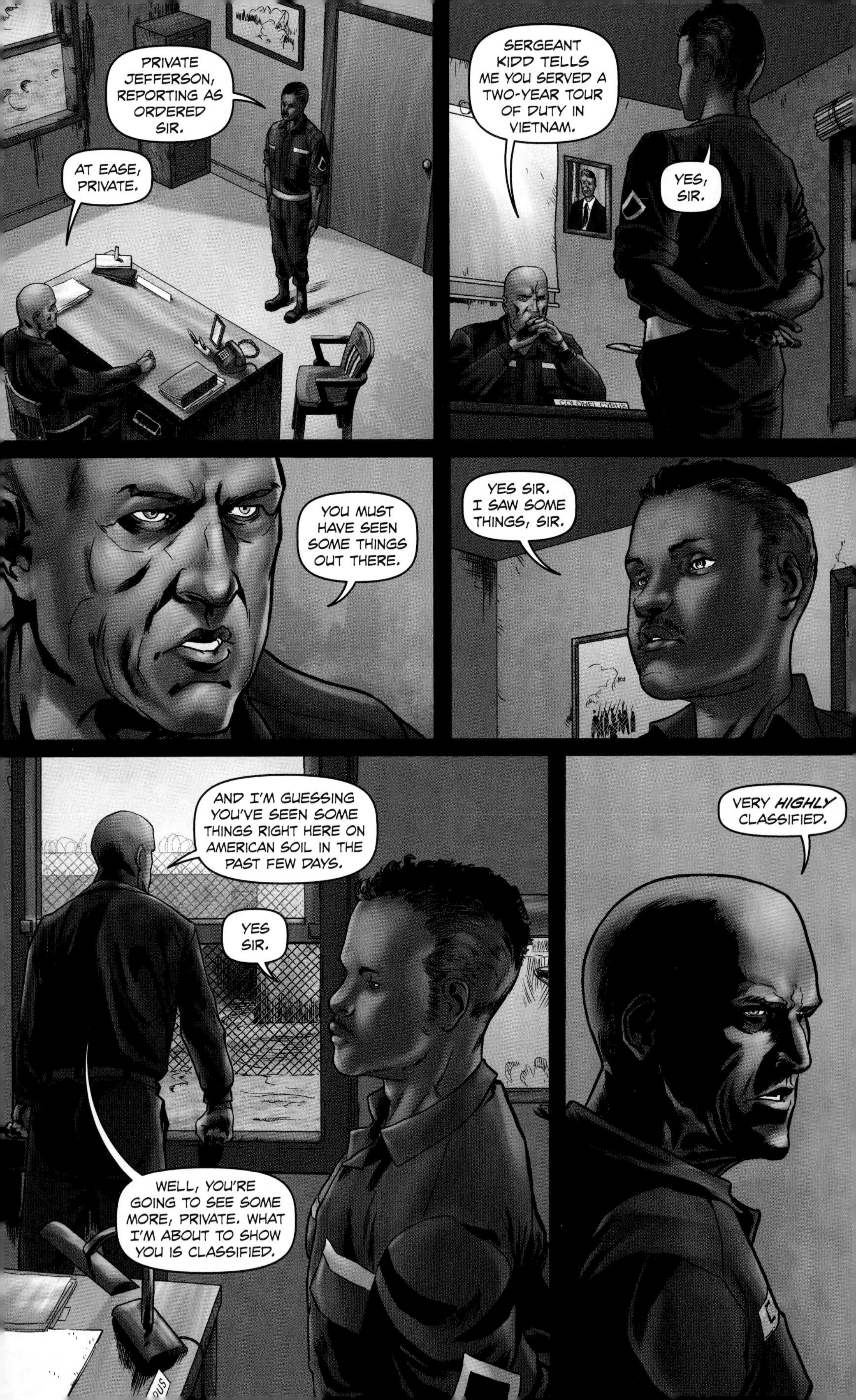
PRIVATE JEFFERSON, REPORTING AS ORDERED SIR.
AT EASE, PRIVATE.
SERGEANT KIDD TELLS ME YOU SERVED A TWO-YEAR TOUR OF DUTY IN VIETNAM.
YES, SIR.
COLONEL CYRUS
YOU MUST HAVE SEEN SOME THINGS OUT THERE.
YES SIR. I SAW SOME THINGS, SIR.
AND I'M GUESSING YOU'VE SEEN SOME THINGS RIGHT HERE ON AMERICAN SOIL IN THE PAST FEW DAYS.
YES SIR.
WELL, YOU'RE GOING TO SEE SOME MORE, PRIVATE. WHAT I'M ABOUT TO SHOW YOU IS CLASSIFIED.
VERY *HIGHLY* CLASSIFIED.

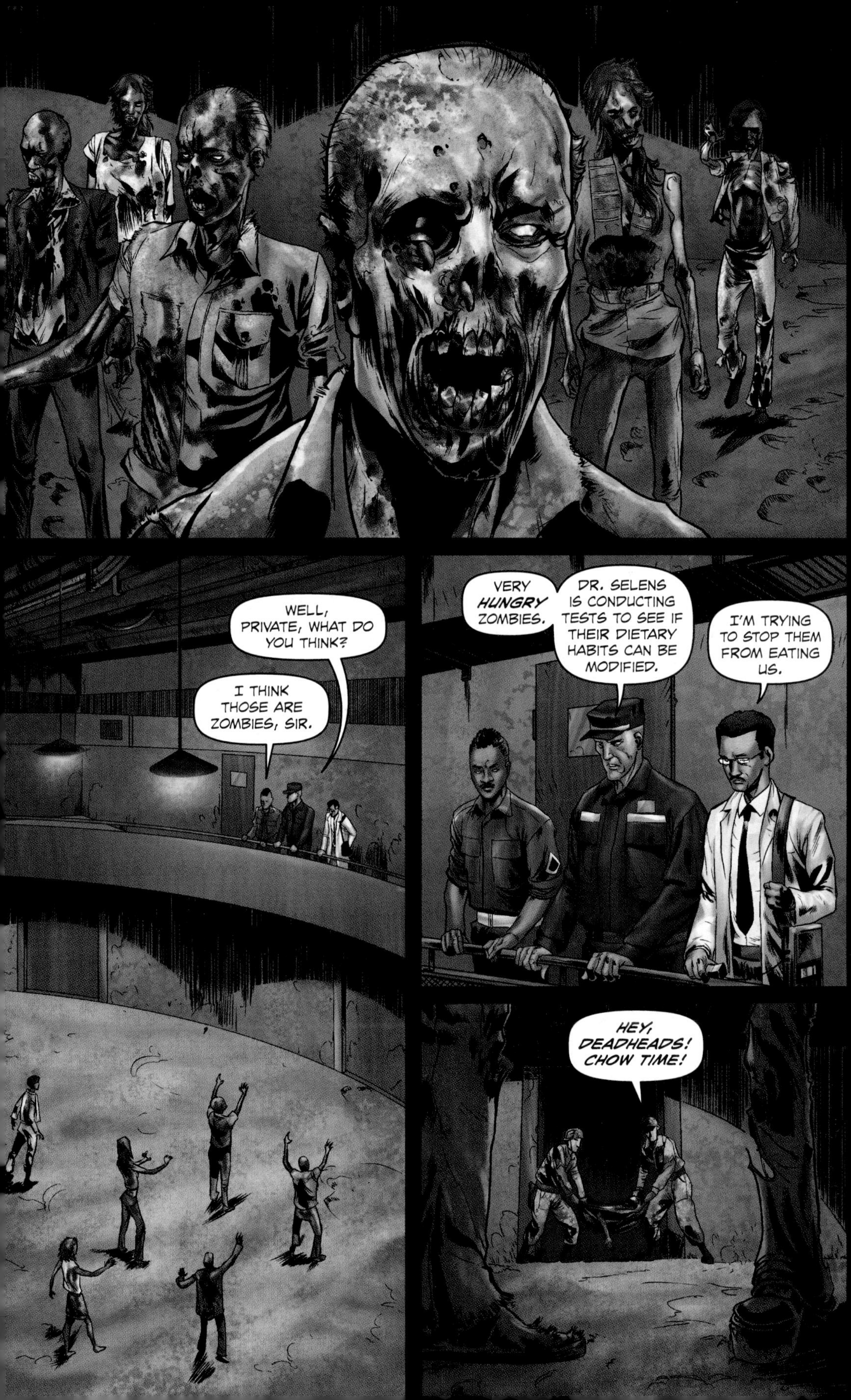
WELL, PRIVATE, WHAT DO YOU THINK?
I THINK THOSE ARE ZOMBIES, SIR.
VERY HUNGRY ZOMBIES.
DR. SELENS IS CONDUCTING TESTS TO SEE IF THEIR DIETARY HABITS CAN BE MODIFIED.
I'M TRYING TO STOP THEM FROM EATING US.
HEY, DEADHEADS! CHOW TIME!

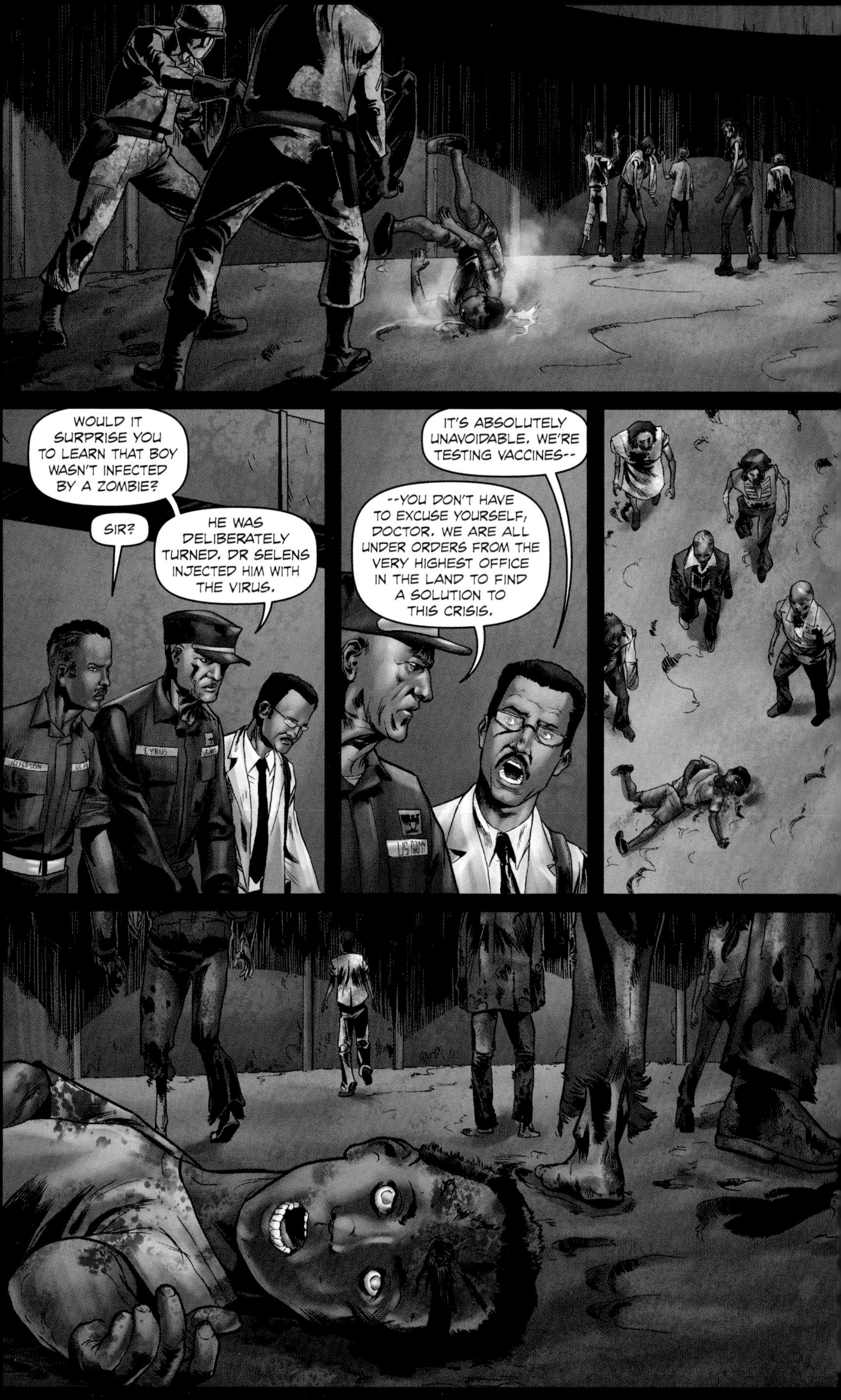
WOULD IT SURPRISE YOU TO LEARN THAT BOY WASN'T INFECTED BY A ZOMBIE?
SIR?
HE WAS DELIBERATELY TURNED. DR SELENS INJECTED HIM WITH THE VIRUS.
JEFFERSON
U.S. ARMY
CYRUS
IT'S ABSOLUTELY UNAVOIDABLE. WE'RE TESTING VACCINES--
--YOU DON'T HAVE TO EXCUSE YOURSELF, DOCTOR. WE ARE ALL UNDER ORDERS FROM THE VERY HIGHEST OFFICE IN THE LAND TO FIND A SOLUTION TO THIS CRISIS.
U.S. ARMY

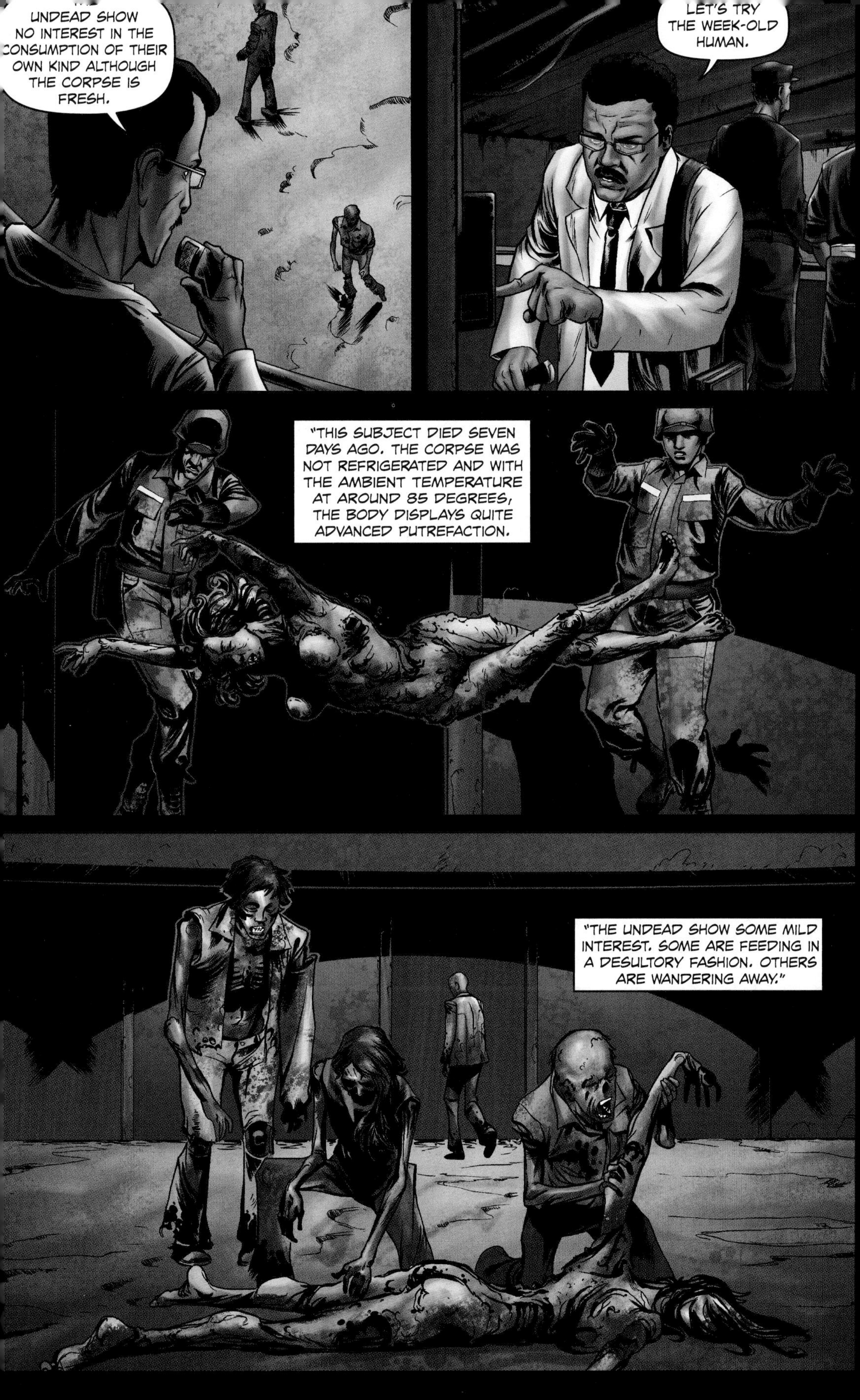
UNDEAD SHOW NO INTEREST IN THE CONSUMPTION OF THEIR OWN KIND ALTHOUGH THE CORPSE IS FRESH.
LET'S TRY THE WEEK-OLD HUMAN.
"THIS SUBJECT DIED SEVEN DAYS AGO. THE CORPSE WAS NOT REFRIGERATED AND WITH THE AMBIENT TEMPERATURE AT AROUND 85 DEGREES, THE BODY DISPLAYS QUITE ADVANCED PUTREFACTION.
"THE UNDEAD SHOW SOME MILD INTEREST. SOME ARE FEEDING IN A DESULTORY FASHION. OTHERS ARE WANDERING AWAY."

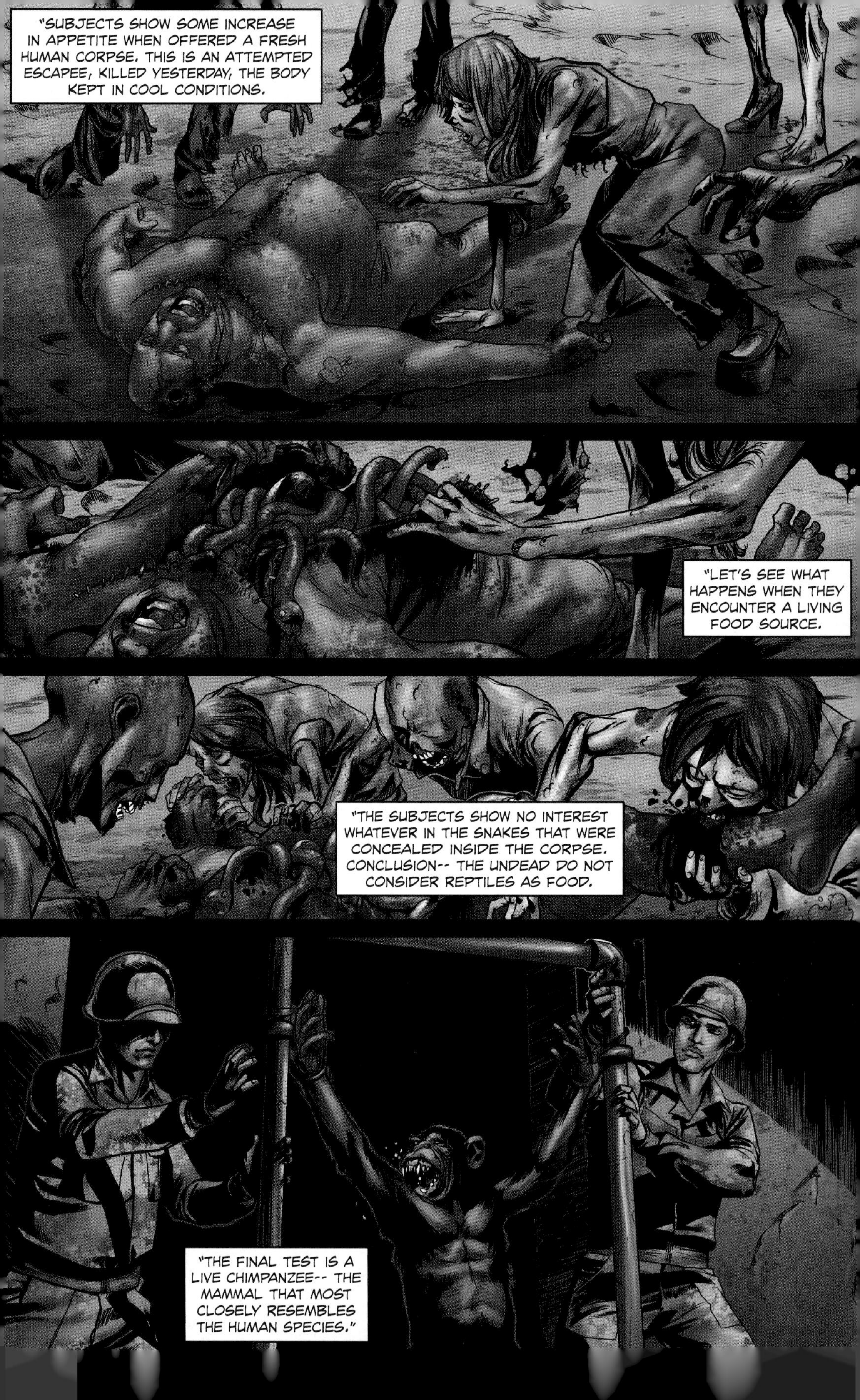
"SUBJECTS SHOW SOME INCREASE IN APPETITE WHEN OFFERED A FRESH HUMAN CORPSE. THIS IS AN ATTEMPTED ESCAPEE, KILLED YESTERDAY, THE BODY KEPT IN COOL CONDITIONS.
"LET'S SEE WHAT HAPPENS WHEN THEY ENCOUNTER A LIVING FOOD SOURCE.
"THE SUBJECTS SHOW NO INTEREST WHATEVER IN THE SNAKES THAT WERE CONCEALED INSIDE THE CORPSE. CONCLUSION-- THE UNDEAD DO NOT CONSIDER REPTILES AS FOOD.
"THE FINAL TEST IS A LIVE CHIMPANZEE-- THE MAMMAL THAT MOST CLOSELY RESEMBLES THE HUMAN SPECIES."

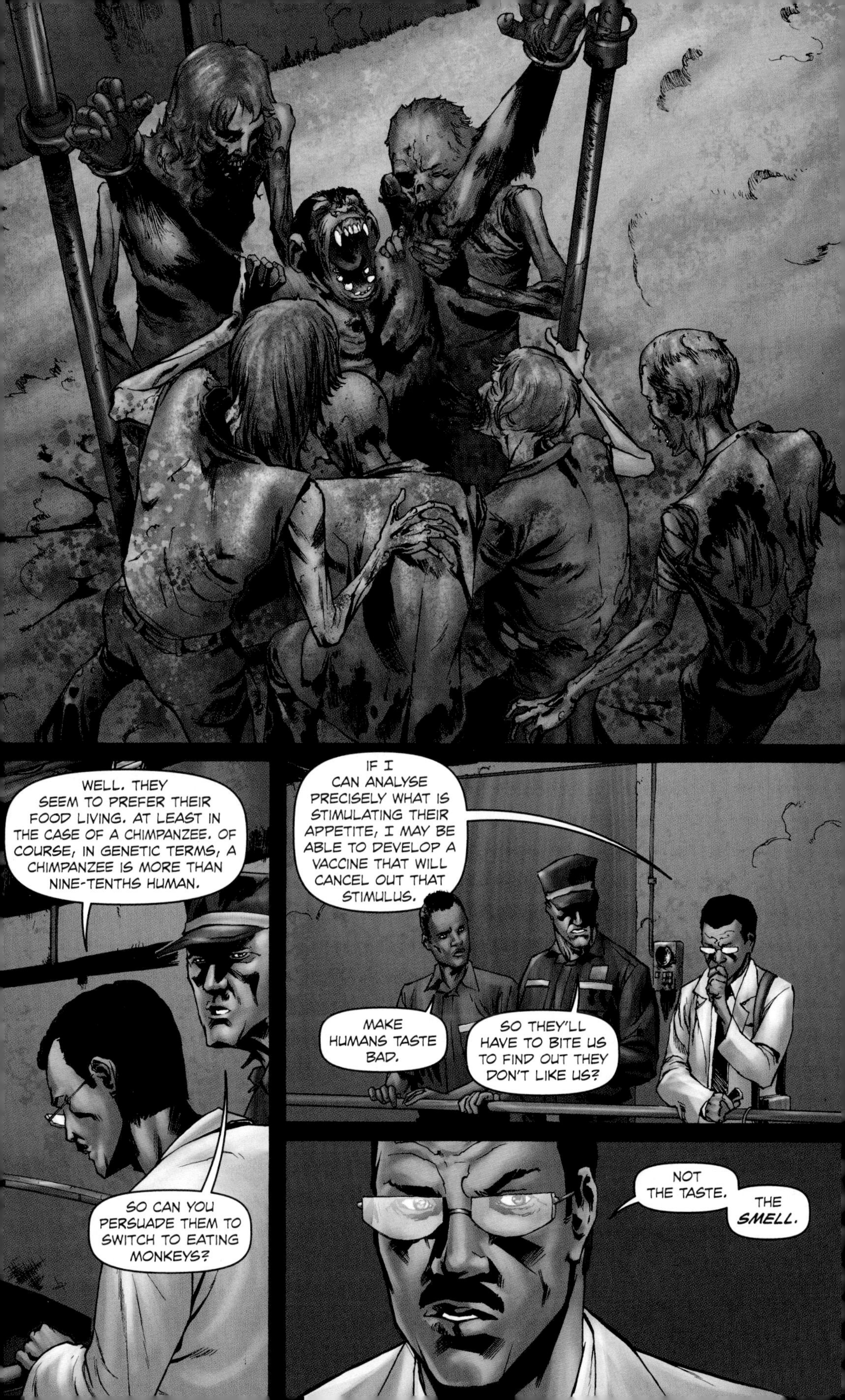

WELL. THEY SEEM TO PREFER THEIR FOOD LIVING. AT LEAST IN THE CASE OF A CHIMPANZEE. OF COURSE, IN GENETIC TERMS, A CHIMPANZEE IS MORE THAN NINE-TENTHS HUMAN.
SO CAN YOU PERSUADE THEM TO SWITCH TO EATING MONKEYS?
IF I CAN ANALYSE PRECISELY WHAT IS STIMULATING THEIR APPETITE, I MAY BE ABLE TO DEVELOP A VACCINE THAT WILL CANCEL OUT THAT STIMULUS.
MAKE HUMANS TASTE BAD.
SO THEY'LL HAVE TO BITE US TO FIND OUT THEY DON'T LIKE US?
NOT THE TASTE.
THE *SMELL*.

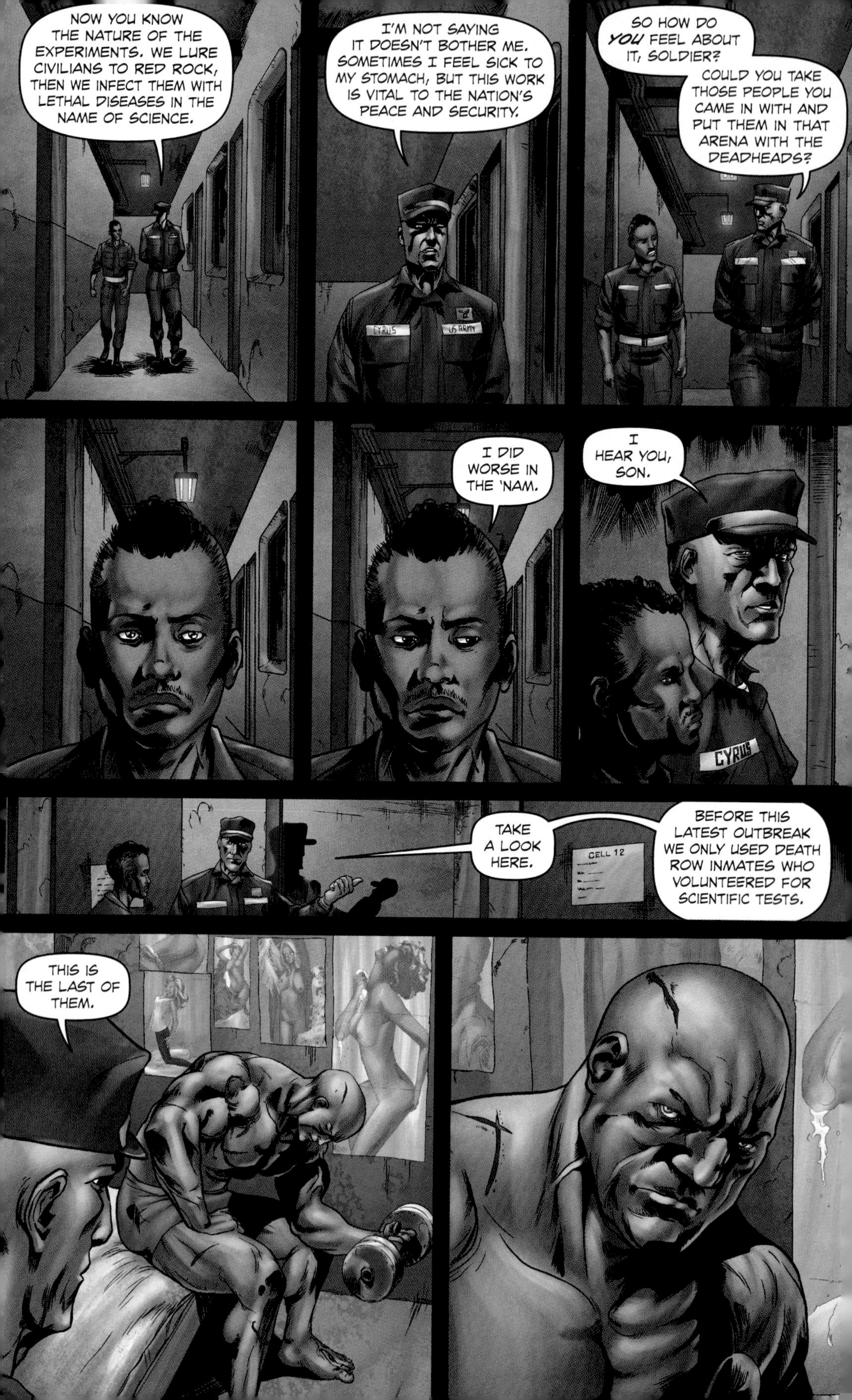
NOW YOU KNOW THE NATURE OF THE EXPERIMENTS. WE LURE CIVILIANS TO RED ROCK, THEN WE INFECT THEM WITH LETHAL DISEASES IN THE NAME OF SCIENCE.
I'M NOT SAYING IT DOESN'T BOTHER ME. SOMETIMES I FEEL SICK TO MY STOMACH, BUT THIS WORK IS VITAL TO THE NATION'S PEACE AND SECURITY.
CYRUS
US ARMY
SO HOW DO *YOU* FEEL ABOUT IT, SOLDIER?
COULD YOU TAKE THOSE PEOPLE YOU CAME IN WITH AND PUT THEM IN THAT ARENA WITH THE DEADHEADS?
I DID WORSE IN THE 'NAM.
I HEAR YOU, SON.
CYRUS
TAKE A LOOK HERE.
BEFORE THIS LATEST OUTBREAK WE ONLY USED DEATH ROW INMATES WHO VOLUNTEERED FOR SCIENTIFIC TESTS.
CELL 12
THIS IS THE LAST OF THEM.

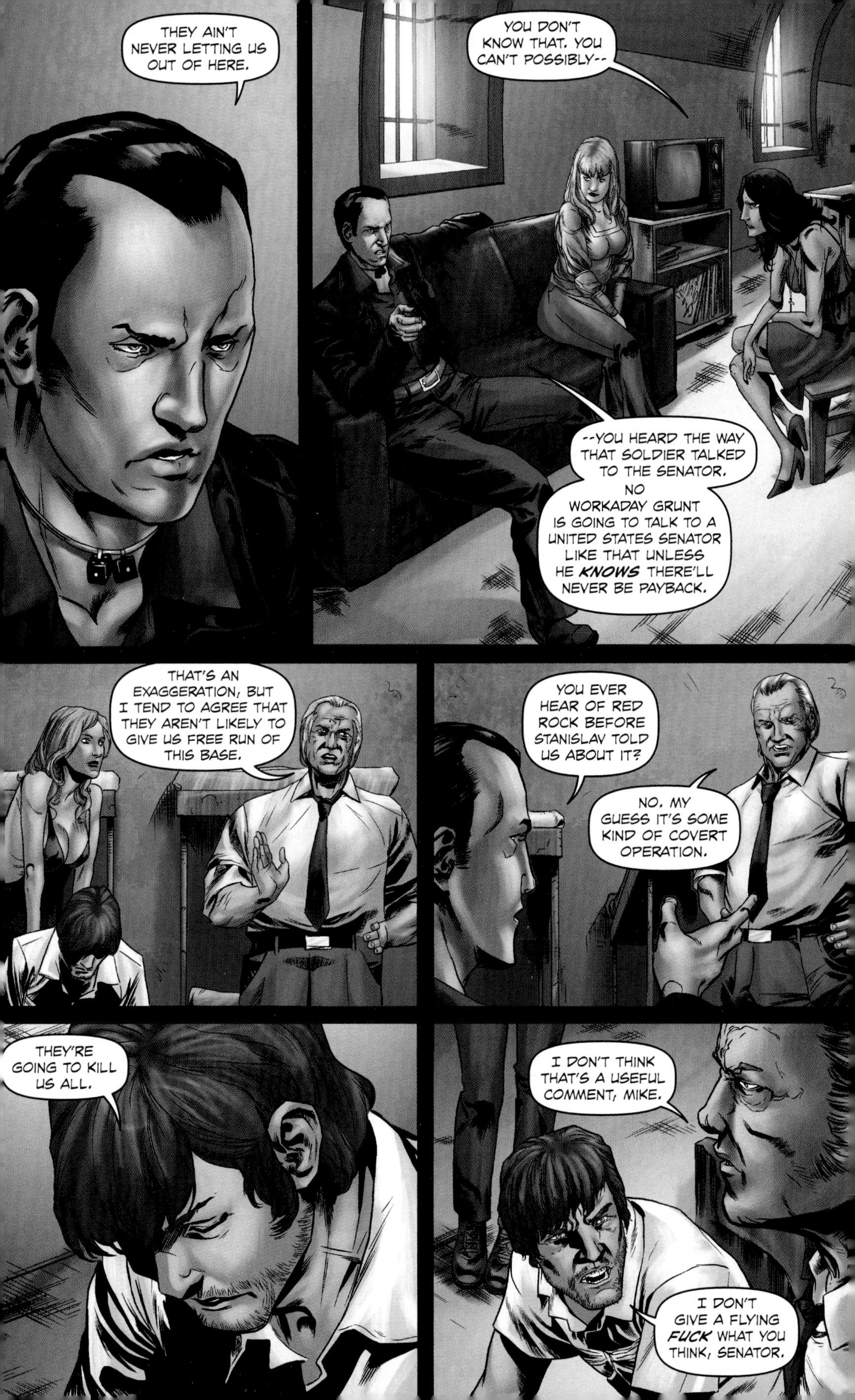
THEY AIN'T NEVER LETTING US OUT OF HERE.
YOU DON'T KNOW THAT. YOU CAN'T POSSIBLY--
--YOU HEARD THE WAY THAT SOLDIER TALKED TO THE SENATOR.
NO WORKADAY GRUNT IS GOING TO TALK TO A UNITED STATES SENATOR LIKE THAT UNLESS HE KNOWS THERE'LL NEVER BE PAYBACK.
THAT'S AN EXAGGERATION, BUT I TEND TO AGREE THAT THEY AREN'T LIKELY TO GIVE US FREE RUN OF THIS BASE.
YOU EVER HEAR OF RED ROCK BEFORE STANISLAV TOLD US ABOUT IT?
NO. MY GUESS IT'S SOME KIND OF COVERT OPERATION.
THEY'RE GOING TO KILL US ALL.
I DON'T THINK THAT'S A USEFUL COMMENT, MIKE.
I DON'T GIVE A FLYING FUCK WHAT YOU THINK, SENATOR.

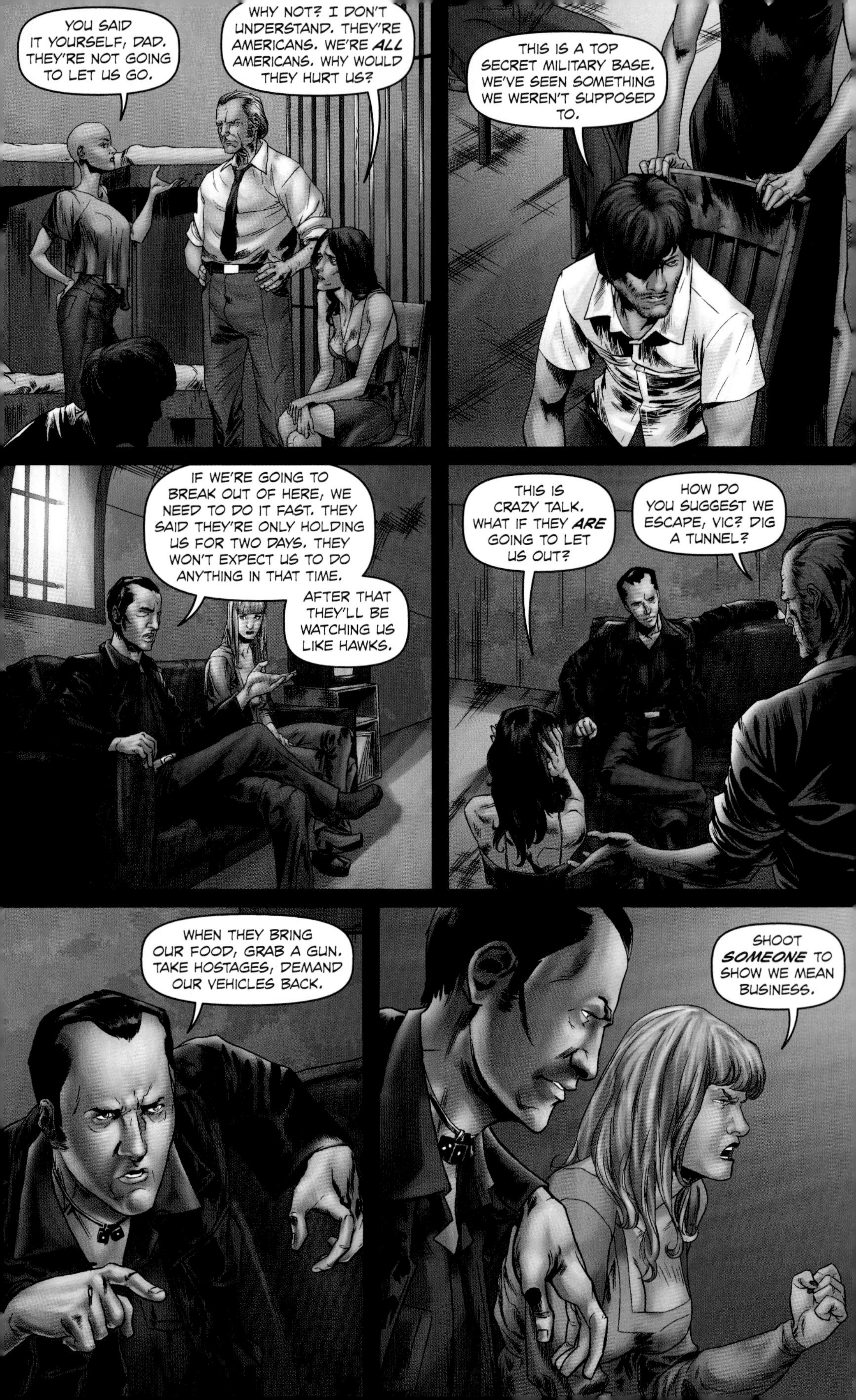
YOU SAID IT YOURSELF, DAD. THEY'RE NOT GOING TO LET US GO.
WHY NOT? I DON'T UNDERSTAND. THEY'RE AMERICANS. WE'RE ALL AMERICANS. WHY WOULD THEY HURT US?
THIS IS A TOP SECRET MILITARY BASE. WE'VE SEEN SOMETHING WE WEREN'T SUPPOSED TO.
IF WE'RE GOING TO BREAK OUT OF HERE, WE NEED TO DO IT FAST. THEY SAID THEY'RE ONLY HOLDING US FOR TWO DAYS. THEY WON'T EXPECT US TO DO ANYTHING IN THAT TIME.
AFTER THAT THEY'LL BE WATCHING US LIKE HAWKS.
THIS IS CRAZY TALK. WHAT IF THEY ARE GOING TO LET US OUT?
HOW DO YOU SUGGEST WE ESCAPE, VIC? DIG A TUNNEL?
WHEN THEY BRING OUR FOOD, GRAB A GUN. TAKE HOSTAGES, DEMAND OUR VEHICLES BACK.
SHOOT SOMEONE TO SHOW WE MEAN BUSINESS.

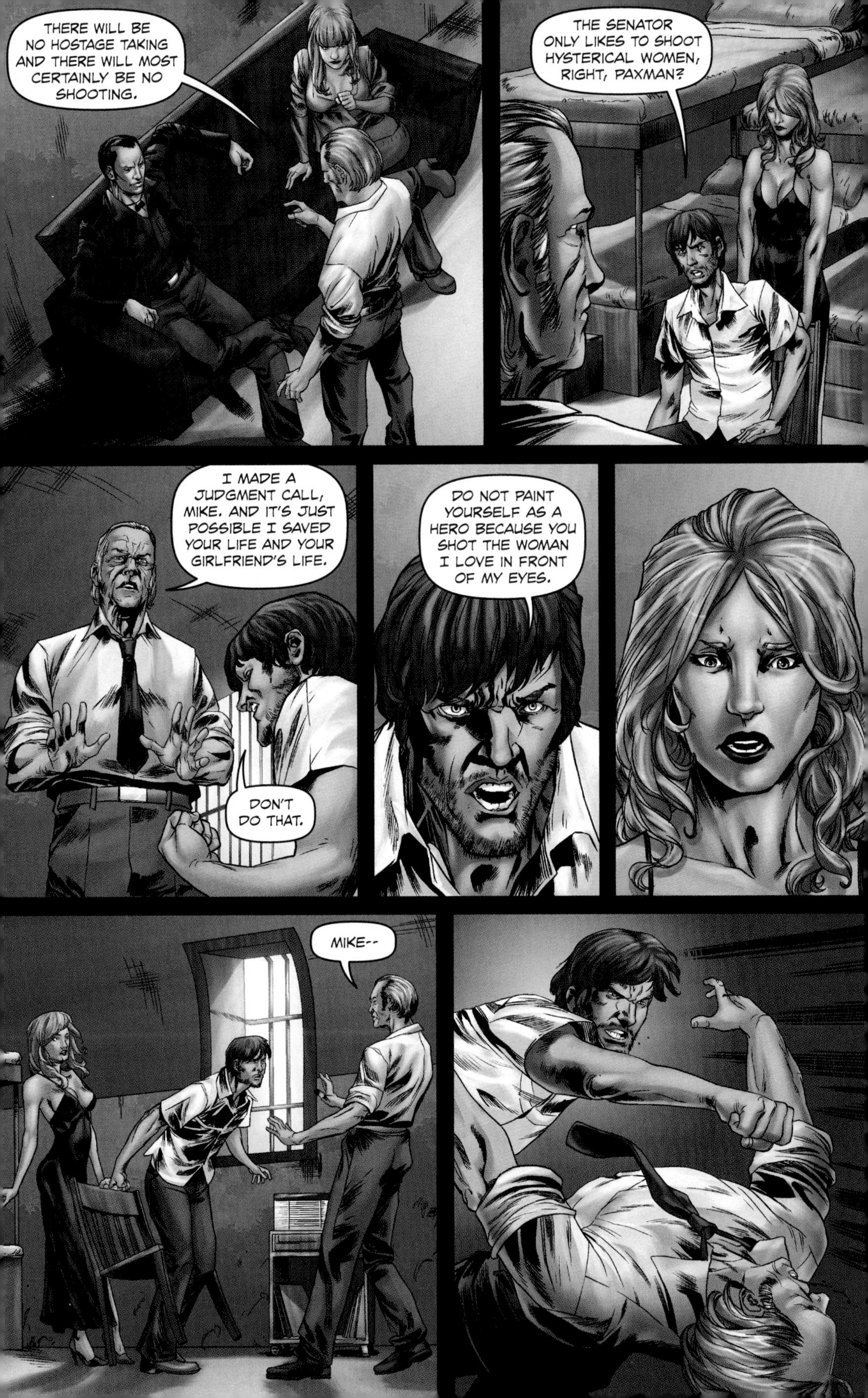
THERE WILL BE NO HOSTAGE TAKING AND THERE WILL MOST CERTAINLY BE NO SHOOTING.
THE SENATOR ONLY LIKES TO SHOOT HYSTERICAL WOMEN, RIGHT, PAXMAN?
I MADE A JUDGMENT CALL, MIKE. AND IT'S JUST POSSIBLE I SAVED YOUR LIFE AND YOUR GIRLFRIEND'S LIFE.
DON'T DO THAT.
DO NOT PAINT YOURSELF AS A HERO BECAUSE YOU SHOT THE WOMAN I LOVE IN FRONT OF MY EYES.
MIKE--

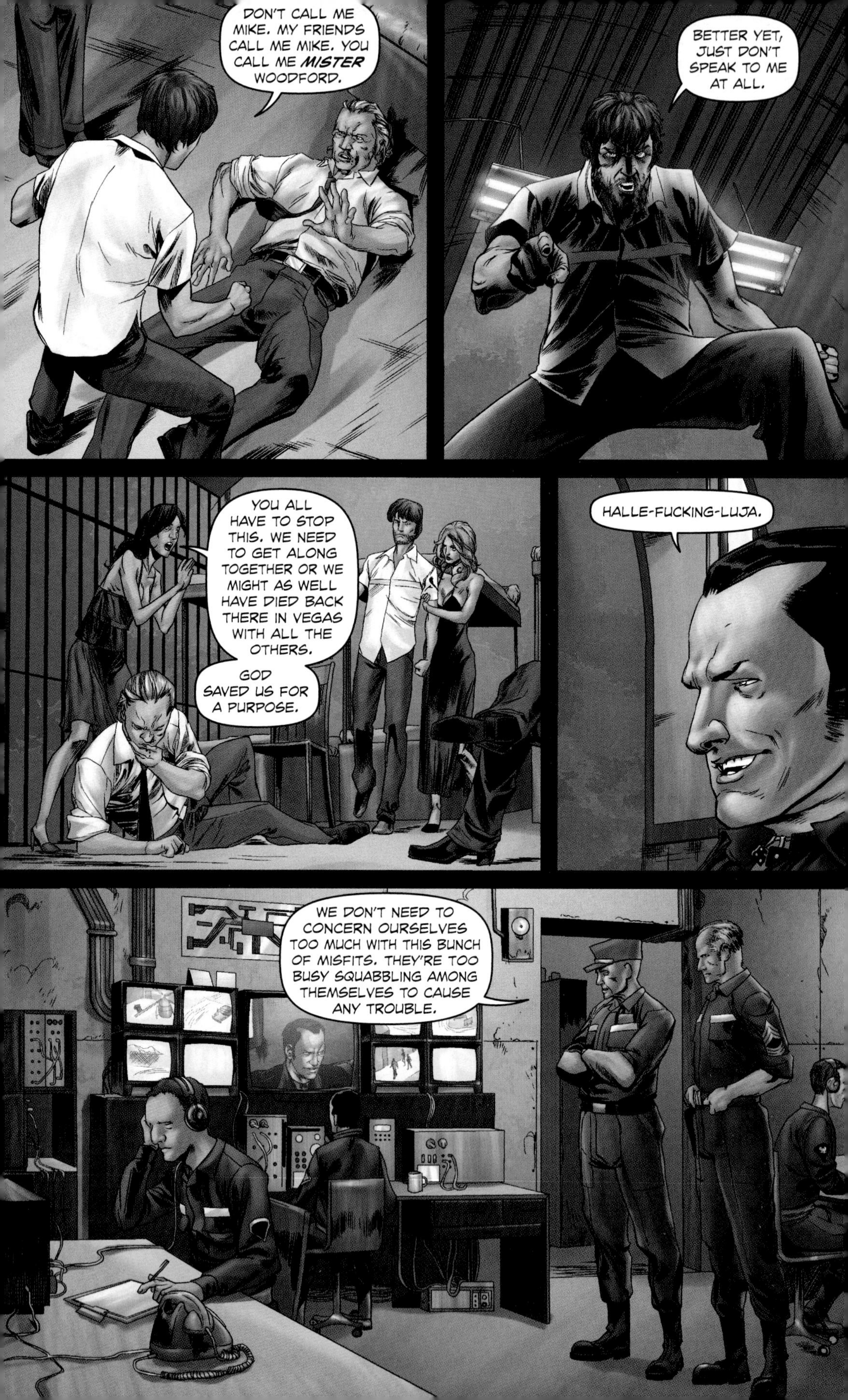
DON'T CALL ME MIKE. MY FRIENDS CALL ME MIKE. YOU CALL ME *MISTER* WOODFORD.
BETTER YET, JUST DON'T SPEAK TO ME AT ALL.
YOU ALL HAVE TO STOP THIS. WE NEED TO GET ALONG TOGETHER OR WE MIGHT AS WELL HAVE DIED BACK THERE IN VEGAS WITH ALL THE OTHERS.
GOD SAVED US FOR A PURPOSE.
HALLE-FUCKING-LUJA.
WE DON'T NEED TO CONCERN OURSELVES TOO MUCH WITH THIS BUNCH OF MISFITS. THEY'RE TOO BUSY SQUABBLING AMONG THEMSELVES TO CAUSE ANY TROUBLE.

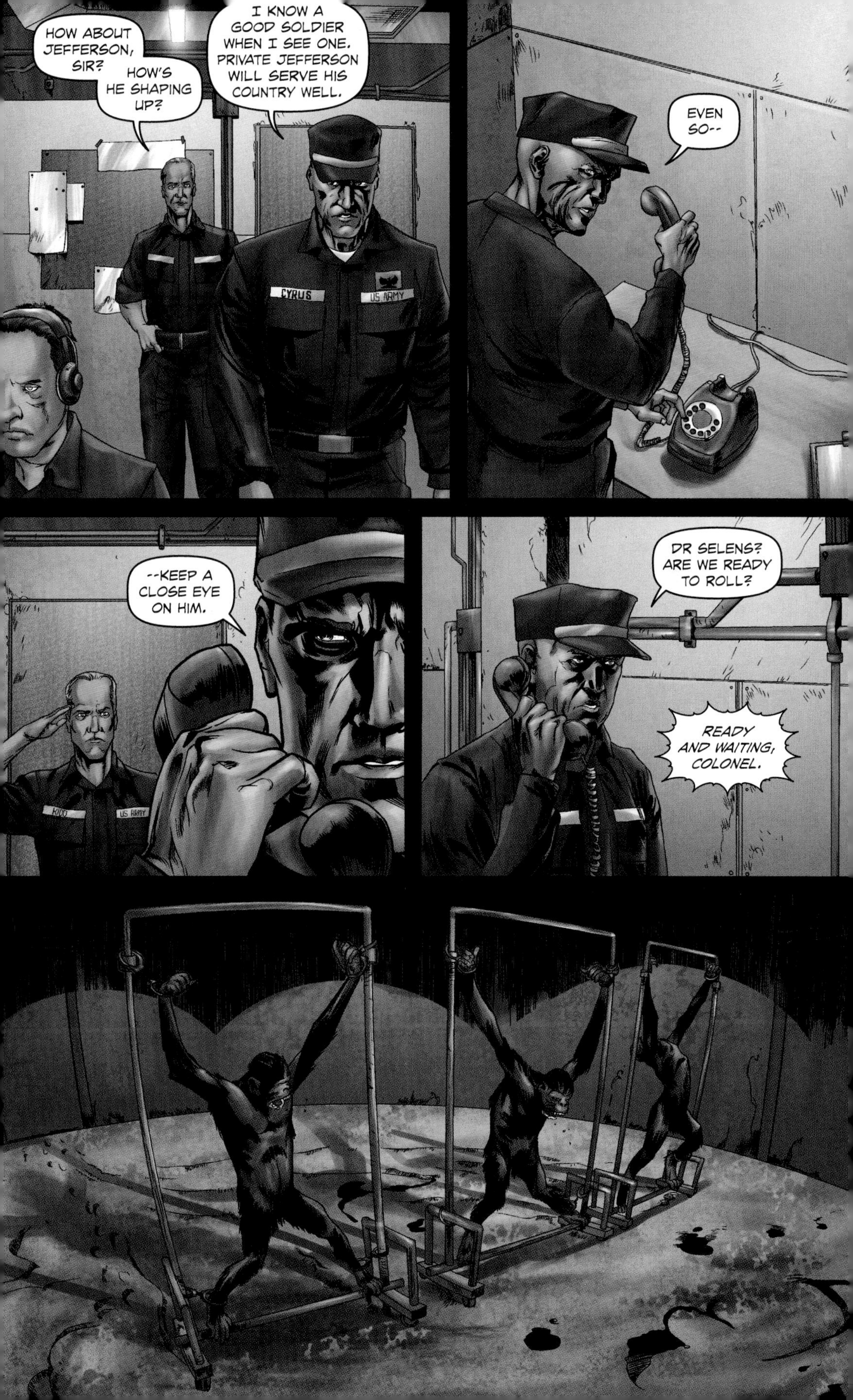
HOW ABOUT JEFFERSON, SIR?
HOW'S HE SHAPING UP?
I KNOW A GOOD SOLDIER WHEN I SEE ONE. PRIVATE JEFFERSON WILL SERVE HIS COUNTRY WELL.
CYRUS
US ARMY
EVEN SO--
--KEEP A CLOSE EYE ON HIM.
KIDD
US ARMY
DR SELENS? ARE WE READY TO ROLL?
READY AND WAITING, COLONEL.

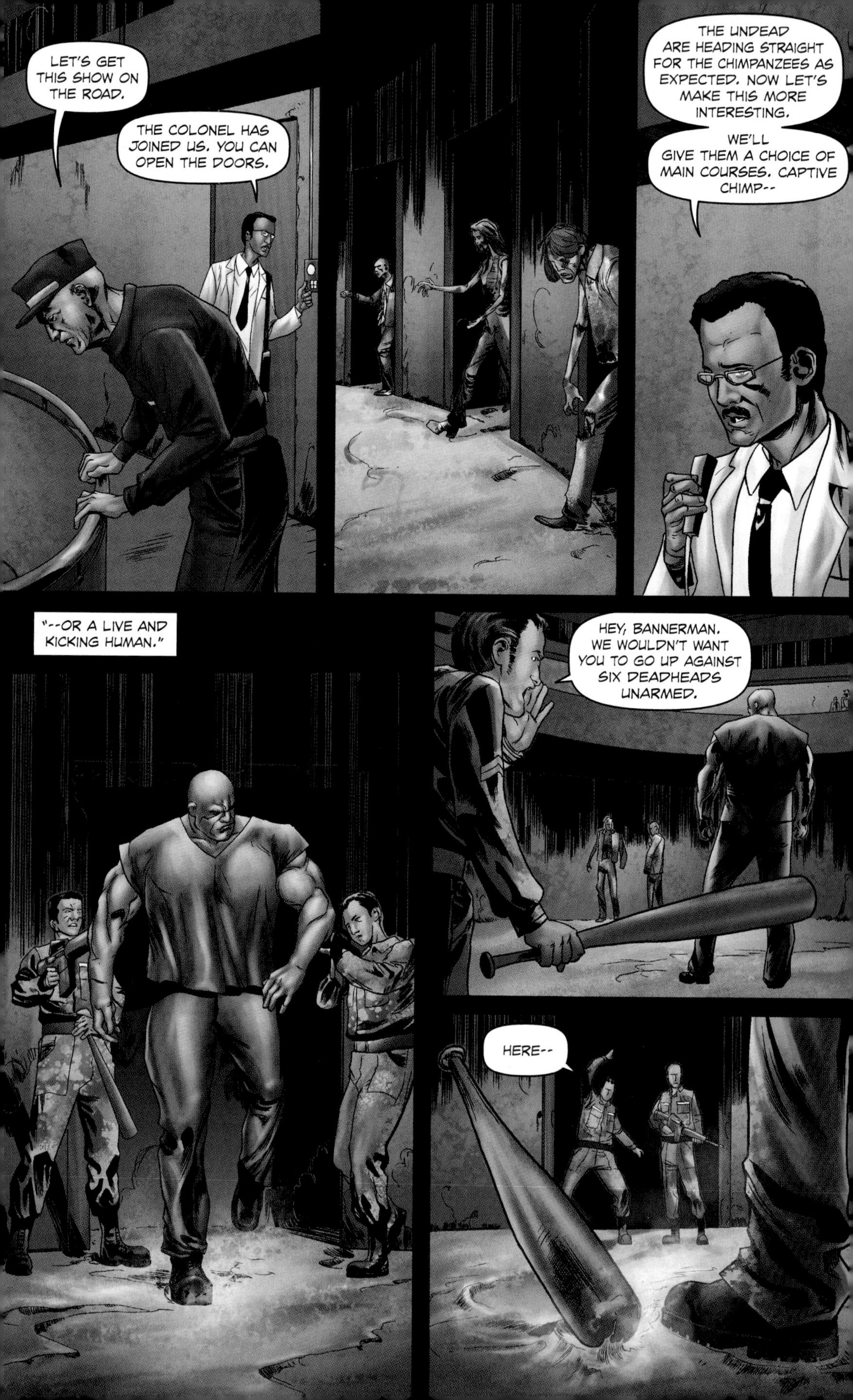
LET'S GET THIS SHOW ON THE ROAD.
THE COLONEL HAS JOINED US. YOU CAN OPEN THE DOORS.
THE UNDEAD ARE HEADING STRAIGHT FOR THE CHIMPANZEES AS EXPECTED. NOW LET'S MAKE THIS MORE INTERESTING.
WE'LL GIVE THEM A CHOICE OF MAIN COURSES. CAPTIVE CHIMP--
"--OR A LIVE AND KICKING HUMAN."
HEY, BANNERMAN. WE WOULDN'T WANT YOU TO GO UP AGAINST SIX DEADHEADS UNARMED.
HERE--

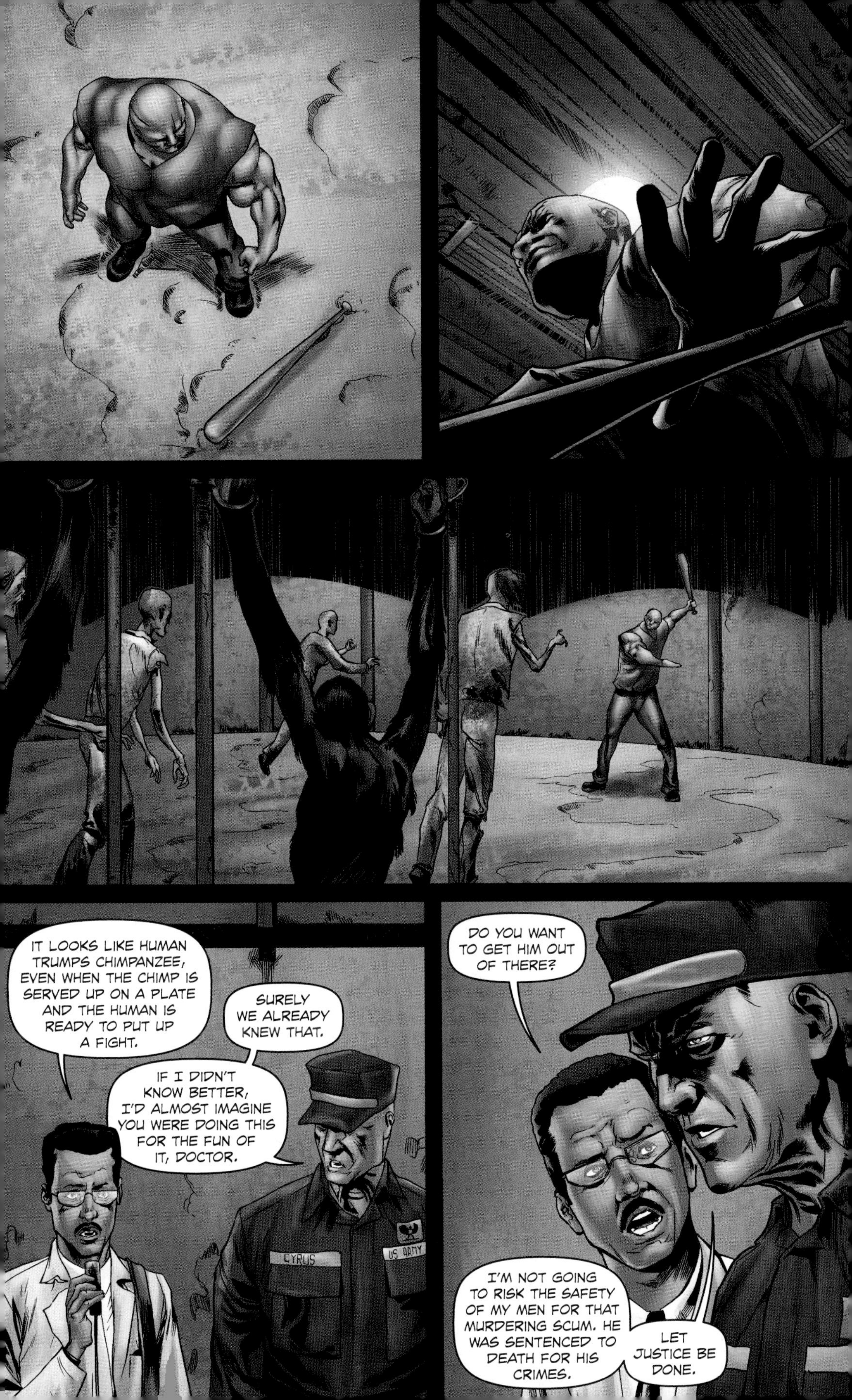
IT LOOKS LIKE HUMAN TRUMPS CHIMPANZEE, EVEN WHEN THE CHIMP IS SERVED UP ON A PLATE AND THE HUMAN IS READY TO PUT UP A FIGHT.
SURELY WE ALREADY KNEW THAT.
IF I DIDN'T KNOW BETTER, I'D ALMOST IMAGINE YOU WERE DOING THIS FOR THE FUN OF IT, DOCTOR.
CYRUS
US ARMY
DO YOU WANT TO GET HIM OUT OF THERE?
I'M NOT GOING TO RISK THE SAFETY OF MY MEN FOR THAT MURDERING SCUM. HE WAS SENTENCED TO DEATH FOR HIS CRIMES.
LET JUSTICE BE DONE.

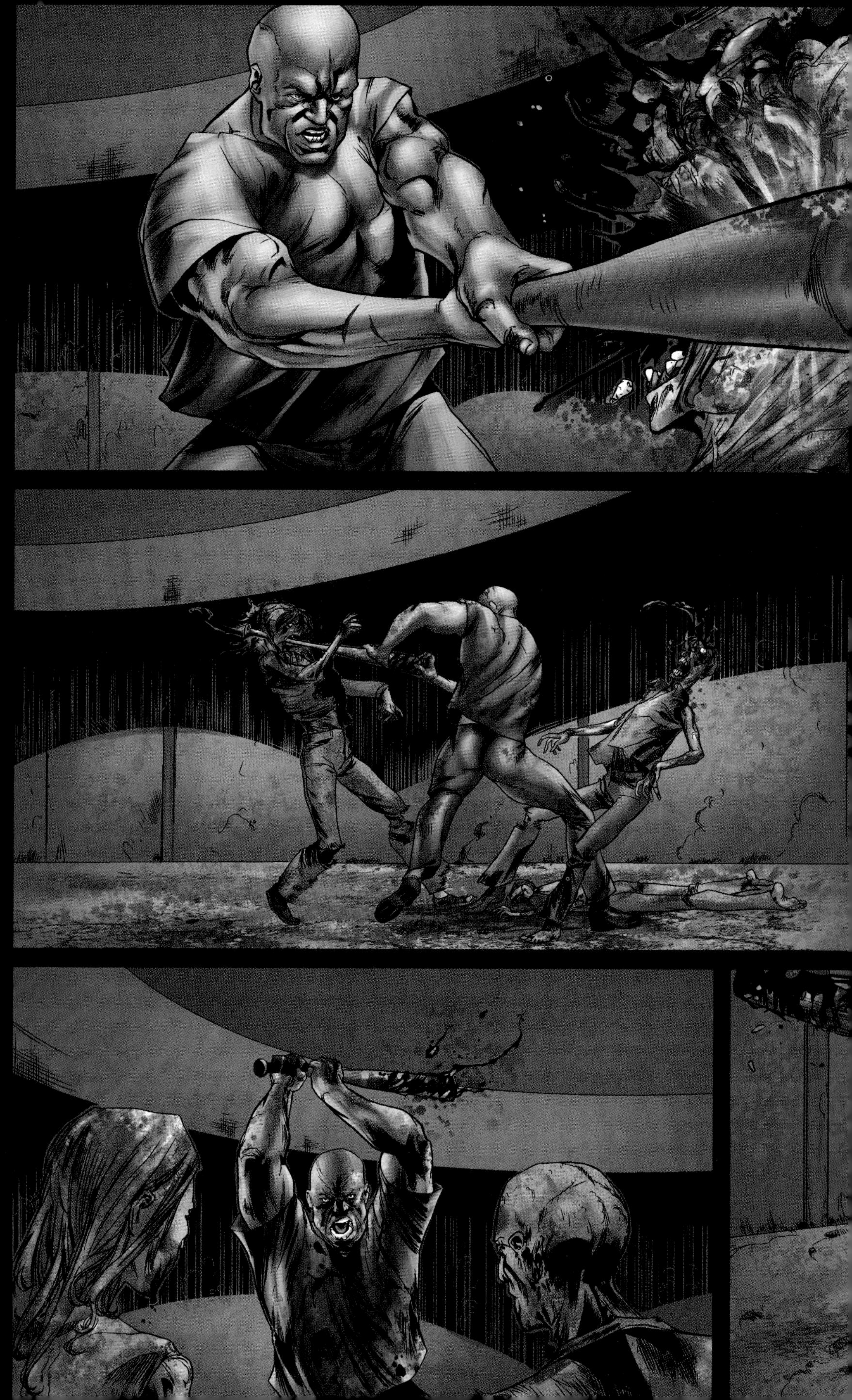

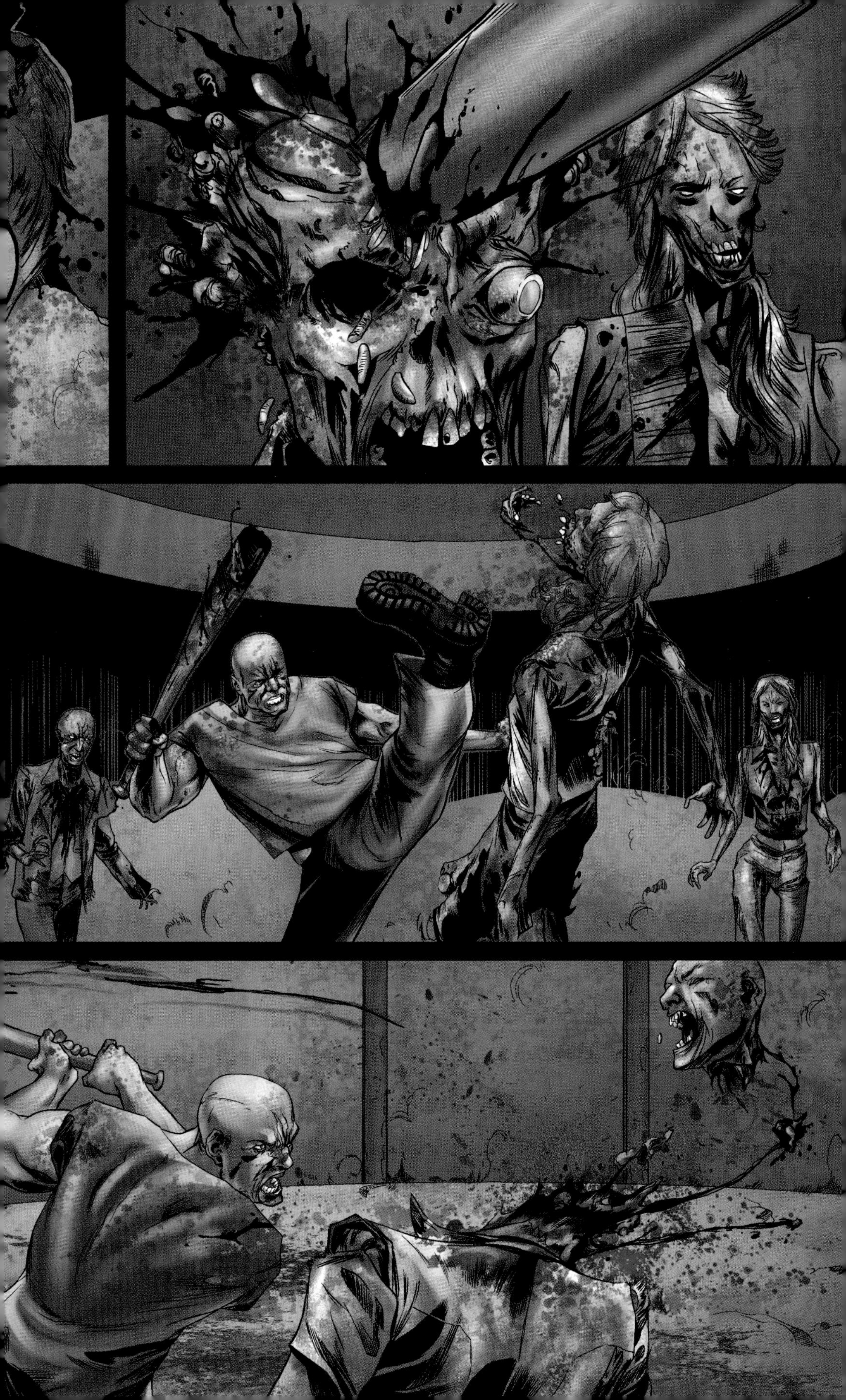

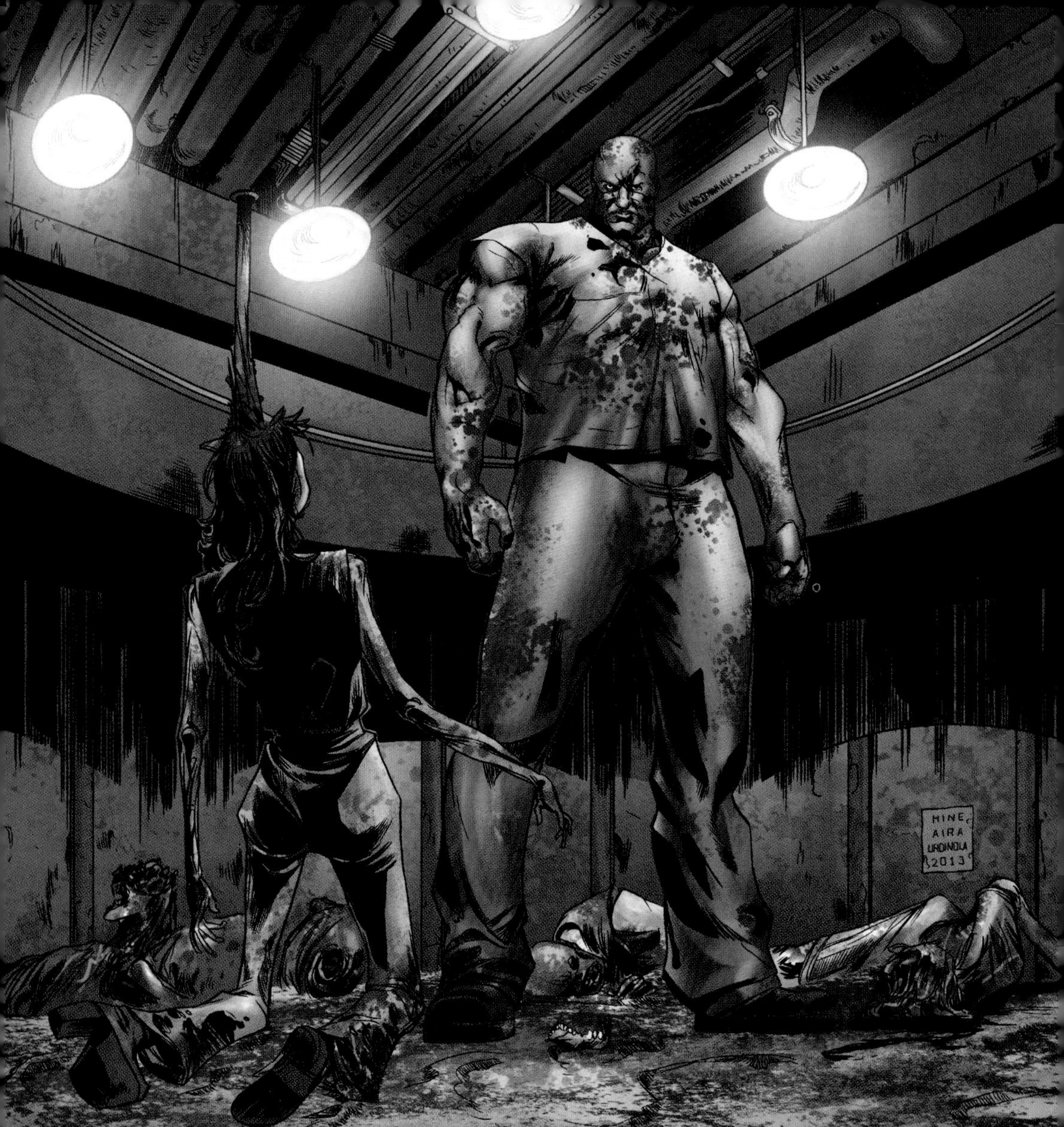
MINE, AIRA URDINOLA 2013

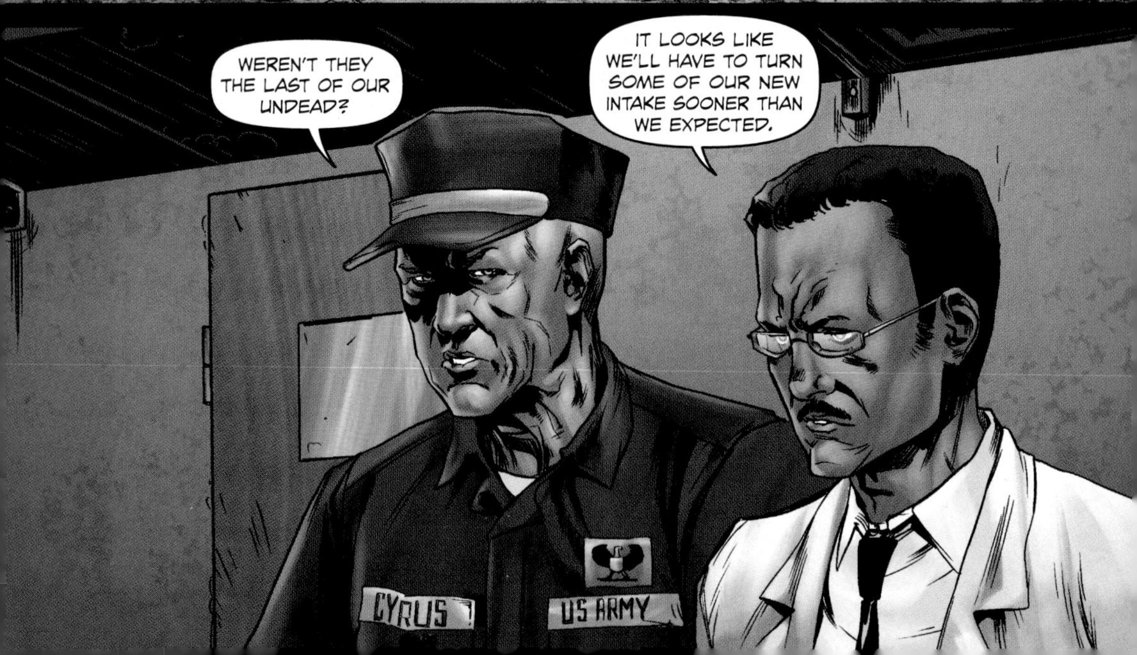
WEREN'T THEY THE LAST OF OUR UNDEAD?
IT LOOKS LIKE WE'LL HAVE TO TURN SOME OF OUR NEW INTAKE SOONER THAN WE EXPECTED.
CYRUS
US ARMY

HUNGRY FOR THE FLESH OF THE LIVIN

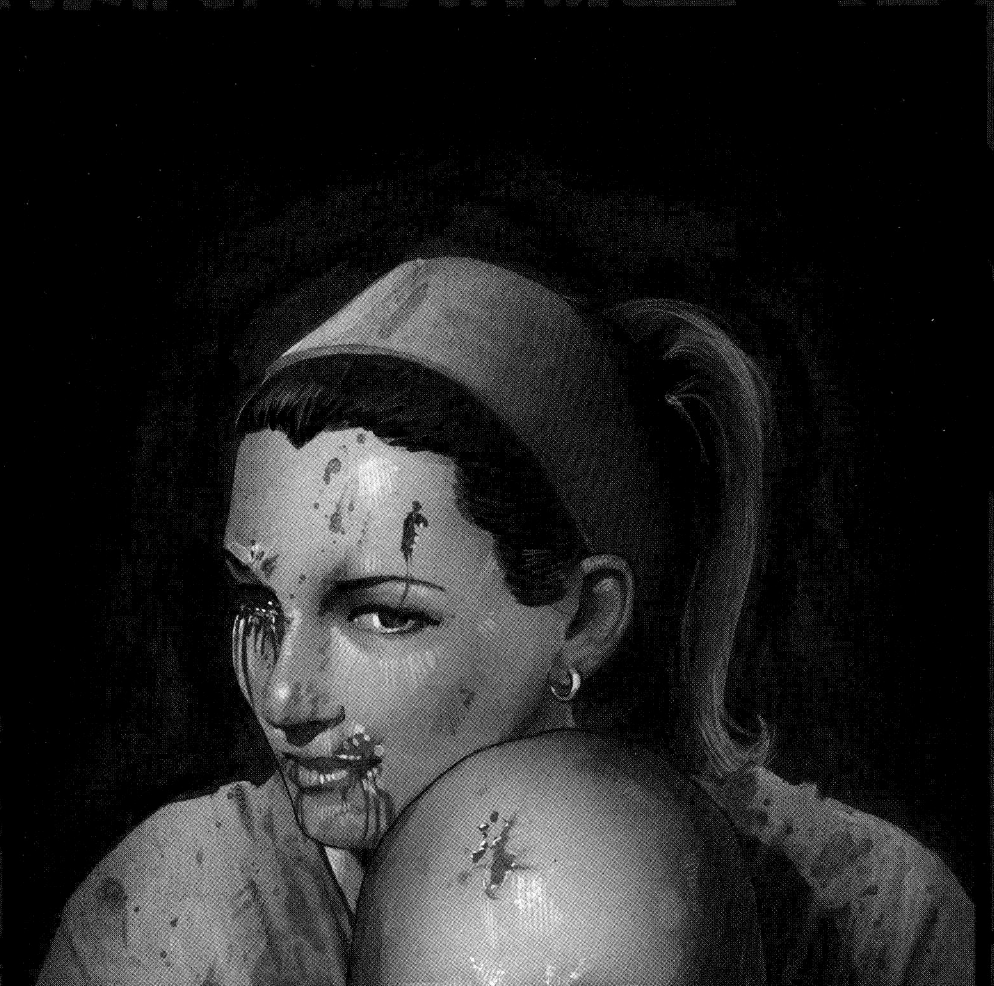

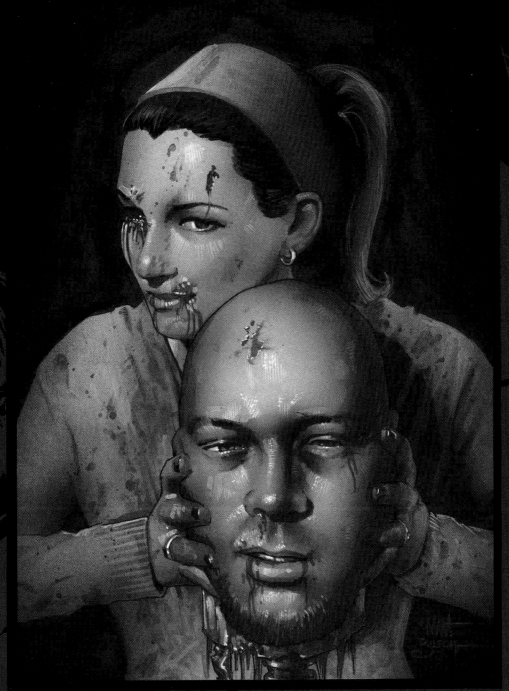

CHAPTER 3

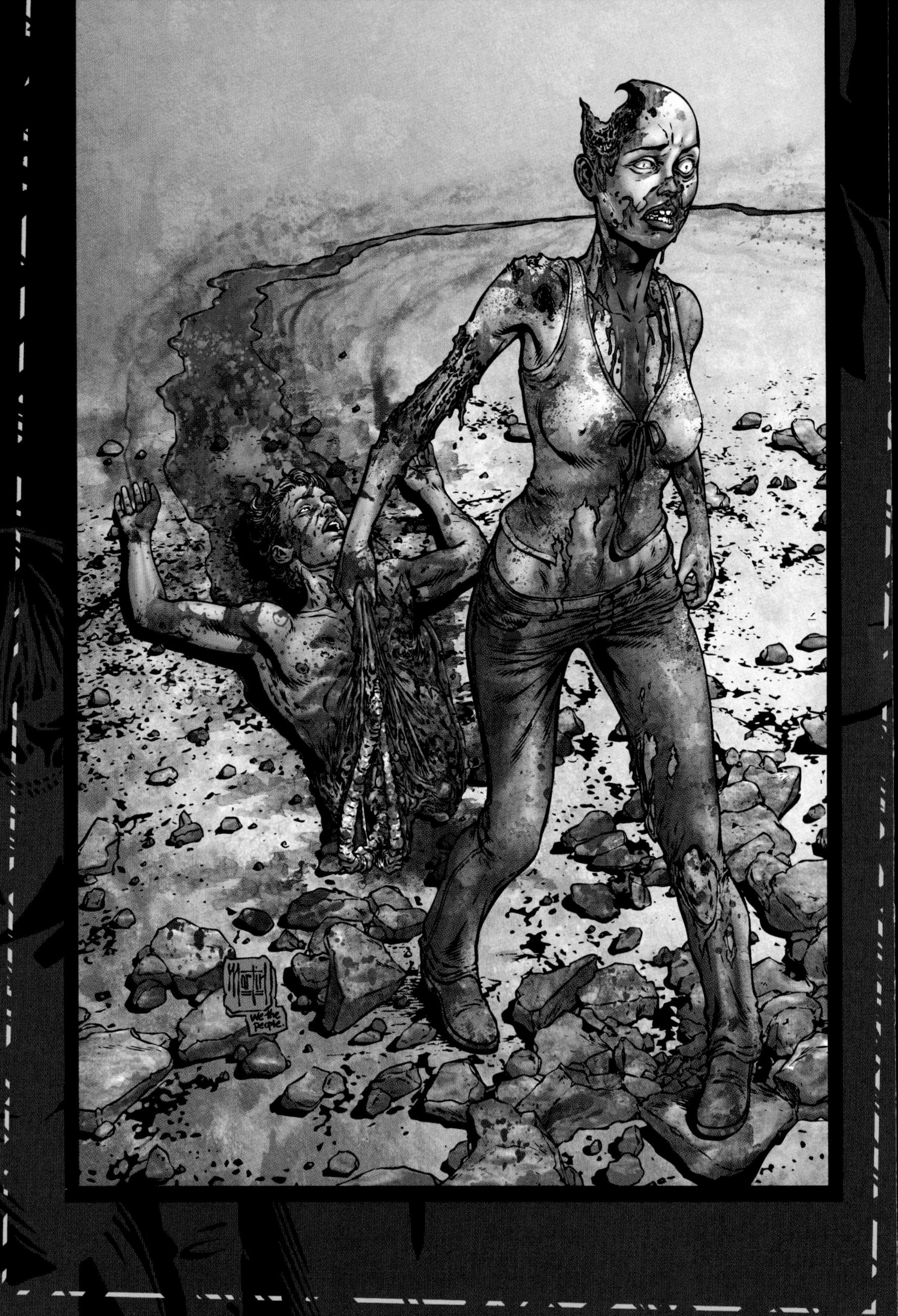
we the people.

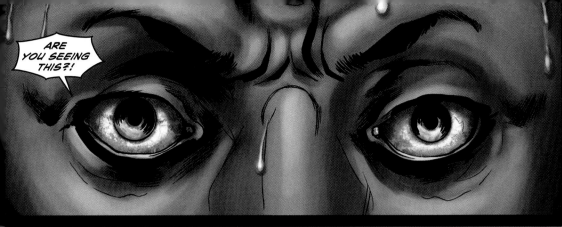

ARE YOU SEEING THIS?!

HOLD YOUR FIRE. WE DON'T WANT THEM DAMAGED.

GODDAMMIT! THERE MUST BE THIRTY OF THEM!

MORE. LOOK BEHIND YOU.

OH SHIT!

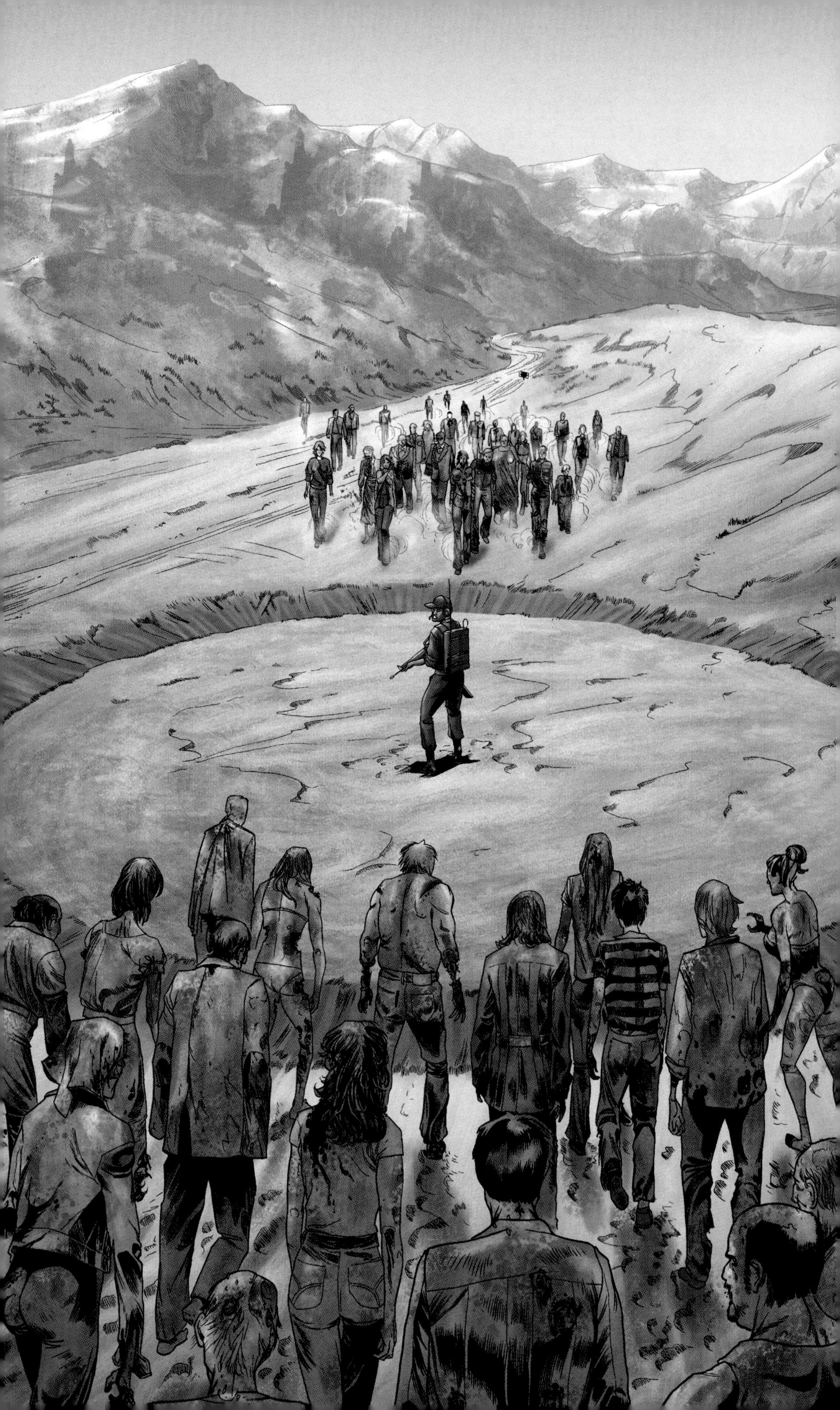

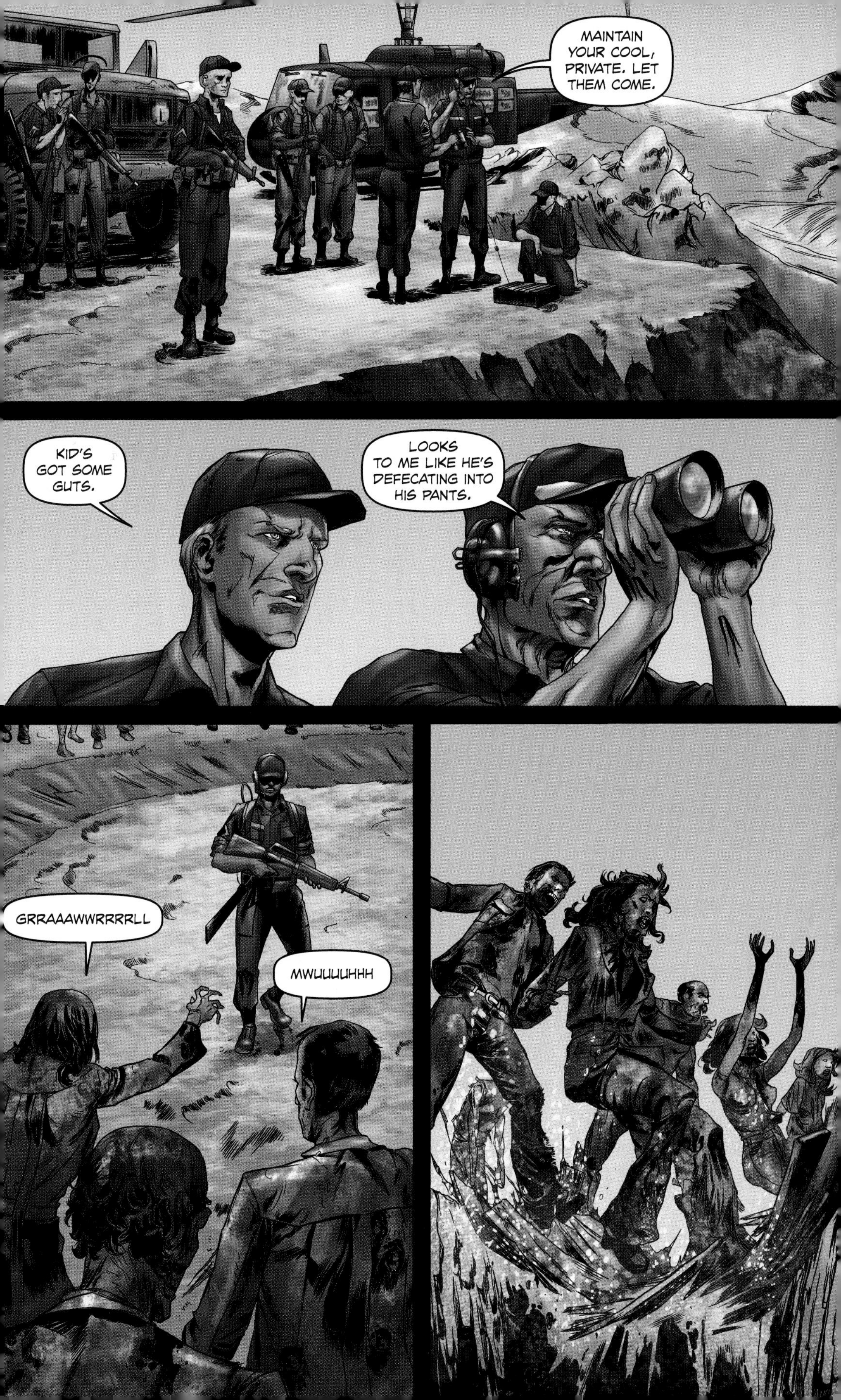
MAINTAIN YOUR COOL, PRIVATE. LET THEM COME.
KID'S GOT SOME GUTS.
LOOKS TO ME LIKE HE'S DEFECATING INTO HIS PANTS.
GRRAAAWWRRRRLL
MWUUUUHHH

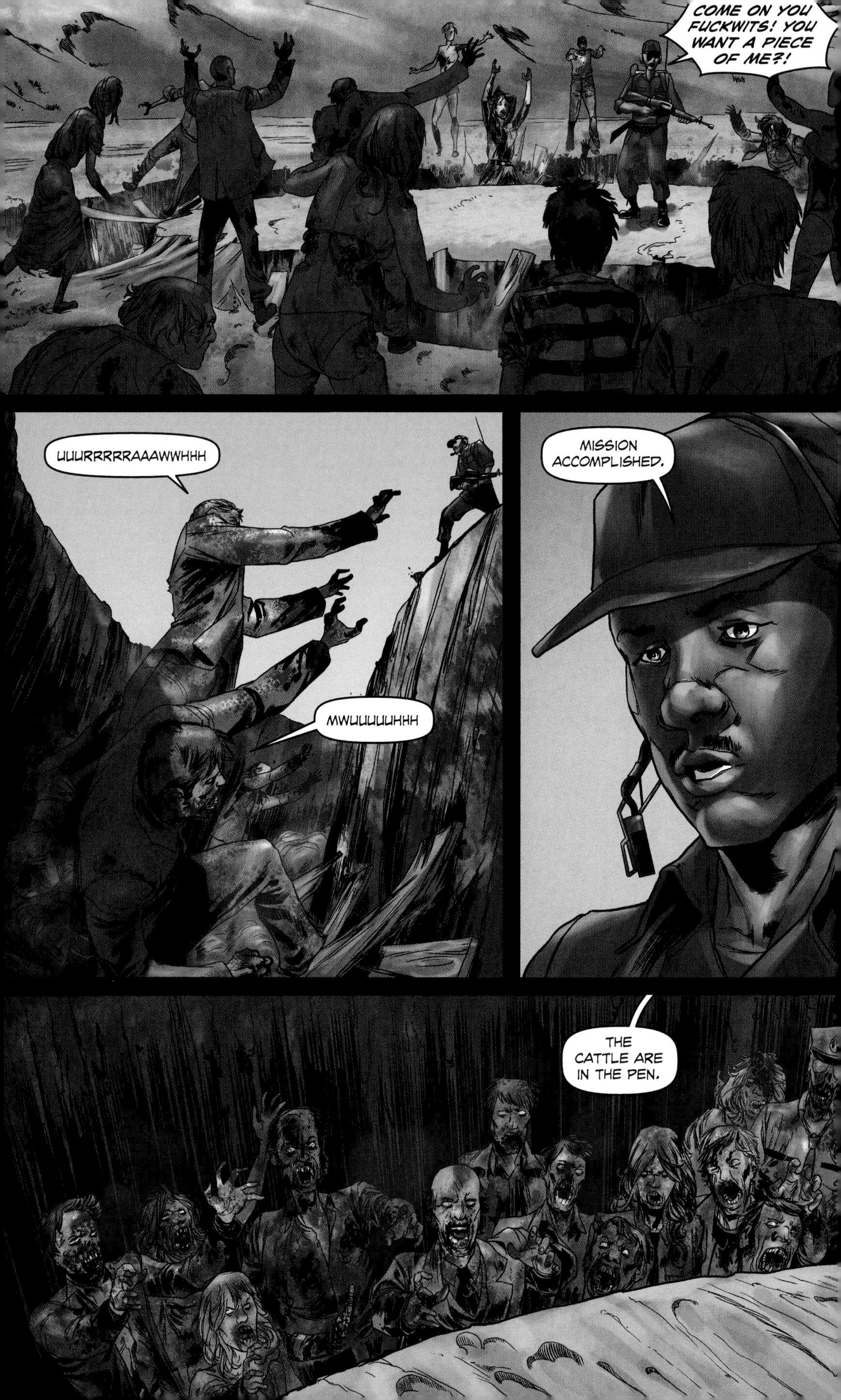
COME ON YOU FUCKWITS! YOU WANT A PIECE OF ME?!
UUURRRRRAAAWWHHH
MWUUUUUHHH
MISSION ACCOMPLISHED.
THE CATTLE ARE IN THE PEN.

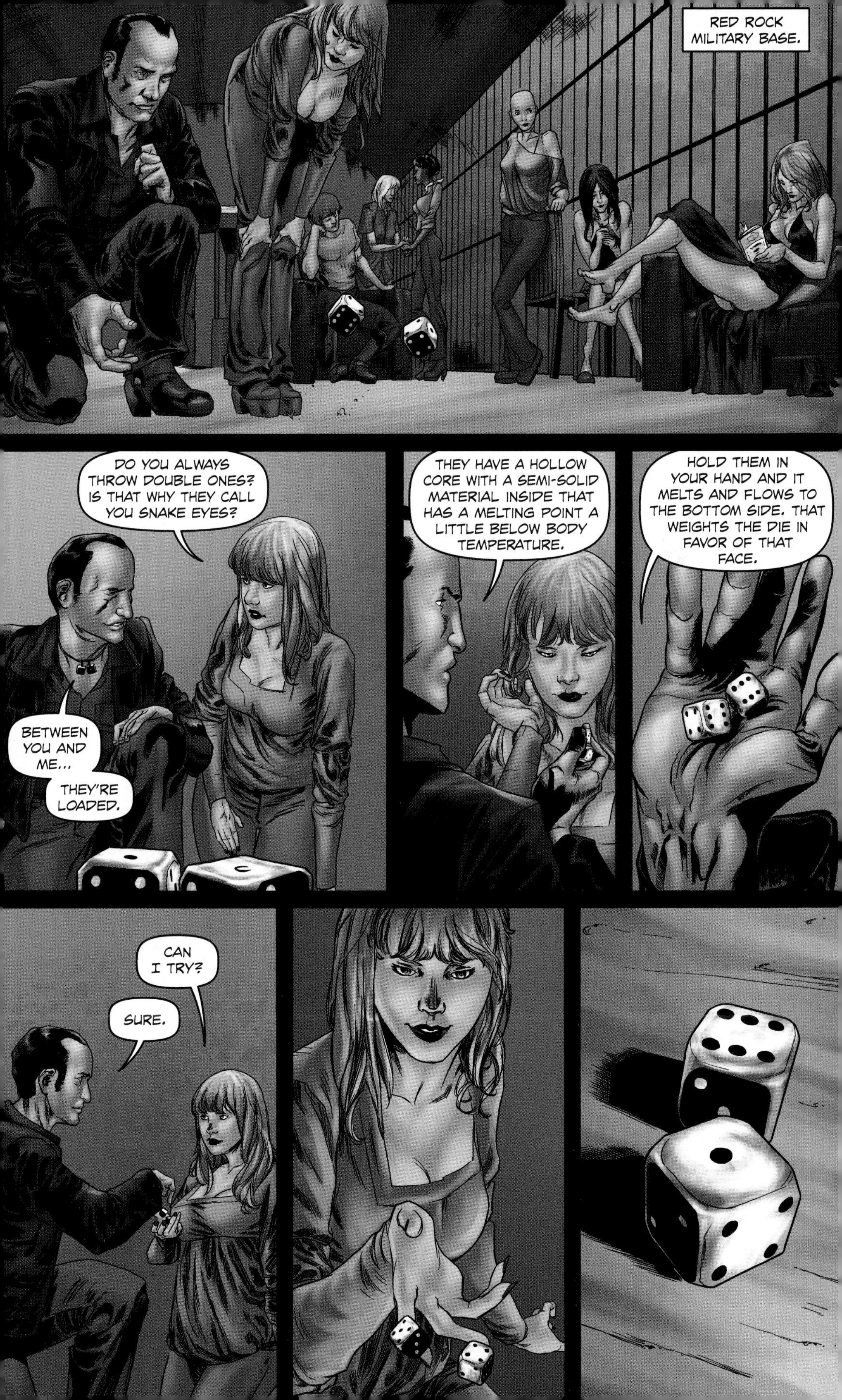
RED ROCK MILITARY BASE.
DO YOU ALWAYS THROW DOUBLE ONES? IS THAT WHY THEY CALL YOU SNAKE EYES?
BETWEEN YOU AND ME...
THEY'RE LOADED.
THEY HAVE A HOLLOW CORE WITH A SEMI-SOLID MATERIAL INSIDE THAT HAS A MELTING POINT A LITTLE BELOW BODY TEMPERATURE.
HOLD THEM IN YOUR HAND AND IT MELTS AND FLOWS TO THE BOTTOM SIDE. THAT WEIGHTS THE DIE IN FAVOR OF THAT FACE.
CAN I TRY?
SURE.

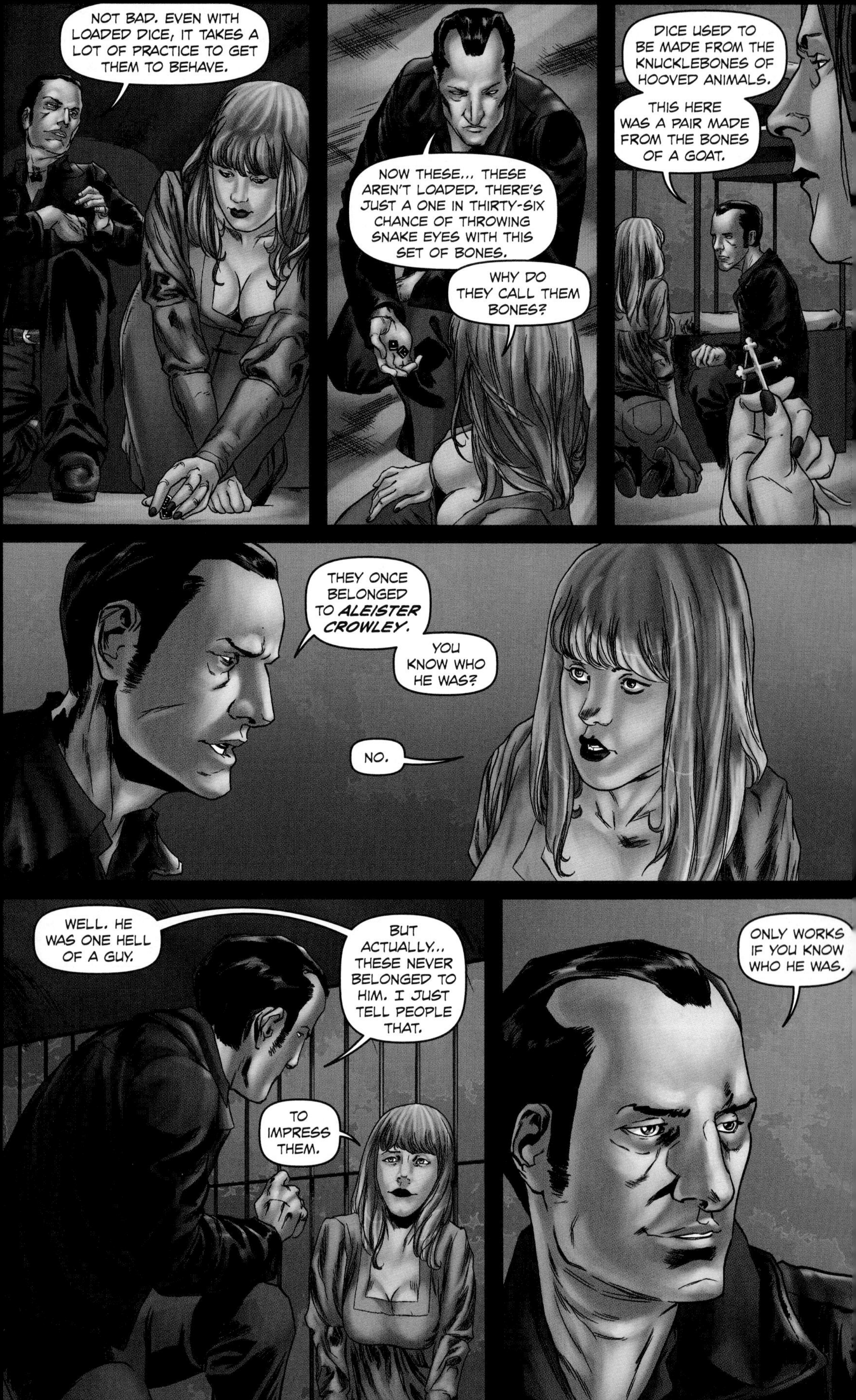
NOT BAD. EVEN WITH LOADED DICE, IT TAKES A LOT OF PRACTICE TO GET THEM TO BEHAVE.
NOW THESE... THESE AREN'T LOADED. THERE'S JUST A ONE IN THIRTY-SIX CHANCE OF THROWING SNAKE EYES WITH THIS SET OF BONES.
WHY DO THEY CALL THEM BONES?
DICE USED TO BE MADE FROM THE KNUCKLEBONES OF HOOVED ANIMALS.
THIS HERE WAS A PAIR MADE FROM THE BONES OF A GOAT.
THEY ONCE BELONGED TO *ALEISTER CROWLEY*.
YOU KNOW WHO HE WAS?
NO.
WELL. HE WAS ONE HELL OF A GUY.
BUT ACTUALLY... THESE NEVER BELONGED TO HIM. I JUST TELL PEOPLE THAT.
TO IMPRESS THEM.
ONLY WORKS IF YOU KNOW WHO HE WAS.

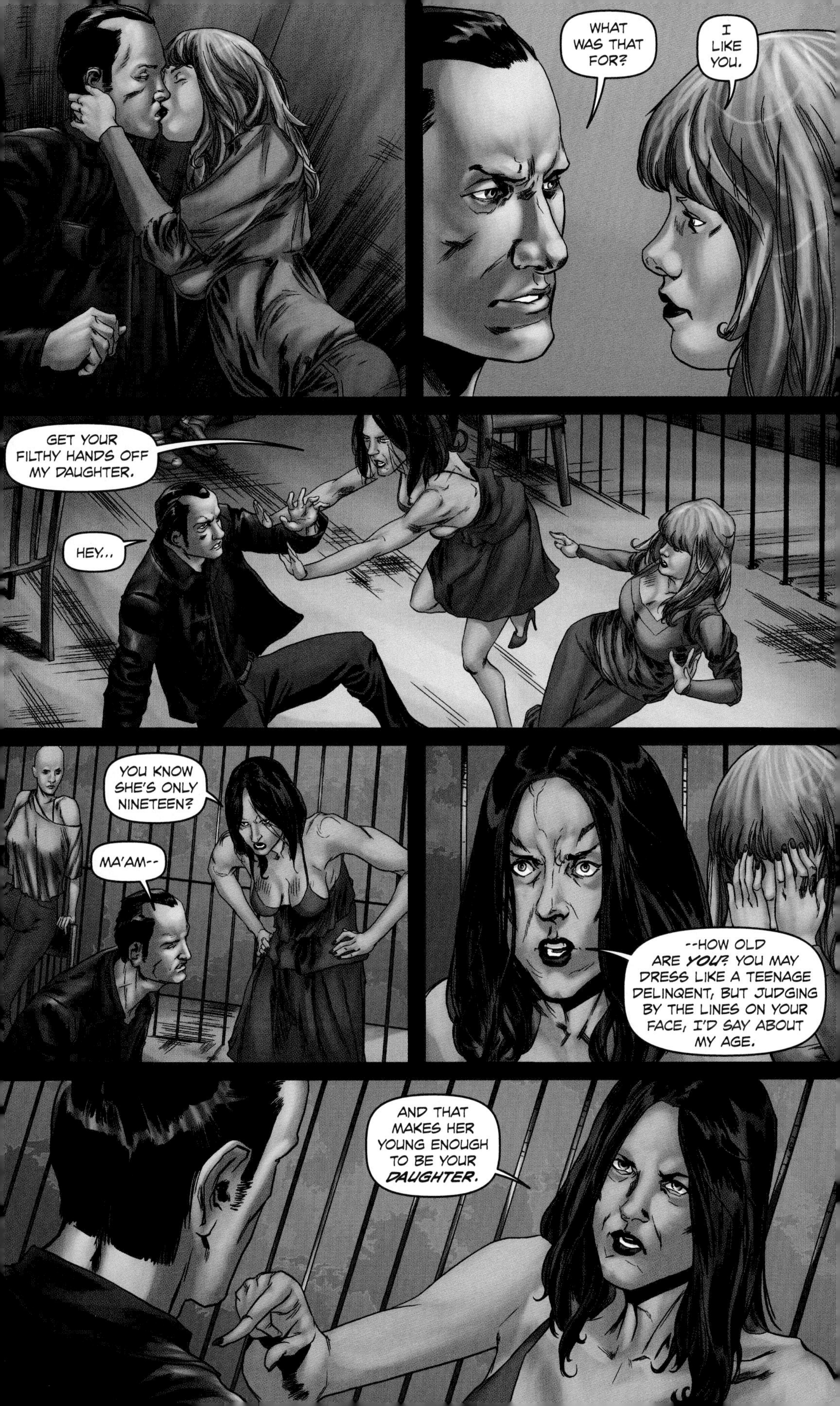
WHAT WAS THAT FOR?
I LIKE YOU.
GET YOUR FILTHY HANDS OFF MY DAUGHTER.
HEY...
YOU KNOW SHE'S ONLY NINETEEN?
MA'AM--
--HOW OLD ARE YOU? YOU MAY DRESS LIKE A TEENAGE DELINQENT, BUT JUDGING BY THE LINES ON YOUR FACE, I'D SAY ABOUT MY AGE.
AND THAT MAKES HER YOUNG ENOUGH TO BE YOUR DAUGHTER.

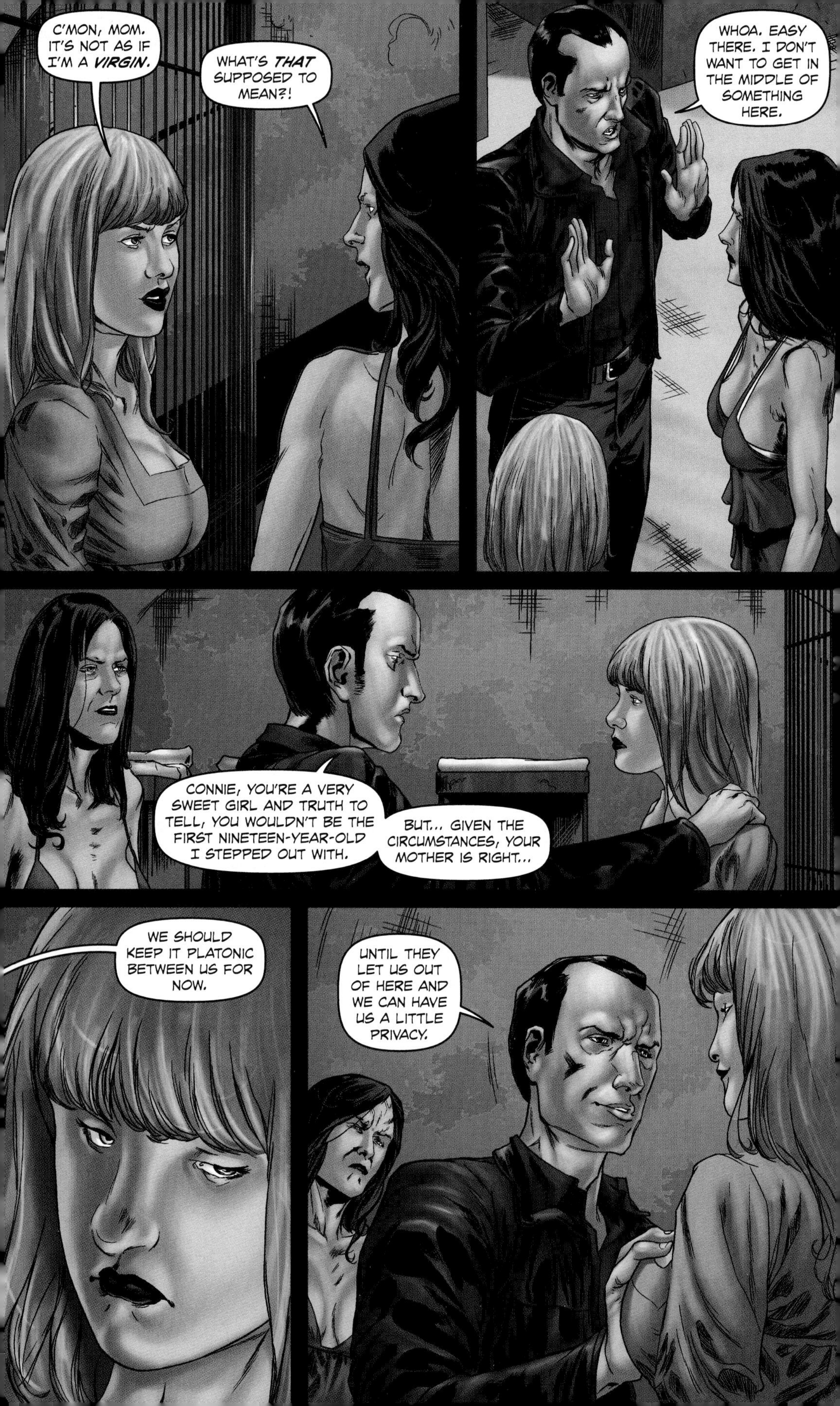

C'MON, MOM. IT'S NOT AS IF I'M A *VIRGIN.*
WHAT'S *THAT* SUPPOSED TO MEAN?!
WHOA. EASY THERE. I DON'T WANT TO GET IN THE MIDDLE OF SOMETHING HERE.
CONNIE, YOU'RE A VERY SWEET GIRL AND TRUTH TO TELL, YOU WOULDN'T BE THE FIRST NINETEEN-YEAR-OLD I STEPPED OUT WITH.
BUT... GIVEN THE CIRCUMSTANCES, YOUR MOTHER IS RIGHT...
WE SHOULD KEEP IT PLATONIC BETWEEN US FOR NOW.
UNTIL THEY LET US OUT OF HERE AND WE CAN HAVE US A LITTLE PRIVACY.

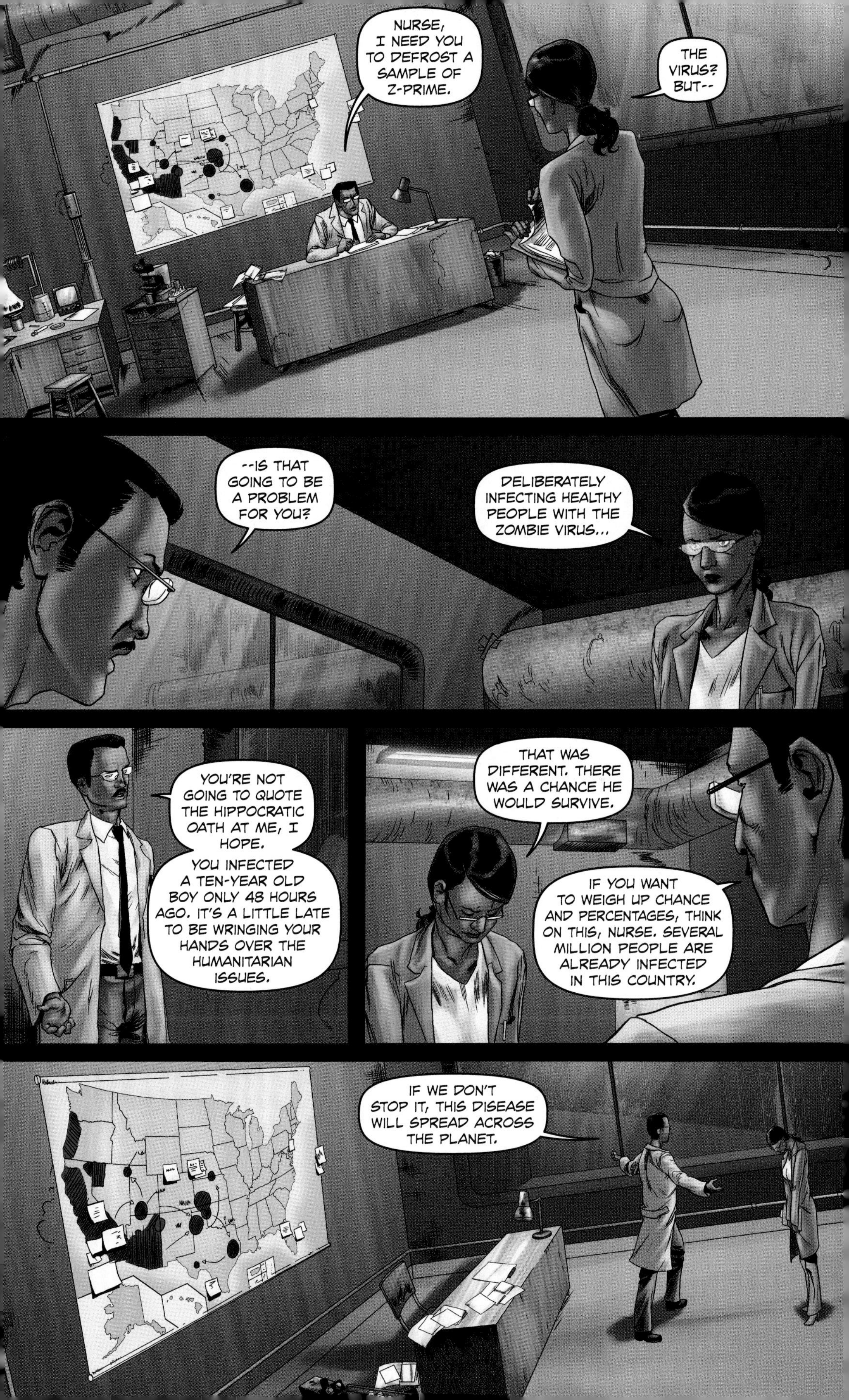
NURSE, I NEED YOU TO DEFROST A SAMPLE OF Z-PRIME.
THE VIRUS? BUT--
--IS THAT GOING TO BE A PROBLEM FOR YOU?
DELIBERATELY INFECTING HEALTHY PEOPLE WITH THE ZOMBIE VIRUS...
YOU'RE NOT GOING TO QUOTE THE HIPPOCRATIC OATH AT ME, I HOPE.
YOU INFECTED A TEN-YEAR OLD BOY ONLY 48 HOURS AGO. IT'S A LITTLE LATE TO BE WRINGING YOUR HANDS OVER THE HUMANITARIAN ISSUES.
THAT WAS DIFFERENT. THERE WAS A CHANCE HE WOULD SURVIVE.
IF YOU WANT TO WEIGH UP CHANCE AND PERCENTAGES, THINK ON THIS, NURSE. SEVERAL MILLION PEOPLE ARE ALREADY INFECTED IN THIS COUNTRY.
IF WE DON'T STOP IT, THIS DISEASE WILL SPREAD ACROSS THE PLANET.

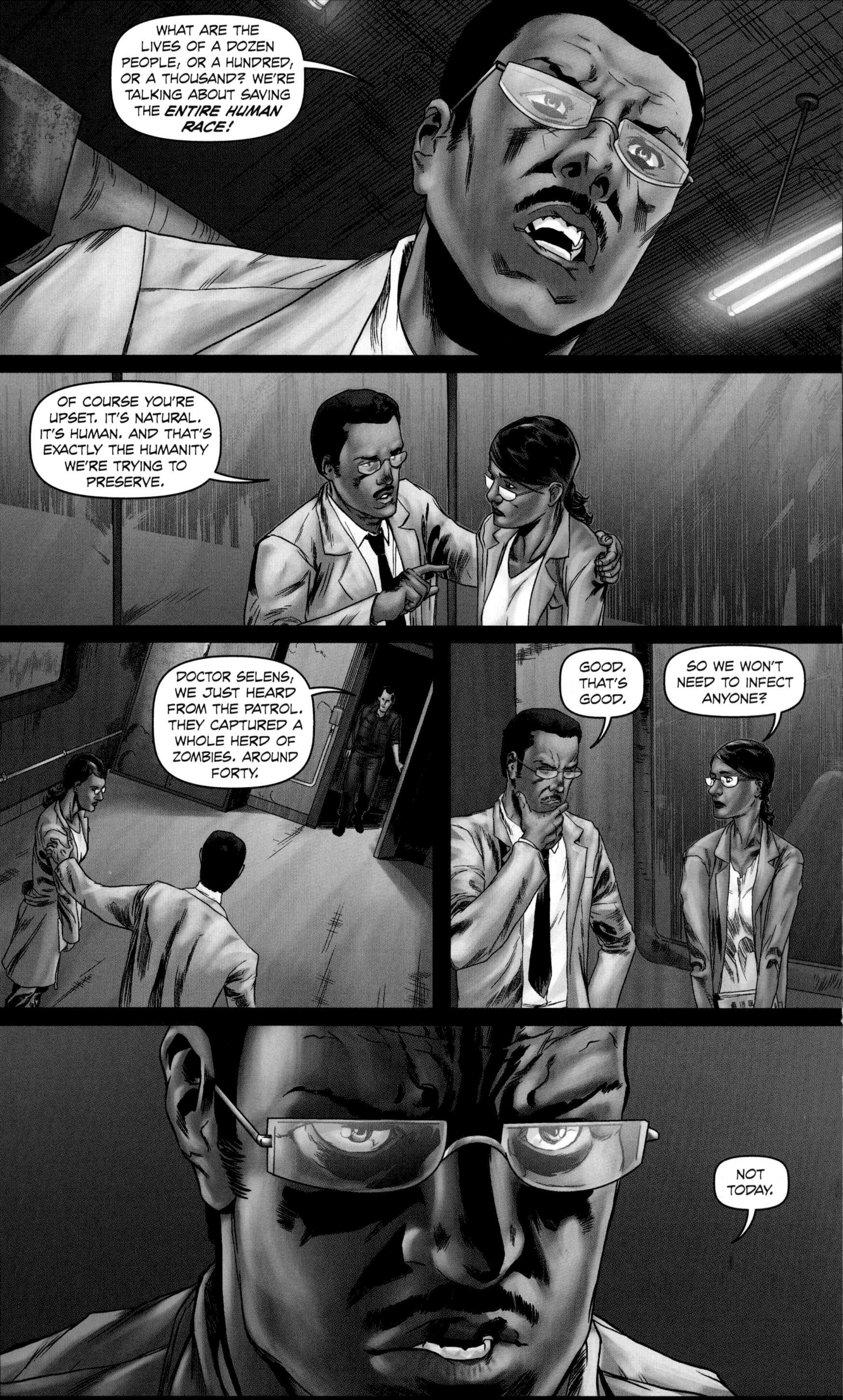
WHAT ARE THE LIVES OF A DOZEN PEOPLE, OR A HUNDRED, OR A THOUSAND? WE'RE TALKING ABOUT SAVING THE ENTIRE HUMAN RACE!
OF COURSE YOU'RE UPSET. IT'S NATURAL. IT'S HUMAN. AND THAT'S EXACTLY THE HUMANITY WE'RE TRYING TO PRESERVE.
DOCTOR SELENS, WE JUST HEARD FROM THE PATROL. THEY CAPTURED A WHOLE HERD OF ZOMBIES. AROUND FORTY.
GOOD. THAT'S GOOD.
SO WE WON'T NEED TO INFECT ANYONE?
NOT TODAY.

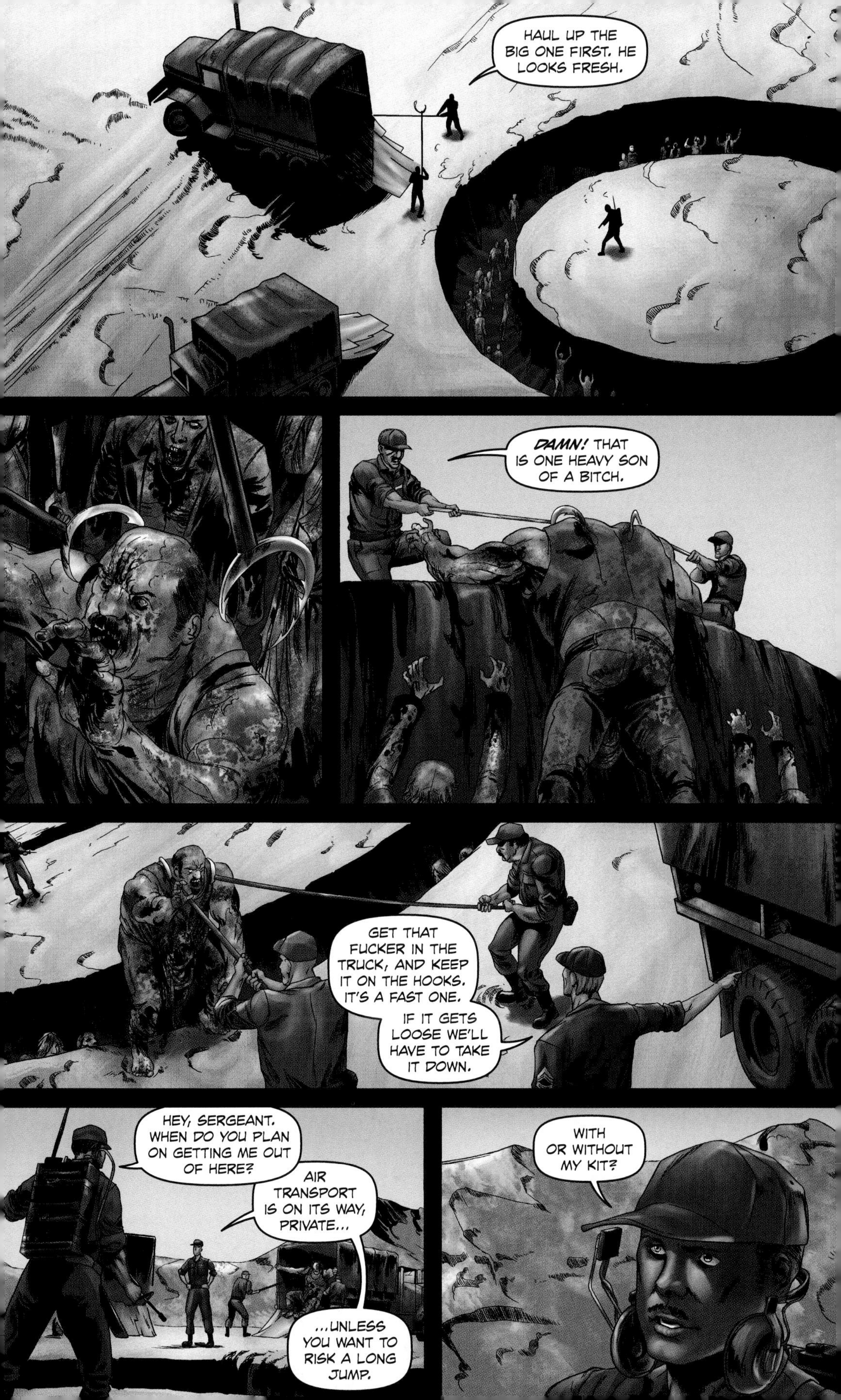
HAUL UP THE BIG ONE FIRST. HE LOOKS FRESH.
DAMN! THAT IS ONE HEAVY SON OF A BITCH.
GET THAT FUCKER IN THE TRUCK, AND KEEP IT ON THE HOOKS. IT'S A FAST ONE.
IF IT GETS LOOSE WE'LL HAVE TO TAKE IT DOWN.
HEY, SERGEANT. WHEN DO YOU PLAN ON GETTING ME OUT OF HERE?
AIR TRANSPORT IS ON ITS WAY, PRIVATE...
...UNLESS YOU WANT TO RISK A LONG JUMP.
WITH OR WITHOUT MY KIT?

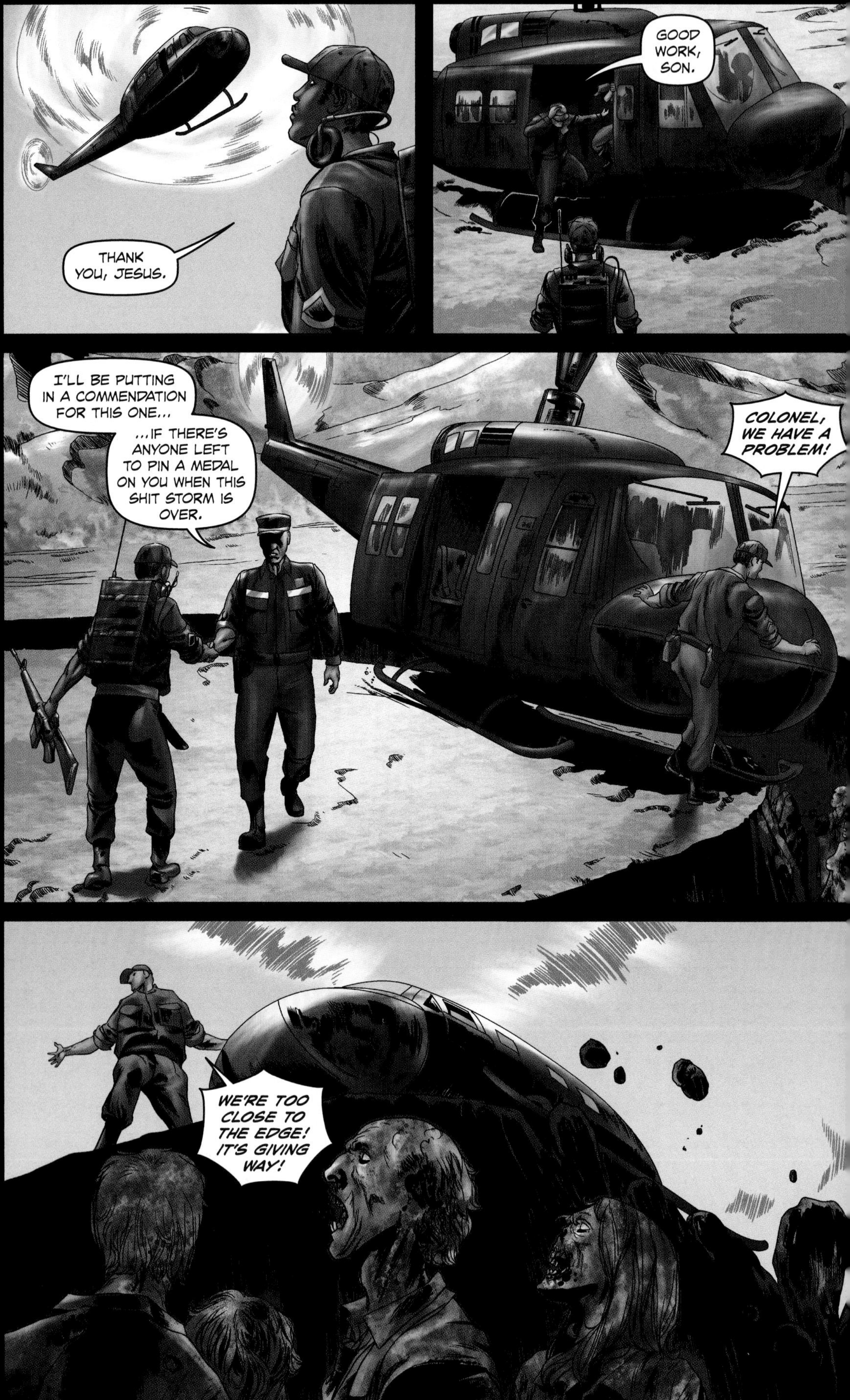
THANK YOU, JESUS.
GOOD WORK, SON.
I'LL BE PUTTING IN A COMMENDATION FOR THIS ONE...
...IF THERE'S ANYONE LEFT TO PIN A MEDAL ON YOU WHEN THIS SHIT STORM IS OVER.
COLONEL, WE HAVE A PROBLEM!
WE'RE TOO CLOSE TO THE EDGE! IT'S GIVING WAY!

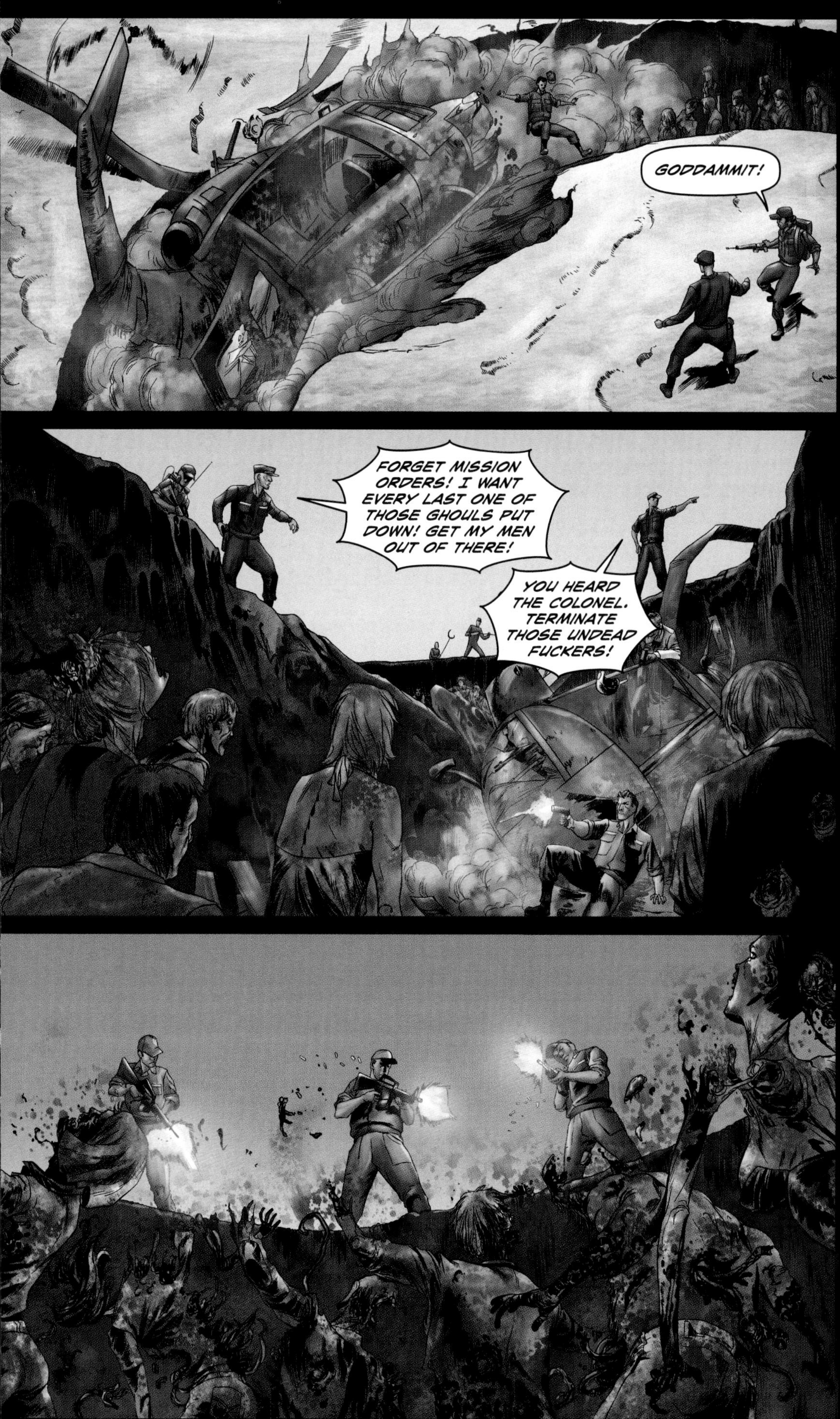
GODDAMMIT!
FORGET MISSION ORDERS! I WANT EVERY LAST ONE OF THOSE GHOULS PUT DOWN! GET MY MEN OUT OF THERE!
YOU HEARD THE COLONEL. TERMINATE THOSE UNDEAD FUCKERS!

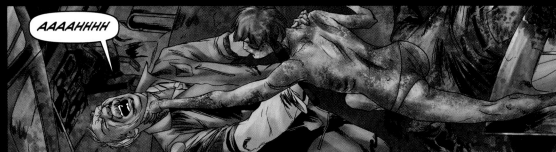

AAAAHHHH

NOOOO!

AIEEEEEE

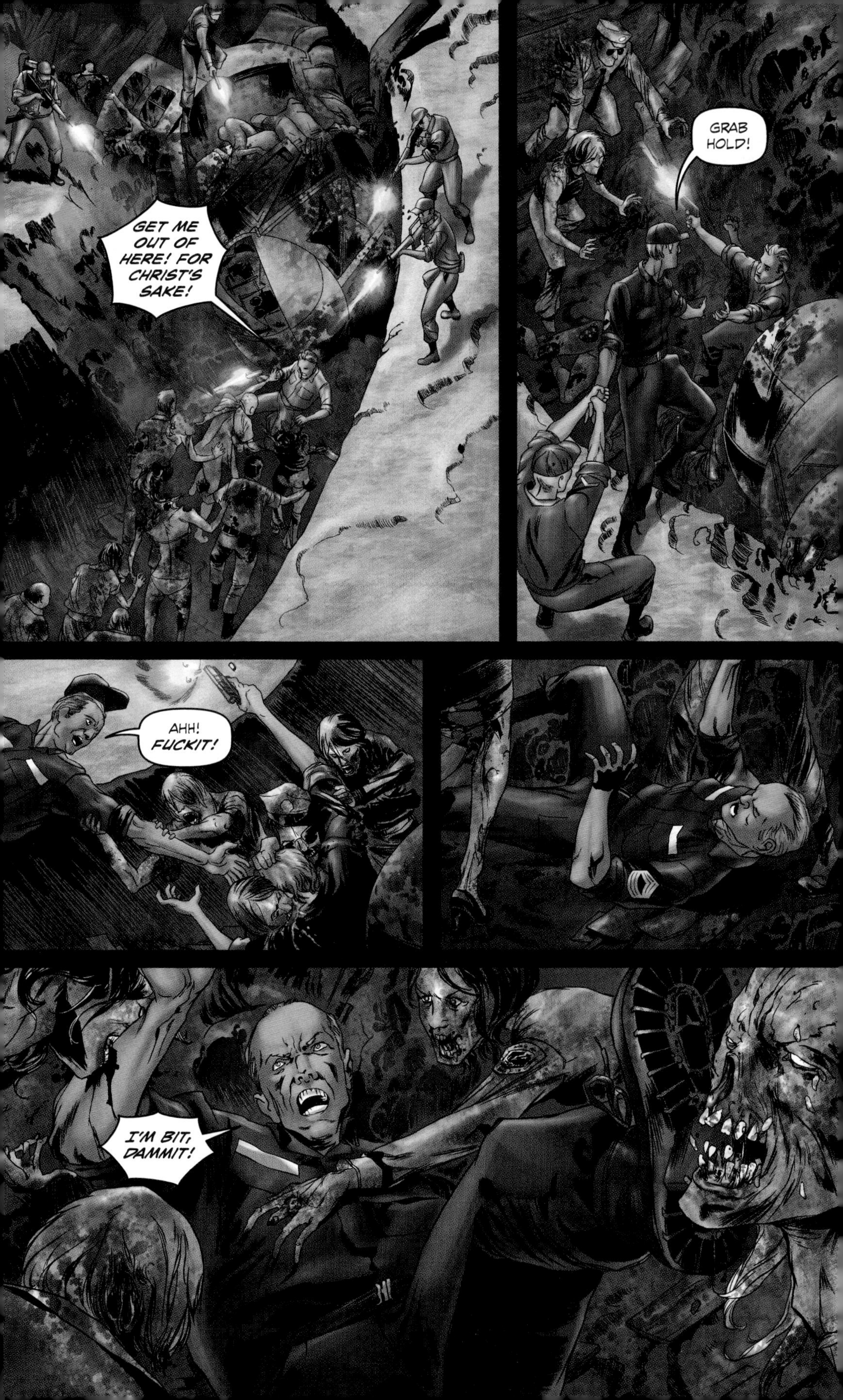
GET ME OUT OF HERE! FOR CHRIST'S SAKE!
GRAB HOLD!
AHH! FUCKIT!
I'M BIT, DAMMIT!

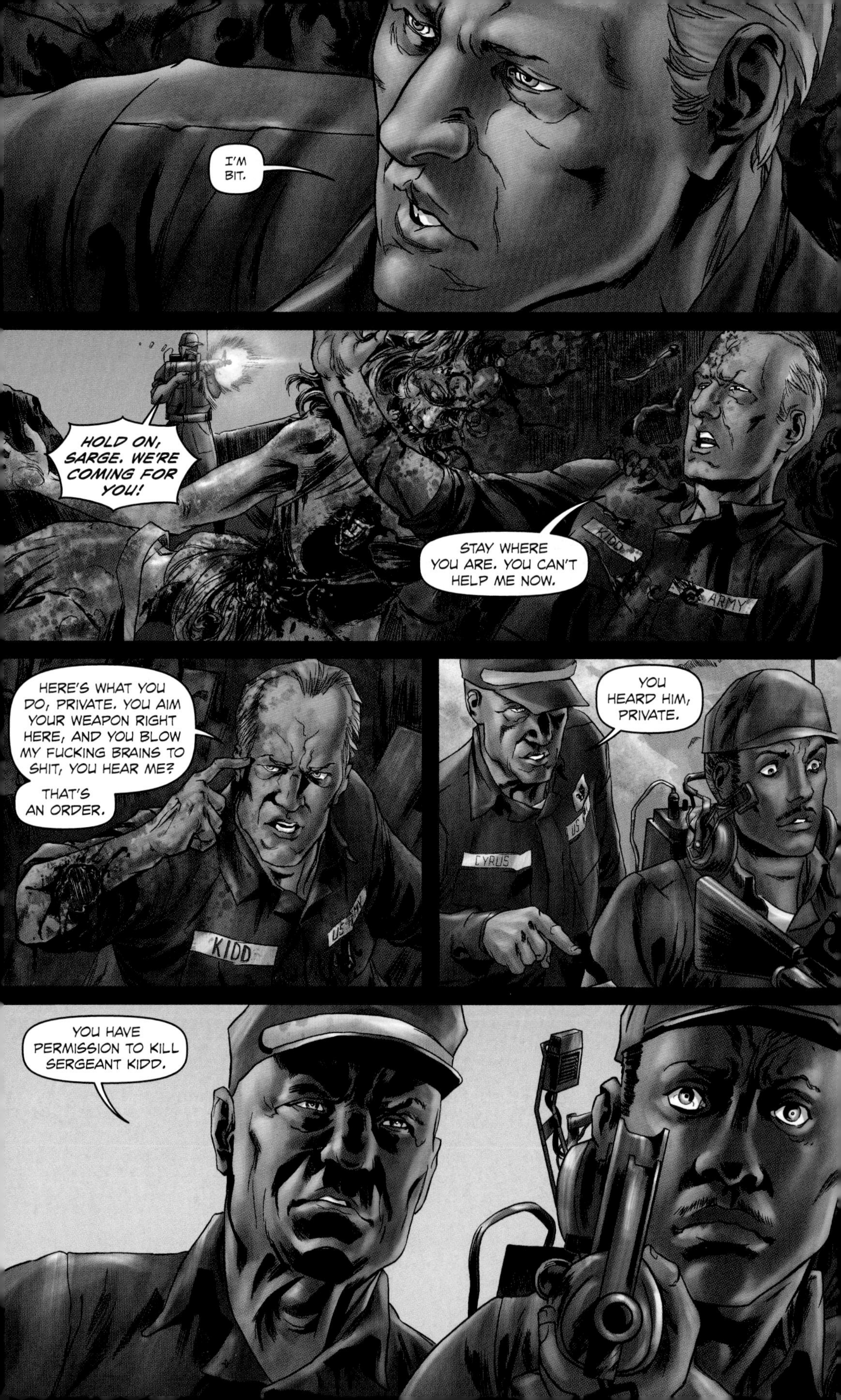
I'M BIT.
HOLD ON, SARGE. WE'RE COMING FOR YOU!
STAY WHERE YOU ARE. YOU CAN'T HELP ME NOW.
KIDD
ARMY
HERE'S WHAT YOU DO, PRIVATE. YOU AIM YOUR WEAPON RIGHT HERE, AND YOU BLOW MY FUCKING BRAINS TO SHIT, YOU HEAR ME?
THAT'S AN ORDER.
KIDD
YOU HEARD HIM, PRIVATE.
CYRUS
YOU HAVE PERMISSION TO KILL SERGEANT KIDD.

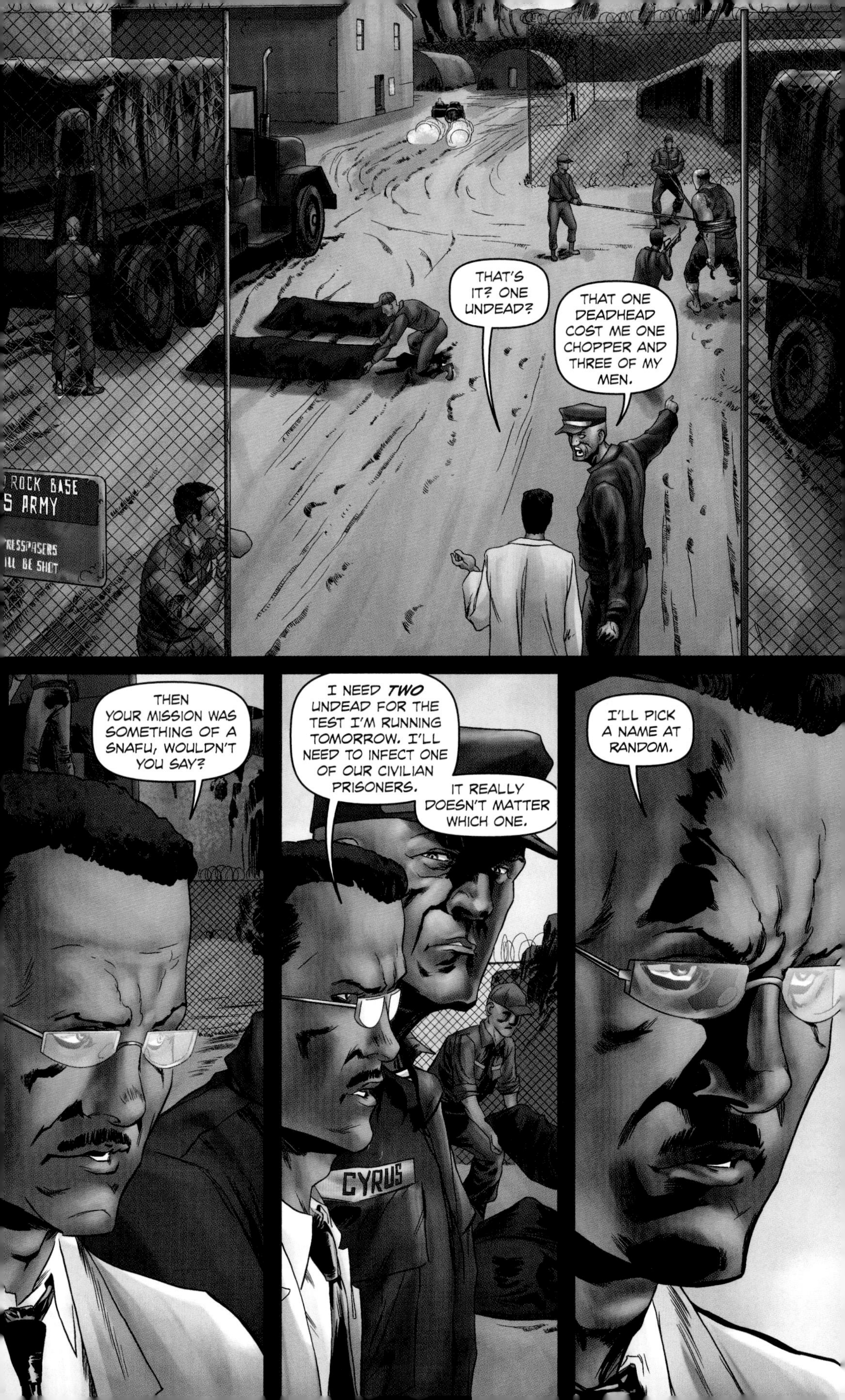
THAT'S IT? ONE UNDEAD?
THAT ONE DEADHEAD COST ME ONE CHOPPER AND THREE OF MY MEN.
THEN YOUR MISSION WAS SOMETHING OF A SNAFU, WOULDN'T YOU SAY?
I NEED *TWO* UNDEAD FOR THE TEST I'M RUNNING TOMORROW. I'LL NEED TO INFECT ONE OF OUR CIVILIAN PRISONERS.
IT REALLY DOESN'T MATTER WHICH ONE.
CYRUS
I'LL PICK A NAME AT RANDOM.

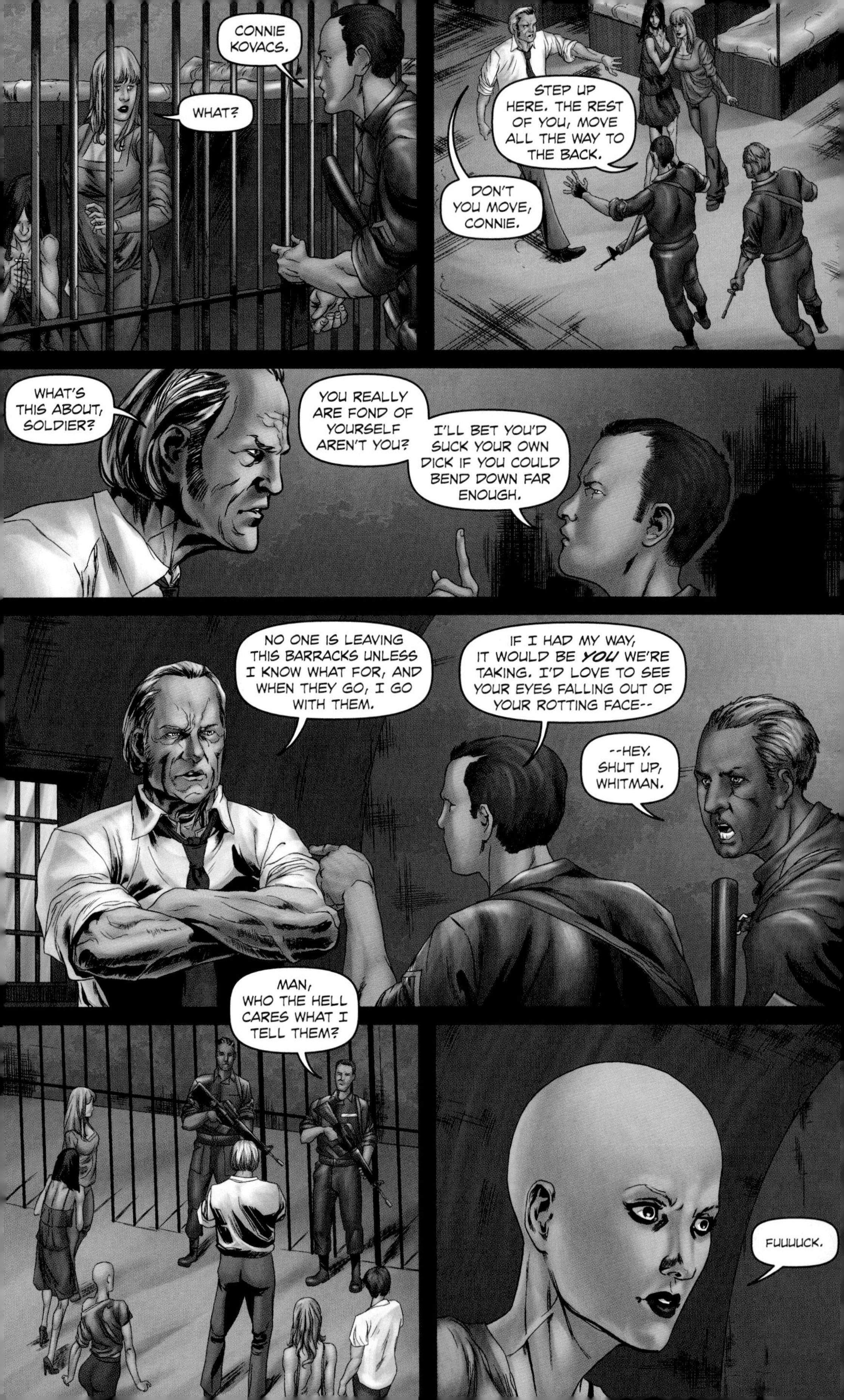
CONNIE KOVACS.
WHAT?
STEP UP HERE. THE REST OF YOU, MOVE ALL THE WAY TO THE BACK.
DON'T YOU MOVE, CONNIE.
WHAT'S THIS ABOUT, SOLDIER?
YOU REALLY ARE FOND OF YOURSELF AREN'T YOU?
I'LL BET YOU'D SUCK YOUR OWN DICK IF YOU COULD BEND DOWN FAR ENOUGH.
NO ONE IS LEAVING THIS BARRACKS UNLESS I KNOW WHAT FOR, AND WHEN THEY GO, I GO WITH THEM.
IF I HAD MY WAY, IT WOULD BE YOU WE'RE TAKING. I'D LOVE TO SEE YOUR EYES FALLING OUT OF YOUR ROTTING FACE--
--HEY. SHUT UP, WHITMAN.
MAN, WHO THE HELL CARES WHAT I TELL THEM?
FUUUUCK.

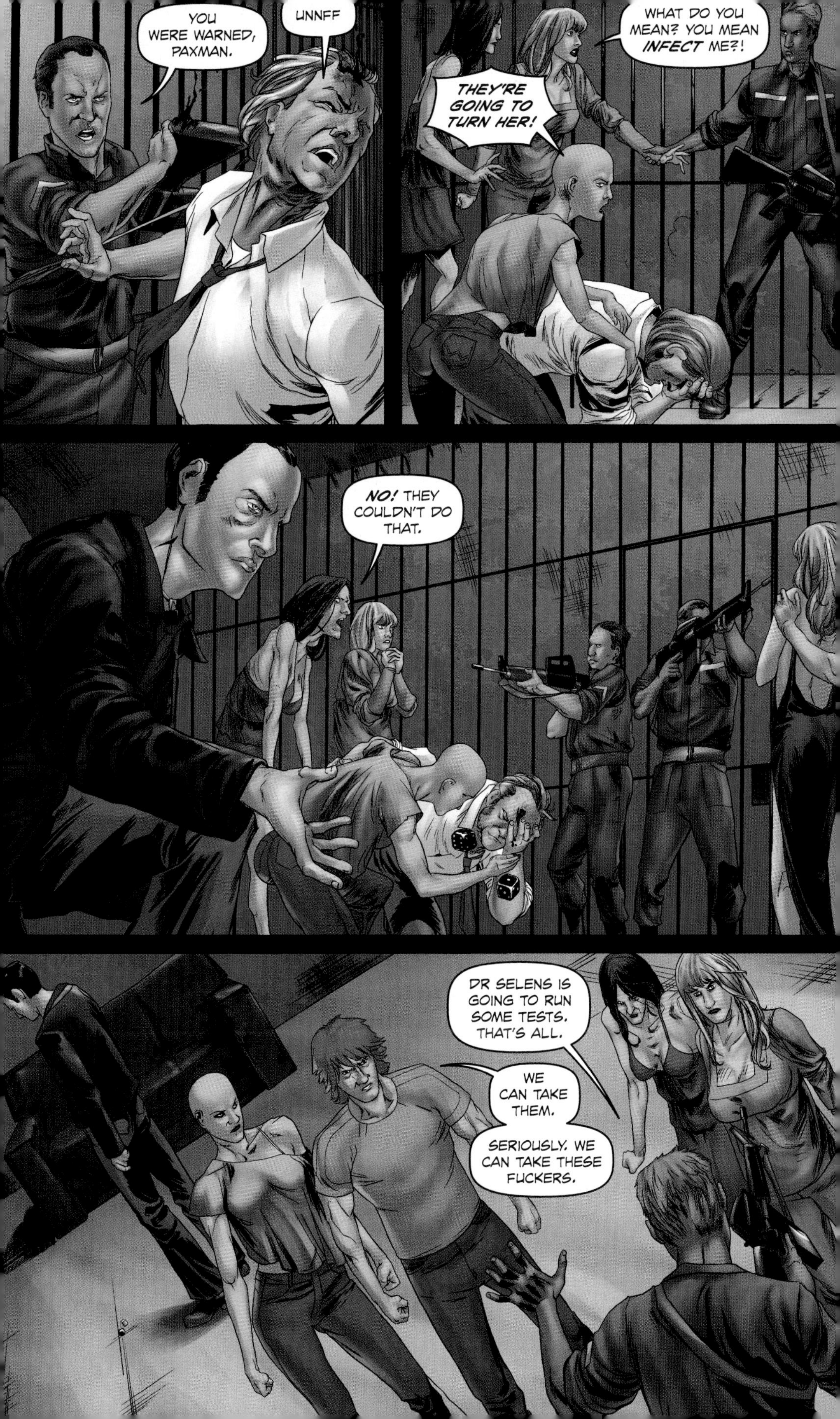
YOU WERE WARNED, PAXMAN.
UNNFF
WHAT DO YOU MEAN? YOU MEAN *INFECT* ME?!
THEY'RE GOING TO TURN HER!
NO! THEY COULDN'T DO THAT.
DR SELENS IS GOING TO RUN SOME TESTS. THAT'S ALL.
WE CAN TAKE THEM.
SERIOUSLY. WE CAN TAKE THESE FUCKERS.

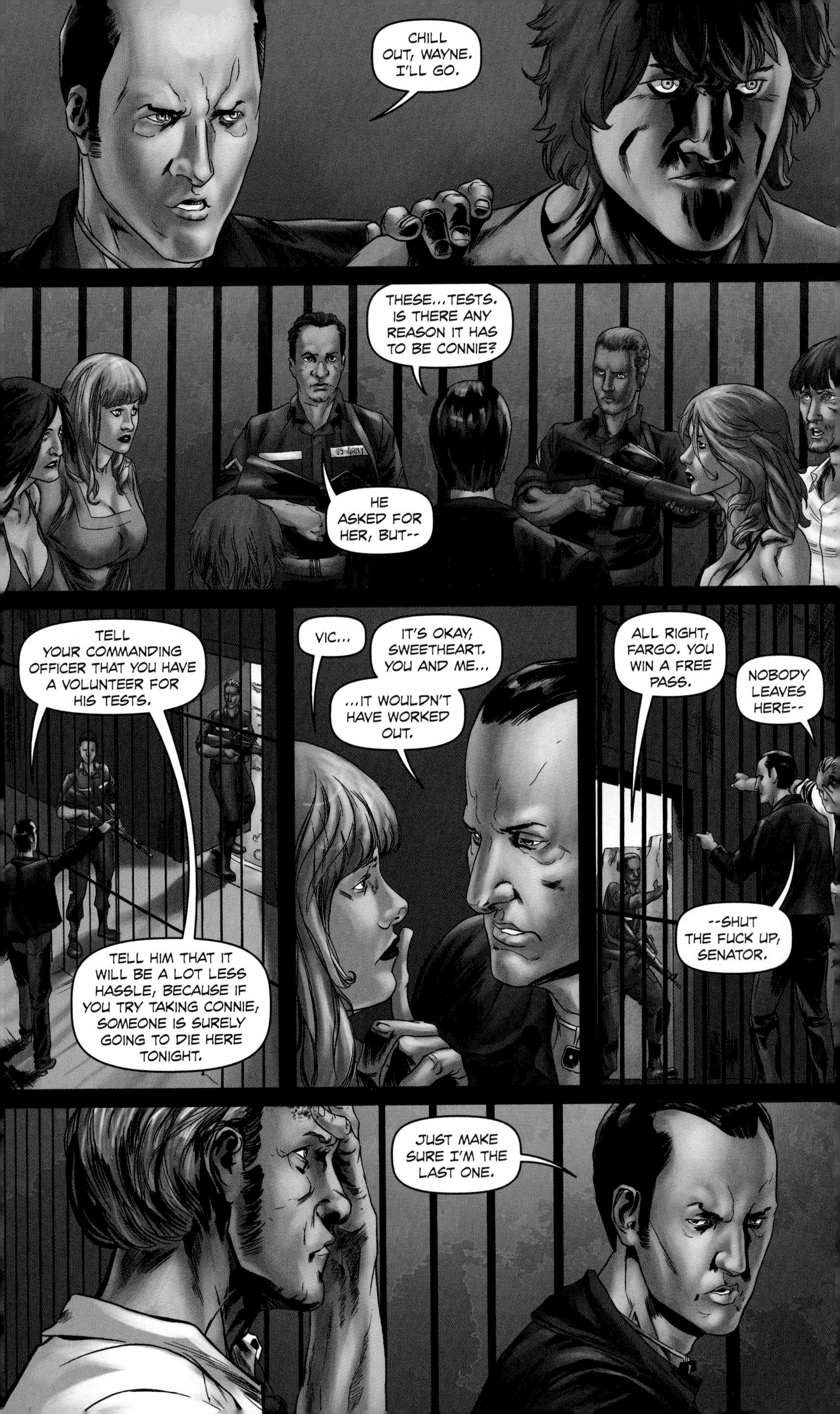
CHILL OUT, WAYNE. I'LL GO.
THESE...TESTS. IS THERE ANY REASON IT HAS TO BE CONNIE?
US ARMY
HE ASKED FOR HER, BUT--
TELL YOUR COMMANDING OFFICER THAT YOU HAVE A VOLUNTEER FOR HIS TESTS.
TELL HIM THAT IT WILL BE A LOT LESS HASSLE, BECAUSE IF YOU TRY TAKING CONNIE, SOMEONE IS SURELY GOING TO DIE HERE TONIGHT.
VIC...
IT'S OKAY, SWEETHEART. YOU AND ME...
...IT WOULDN'T HAVE WORKED OUT.
ALL RIGHT, FARGO. YOU WIN A FREE PASS.
NOBODY LEAVES HERE--
--SHUT THE FUCK UP, SENATOR.
JUST MAKE SURE I'M THE LAST ONE.

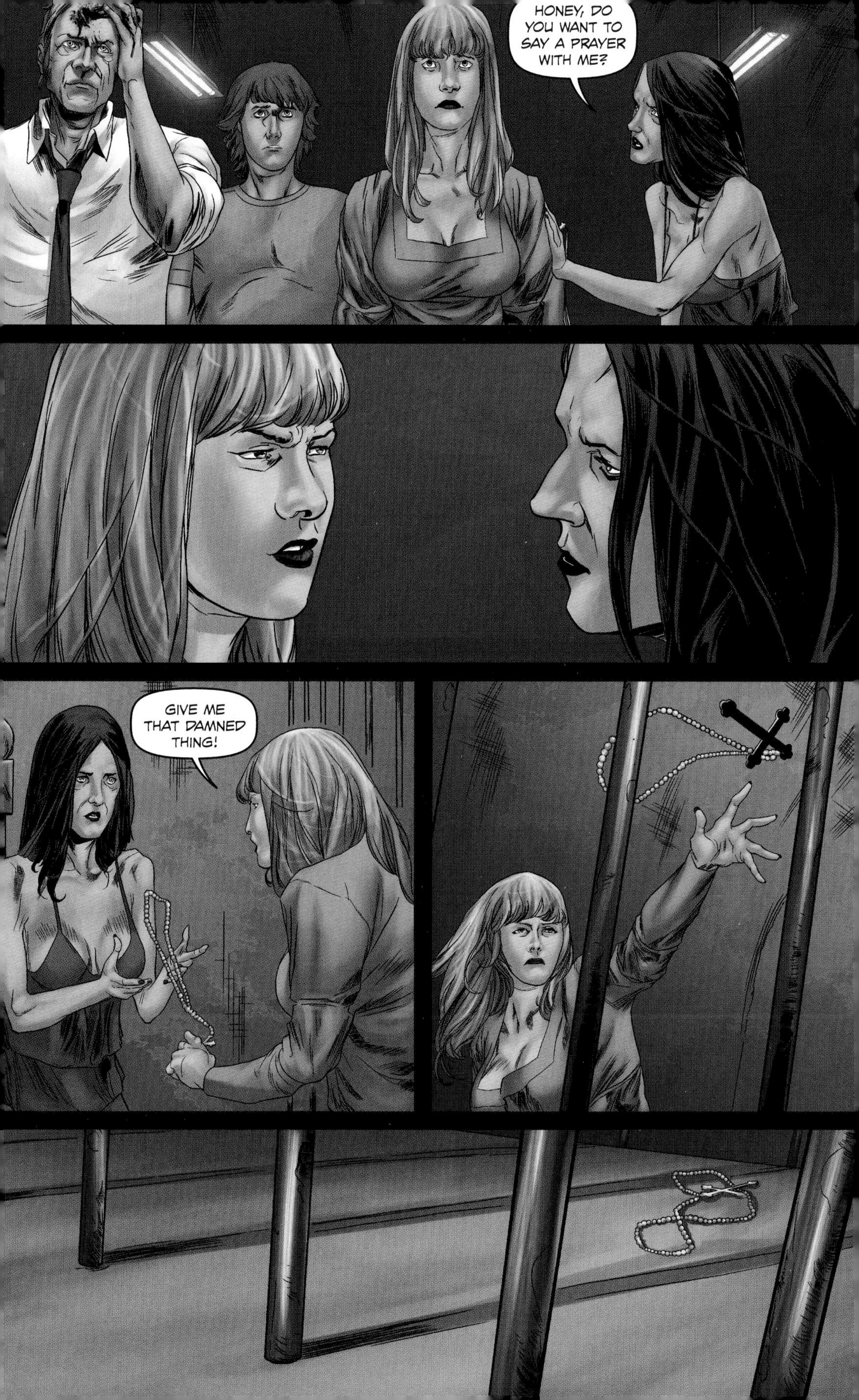
HONEY, DO YOU WANT TO SAY A PRAYER WITH ME?
GIVE ME THAT DAMNED THING!

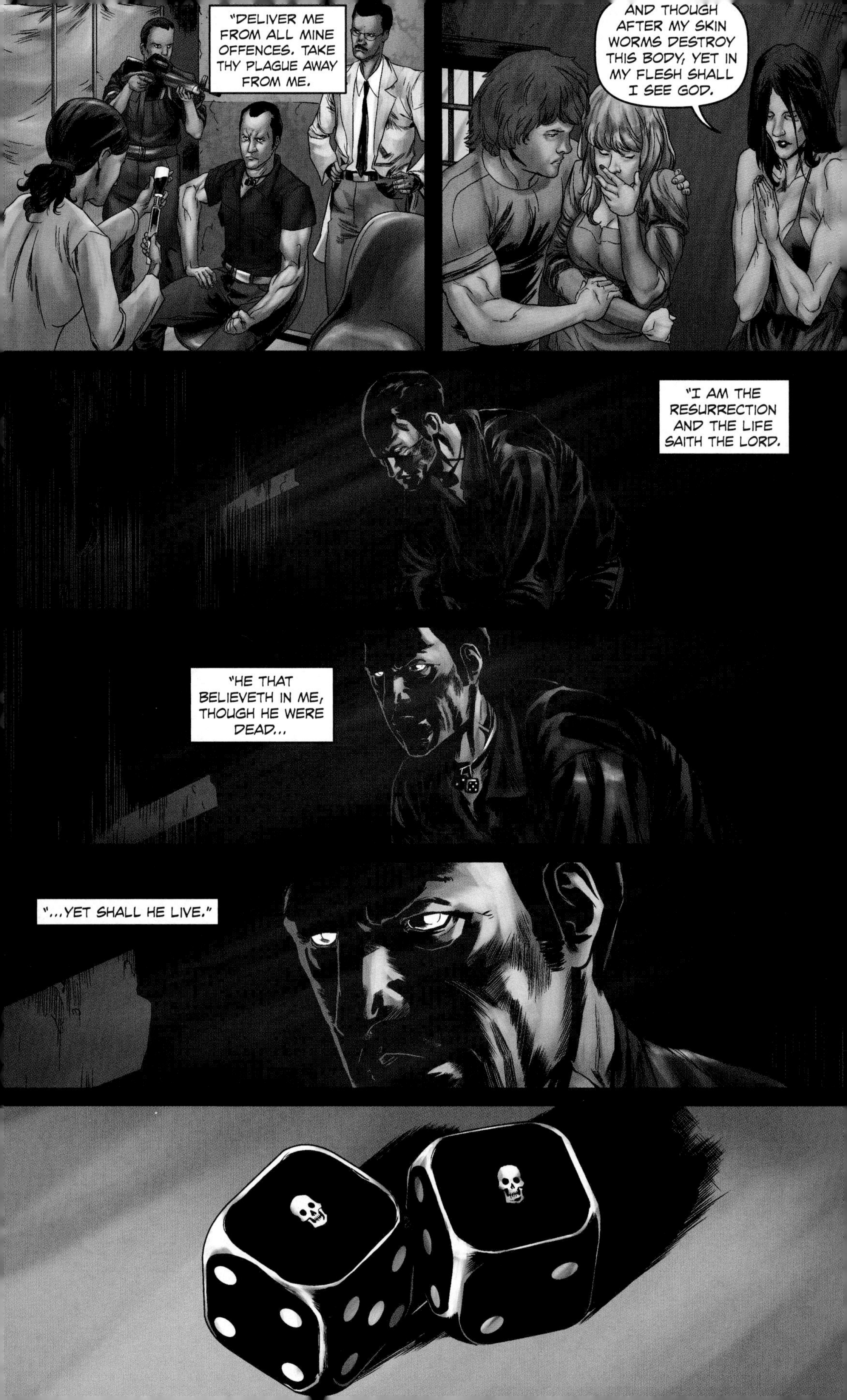
"DELIVER ME FROM ALL MINE OFFENCES. TAKE THY PLAGUE AWAY FROM ME.
AND THOUGH AFTER MY SKIN WORMS DESTROY THIS BODY, YET IN MY FLESH SHALL I SEE GOD.
"I AM THE RESURRECTION AND THE LIFE SAITH THE LORD.
"HE THAT BELIEVETH IN ME, THOUGH HE WERE DEAD...
"...YET SHALL HE LIVE."

HUNGRY FOR THE FLESH OF THE LIVING

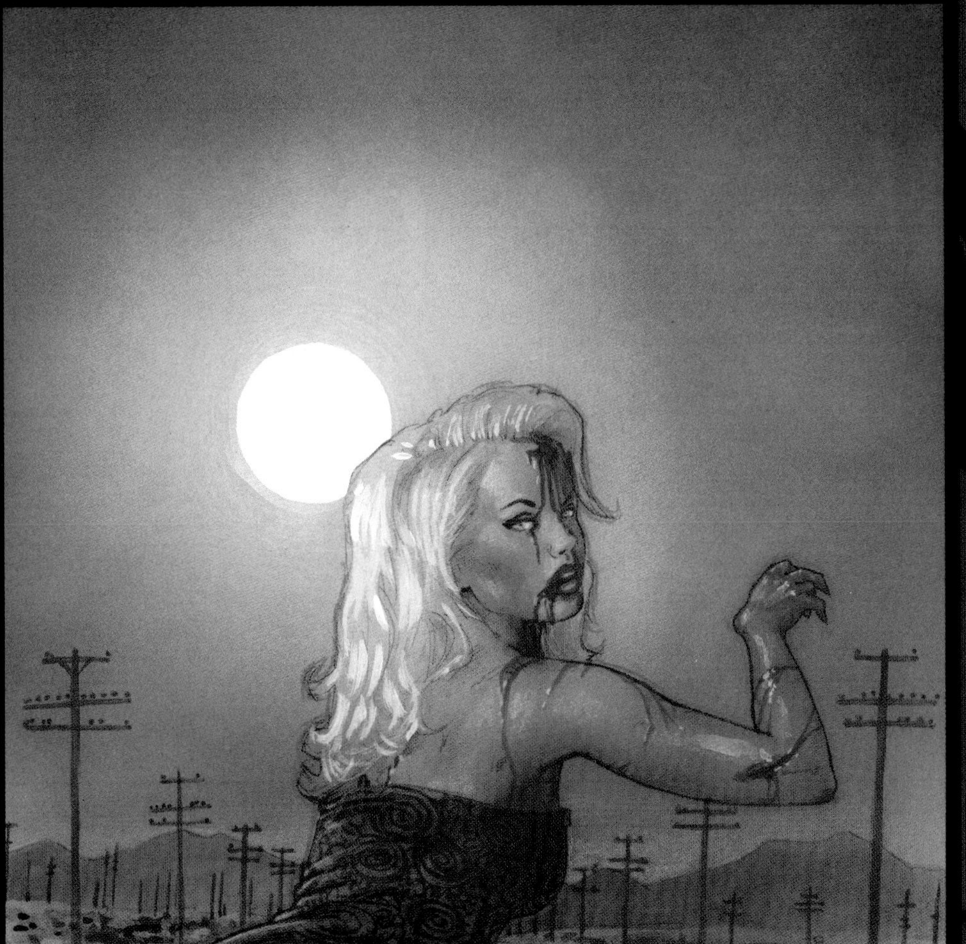

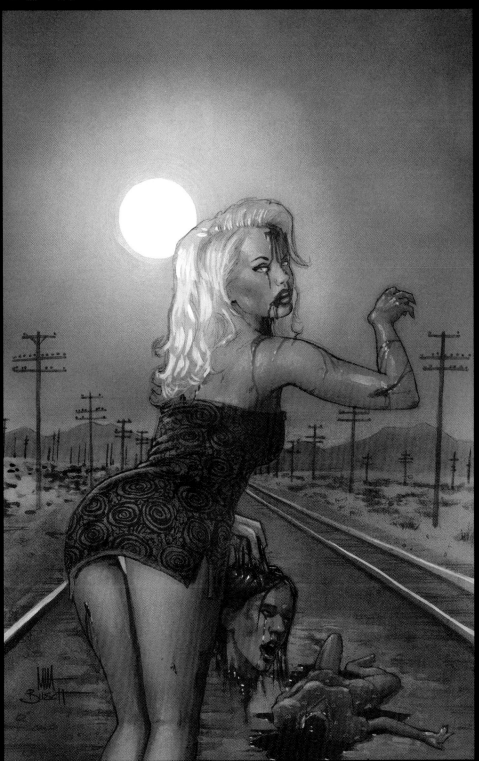

CHAPTER 4

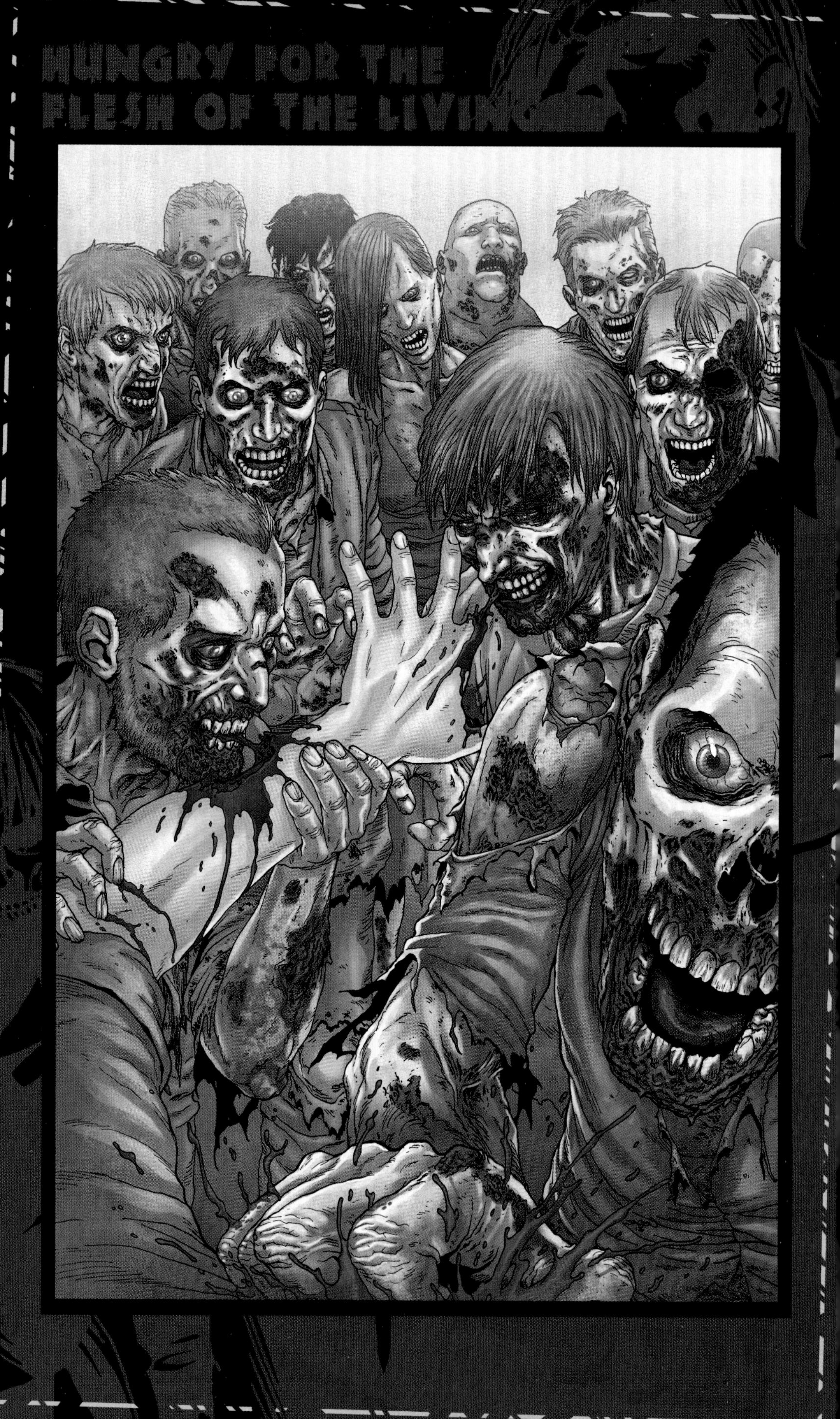
HUNGRY FOR THE
FLESH OF THE LIVING

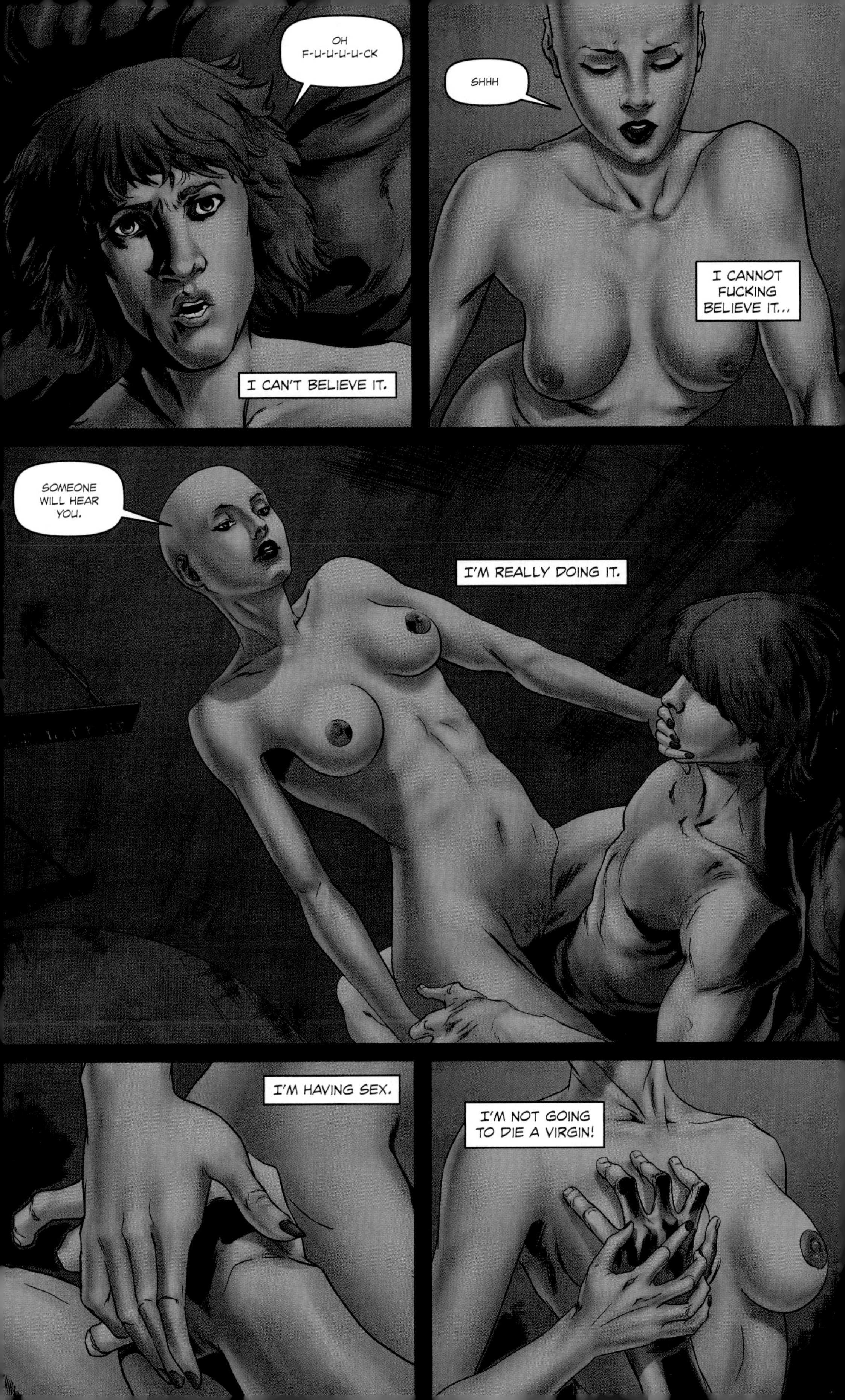
OH F-U-U-U-U-CK
I CAN'T BELIEVE IT.
SHHH
I CANNOT FUCKING BELIEVE IT...
SOMEONE WILL HEAR YOU.
I'M REALLY DOING IT.
I'M HAVING SEX.
I'M NOT GOING TO DIE A VIRGIN!

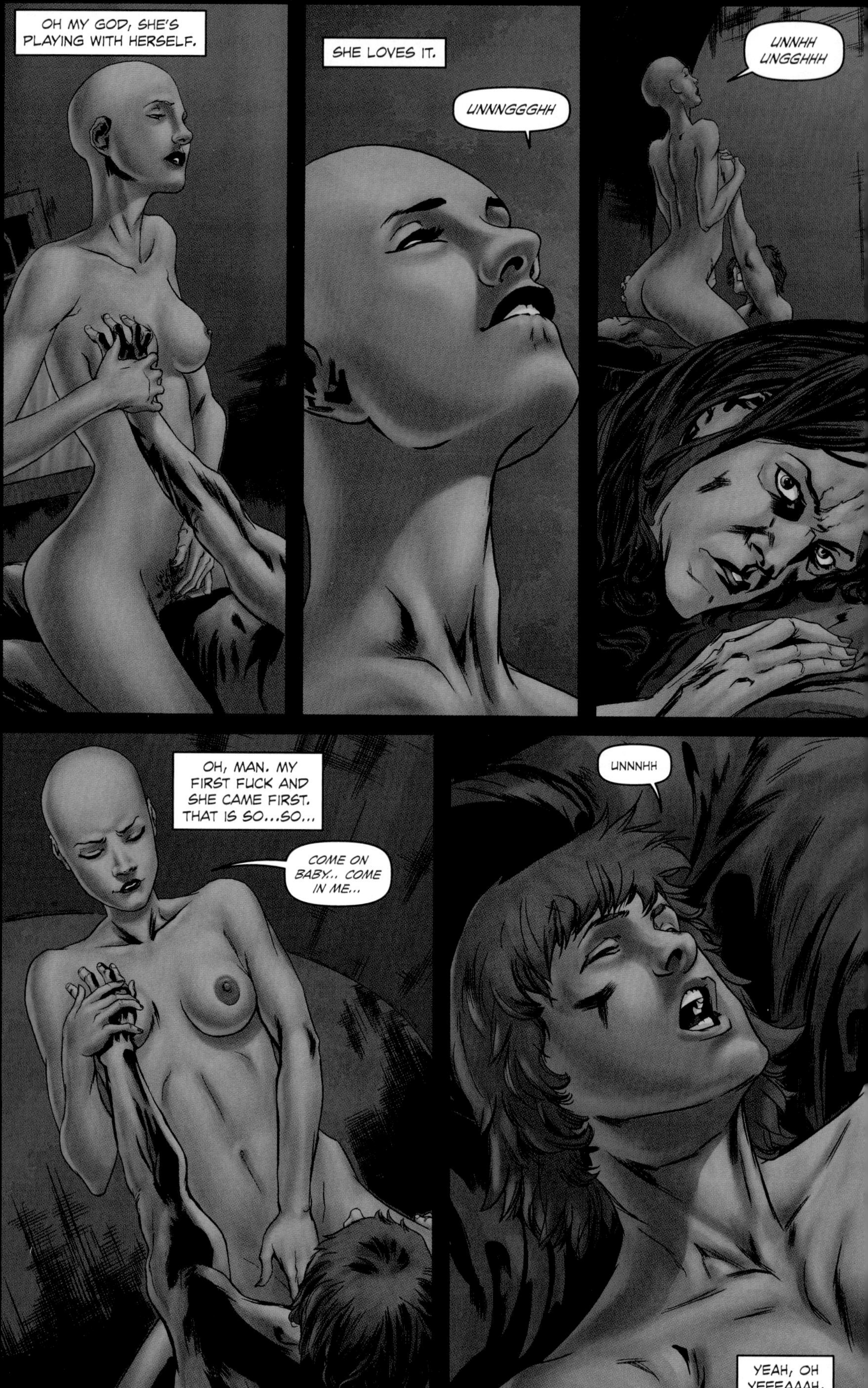
OH MY GOD, SHE'S PLAYING WITH HERSELF.
SHE LOVES IT.
UNNNGGGHH
UNNHH UNGGHHH
OH, MAN. MY FIRST FUCK AND SHE CAME FIRST. THAT IS SO...SO...
COME ON BABY... COME IN ME...
UNNNHH
YEAH, OH YEEEAAAH, I'M C-C-C

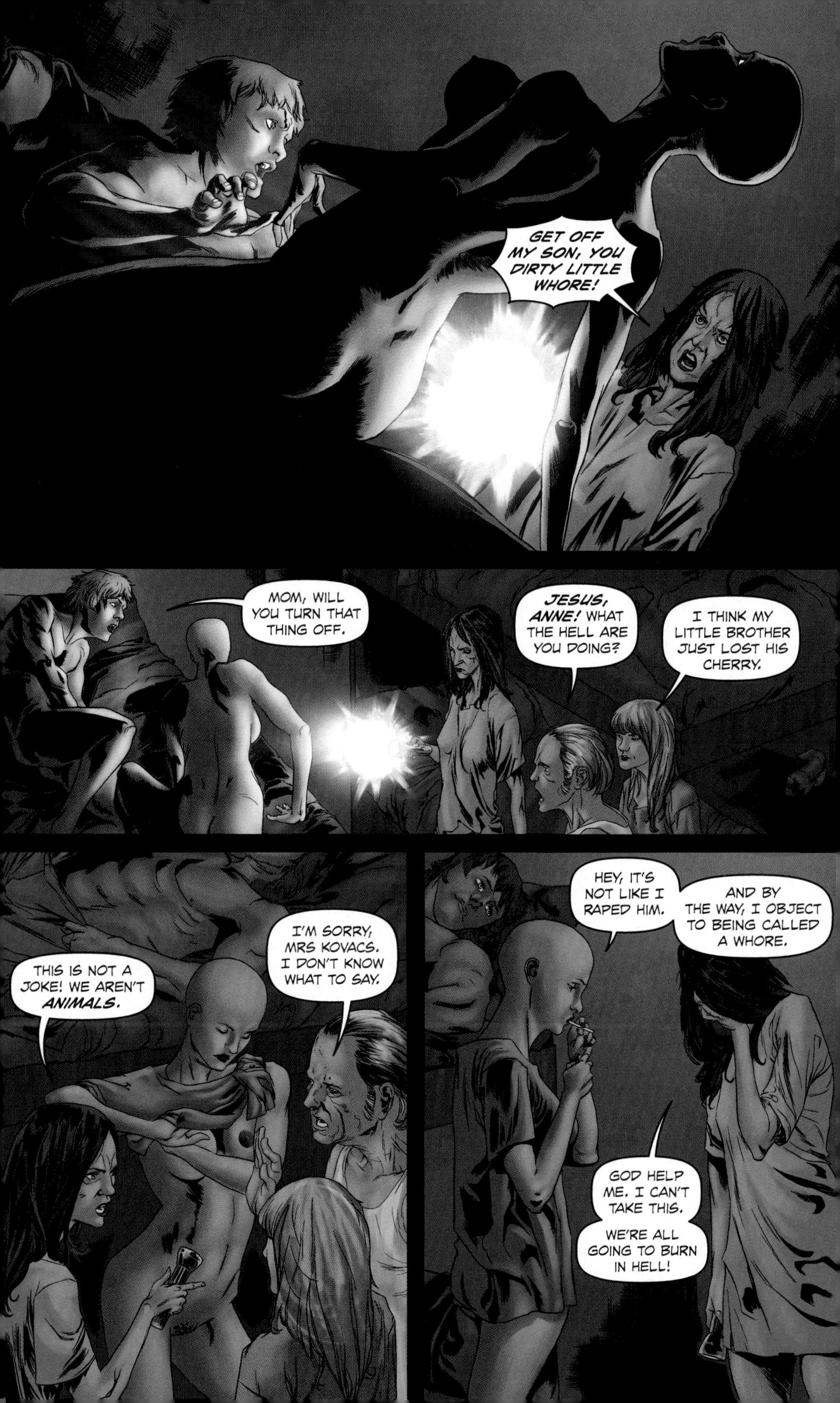
GET OFF MY SON, YOU DIRTY LITTLE WHORE!
MOM, WILL YOU TURN THAT THING OFF.
JESUS, ANNE! WHAT THE HELL ARE YOU DOING?
I THINK MY LITTLE BROTHER JUST LOST HIS CHERRY.
THIS IS NOT A JOKE! WE AREN'T ANIMALS.
I'M SORRY, MRS KOVACS. I DON'T KNOW WHAT TO SAY.
HEY, IT'S NOT LIKE I RAPED HIM.
AND BY THE WAY, I OBJECT TO BEING CALLED A WHORE.
GOD HELP ME. I CAN'T TAKE THIS.
WE'RE ALL GOING TO BURN IN HELL!

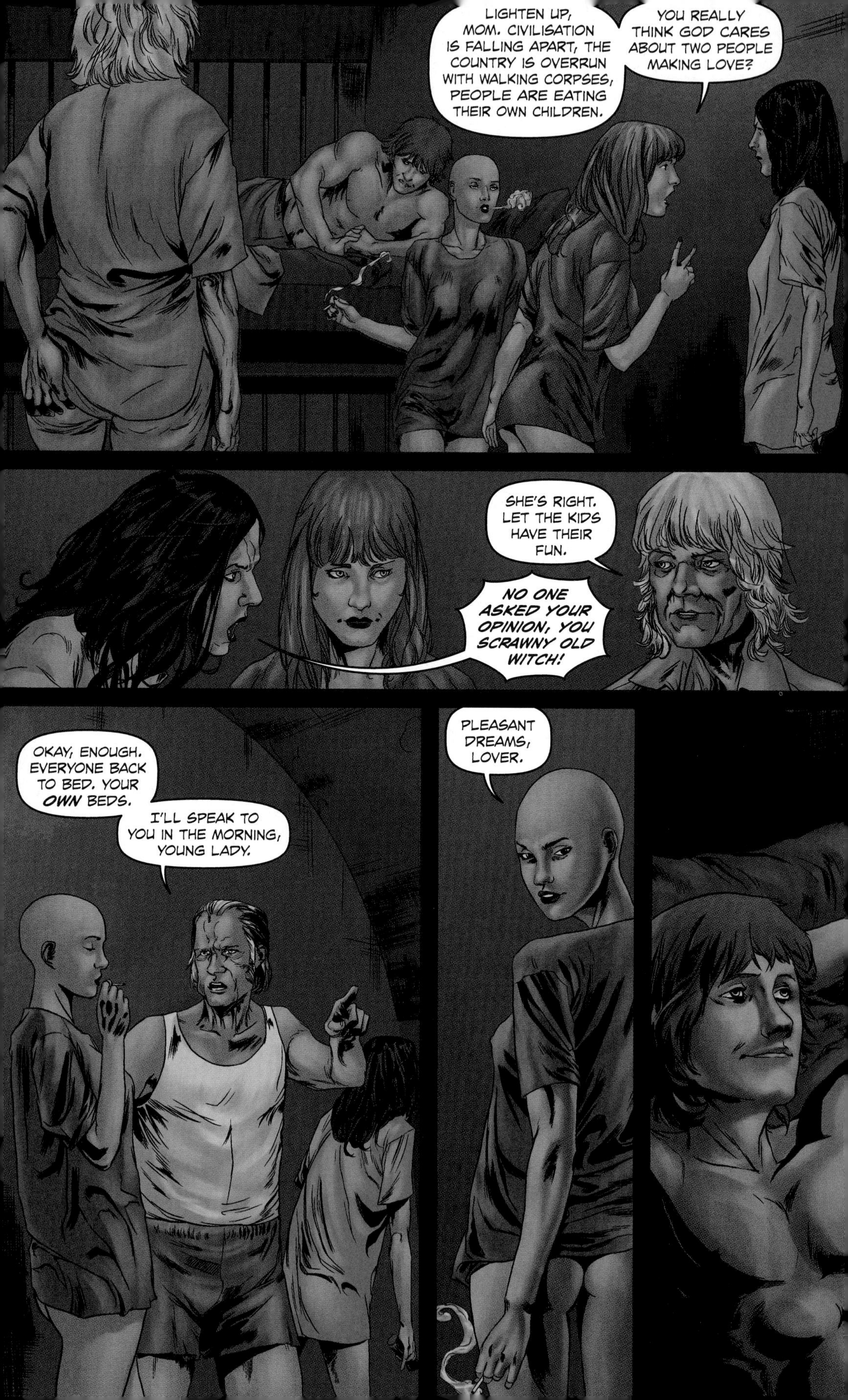
LIGHTEN UP, MOM. CIVILISATION IS FALLING APART, THE COUNTRY IS OVERRUN WITH WALKING CORPSES, PEOPLE ARE EATING THEIR OWN CHILDREN.
YOU REALLY THINK GOD CARES ABOUT TWO PEOPLE MAKING LOVE?
SHE'S RIGHT. LET THE KIDS HAVE THEIR FUN.
NO ONE ASKED YOUR OPINION, YOU SCRAWNY OLD WITCH!
OKAY, ENOUGH. EVERYONE BACK TO BED. YOUR OWN BEDS.
I'LL SPEAK TO YOU IN THE MORNING, YOUNG LADY.
PLEASANT DREAMS, LOVER.

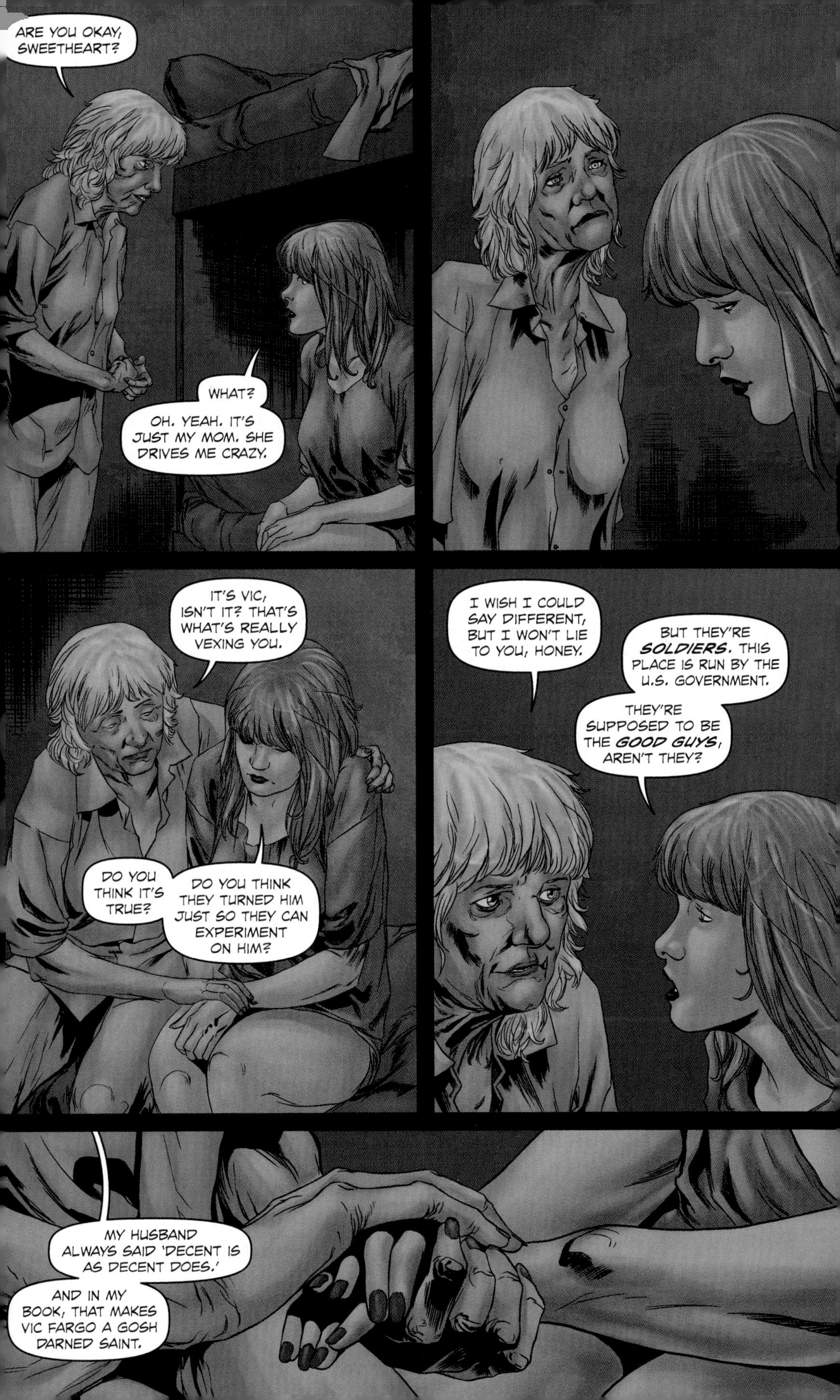
ARE YOU OKAY, SWEETHEART?
WHAT?
OH. YEAH. IT'S JUST MY MOM. SHE DRIVES ME CRAZY.
IT'S VIC, ISN'T IT? THAT'S WHAT'S REALLY VEXING YOU.
DO YOU THINK IT'S TRUE?
DO YOU THINK THEY TURNED HIM JUST SO THEY CAN EXPERIMENT ON HIM?
I WISH I COULD SAY DIFFERENT, BUT I WON'T LIE TO YOU, HONEY.
BUT THEY'RE SOLDIERS. THIS PLACE IS RUN BY THE U.S. GOVERNMENT.
THEY'RE SUPPOSED TO BE THE GOOD GUYS, AREN'T THEY?
MY HUSBAND ALWAYS SAID 'DECENT IS AS DECENT DOES.'
AND IN MY BOOK, THAT MAKES VIC FARGO A GOSH DARNED SAINT.

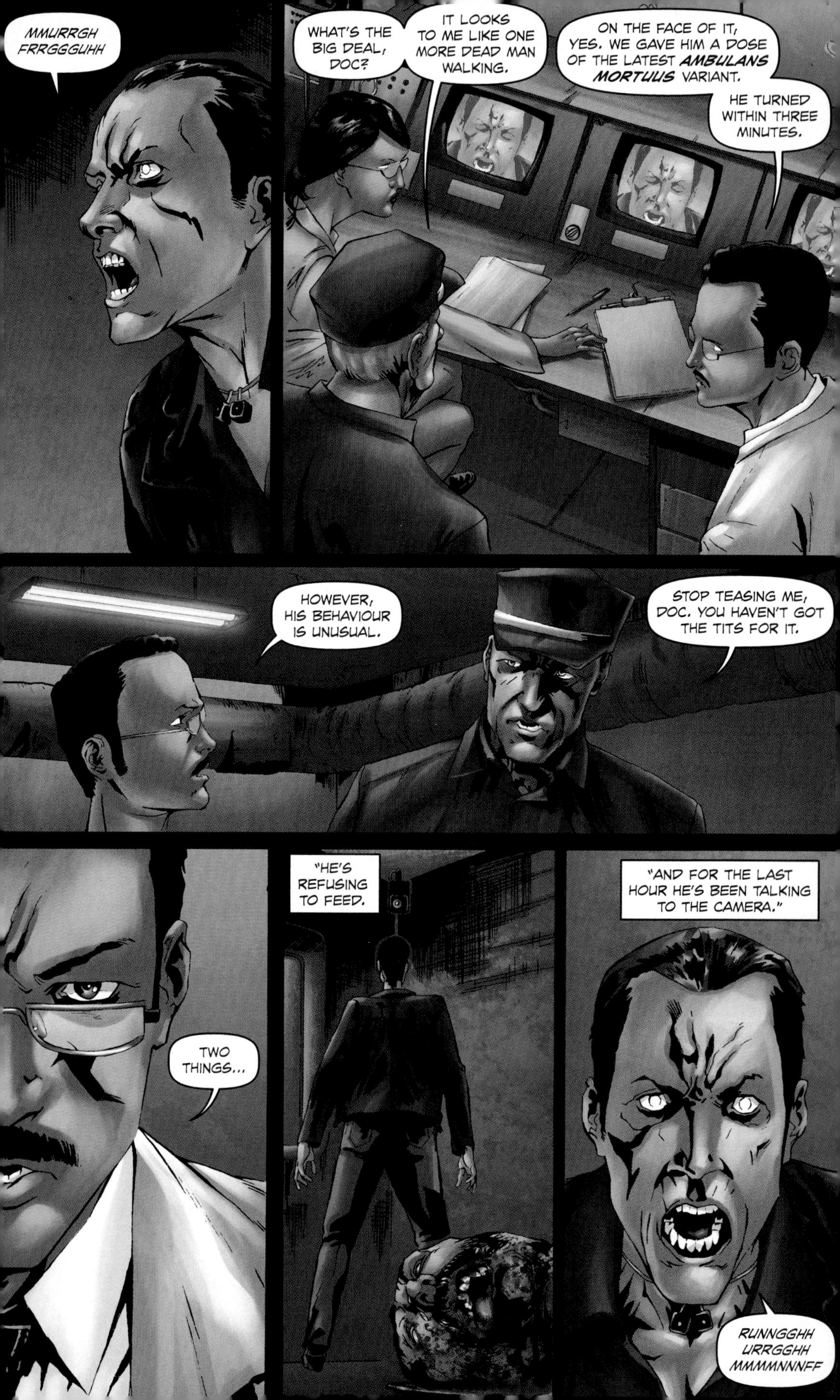
MMURRGH FRRGGGUHH
WHAT'S THE BIG DEAL, DOC?
IT LOOKS TO ME LIKE ONE MORE DEAD MAN WALKING.
ON THE FACE OF IT, YES. WE GAVE HIM A DOSE OF THE LATEST AMBULANS MORTUUS VARIANT.
HE TURNED WITHIN THREE MINUTES.
HOWEVER, HIS BEHAVIOUR IS UNUSUAL.
STOP TEASING ME, DOC. YOU HAVEN'T GOT THE TITS FOR IT.
TWO THINGS...
"HE'S REFUSING TO FEED.
"AND FOR THE LAST HOUR HE'S BEEN TALKING TO THE CAMERA."
RUNNGGHH URRGGHH MMMMNNNFF

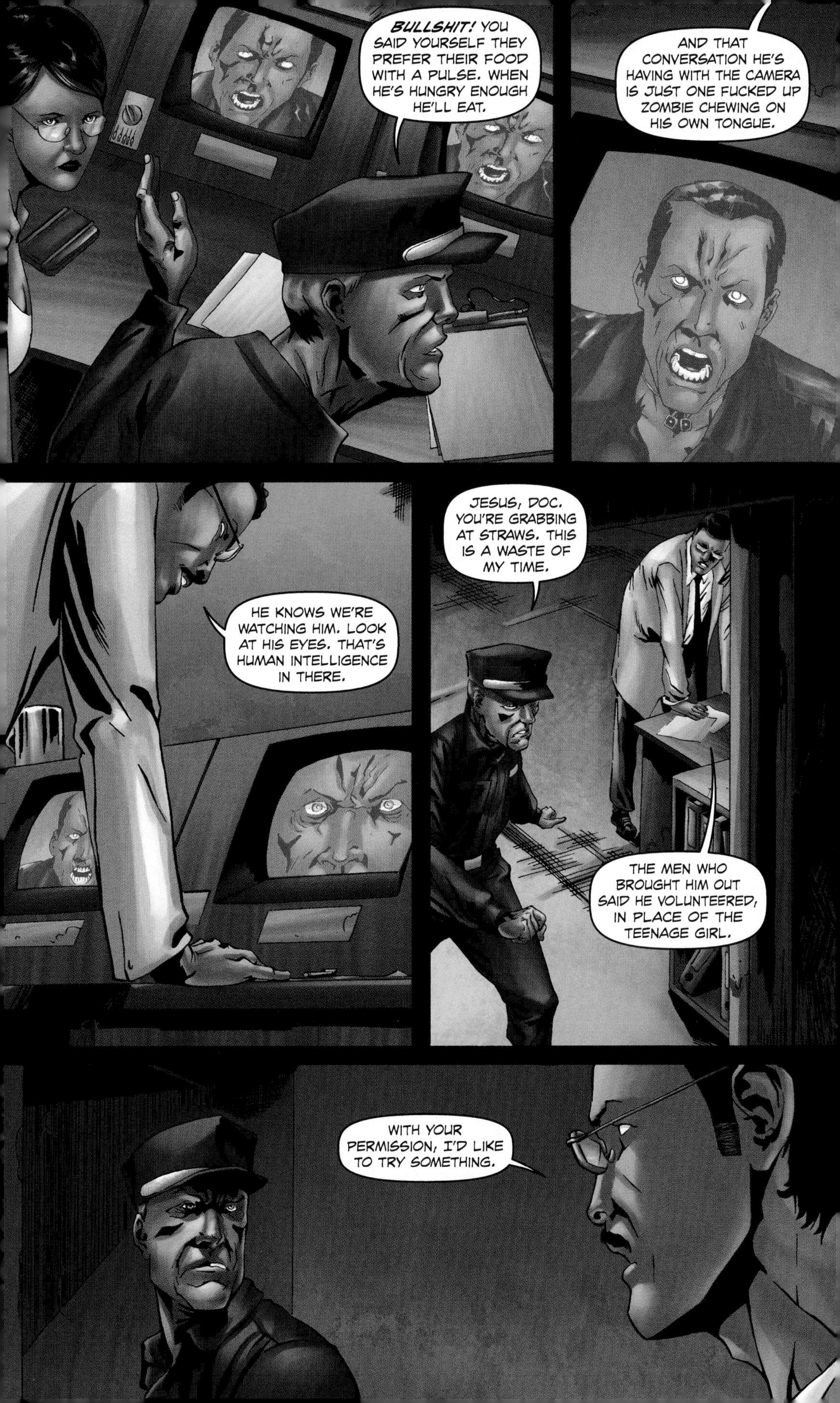
BULLSHIT! YOU SAID YOURSELF THEY PREFER THEIR FOOD WITH A PULSE. WHEN HE'S HUNGRY ENOUGH HE'LL EAT.
AND THAT CONVERSATION HE'S HAVING WITH THE CAMERA IS JUST ONE FUCKED UP ZOMBIE CHEWING ON HIS OWN TONGUE.
HE KNOWS WE'RE WATCHING HIM. LOOK AT HIS EYES. THAT'S HUMAN INTELLIGENCE IN THERE.
JESUS, DOC. YOU'RE GRABBING AT STRAWS. THIS IS A WASTE OF MY TIME.
THE MEN WHO BROUGHT HIM OUT SAID HE VOLUNTEERED, IN PLACE OF THE TEENAGE GIRL.
WITH YOUR PERMISSION, I'D LIKE TO TRY SOMETHING.

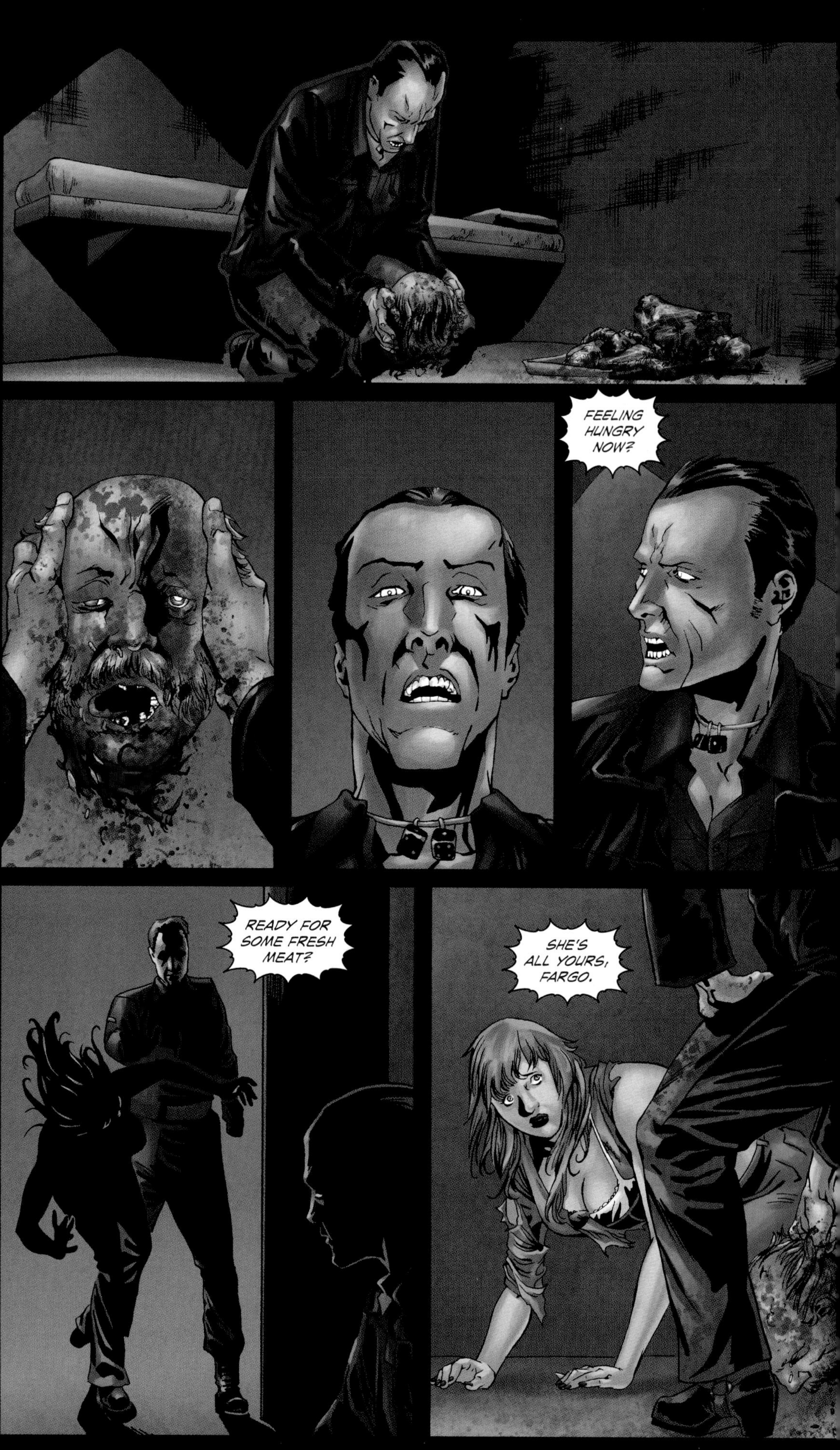
FEELING HUNGRY NOW?
READY FOR SOME FRESH MEAT?
SHE'S ALL YOURS, FARGO.

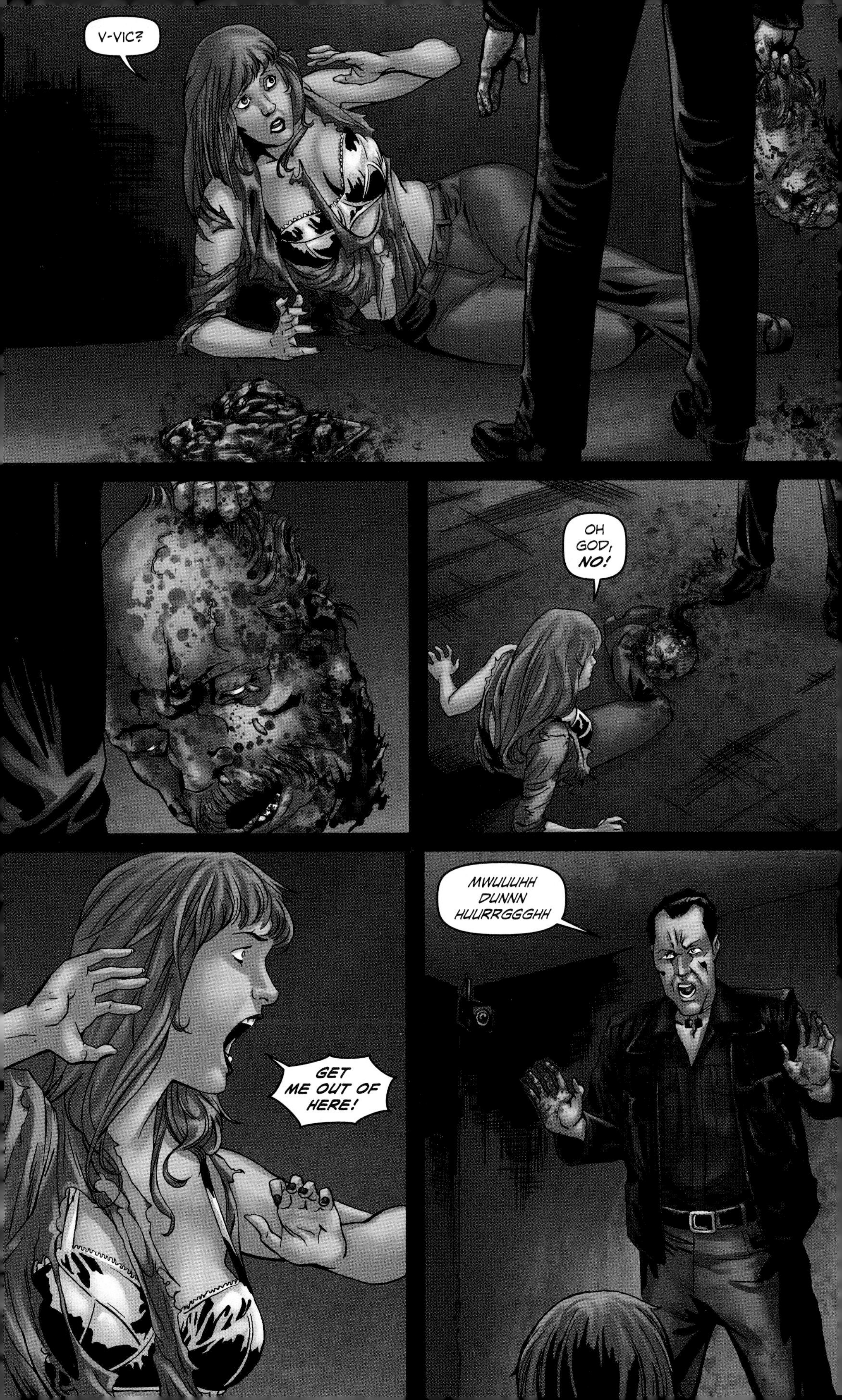
V-VIC?
OH GOD, NO!
GET ME OUT OF HERE!
MWUUUHH DUNNN HUURRGGGHH

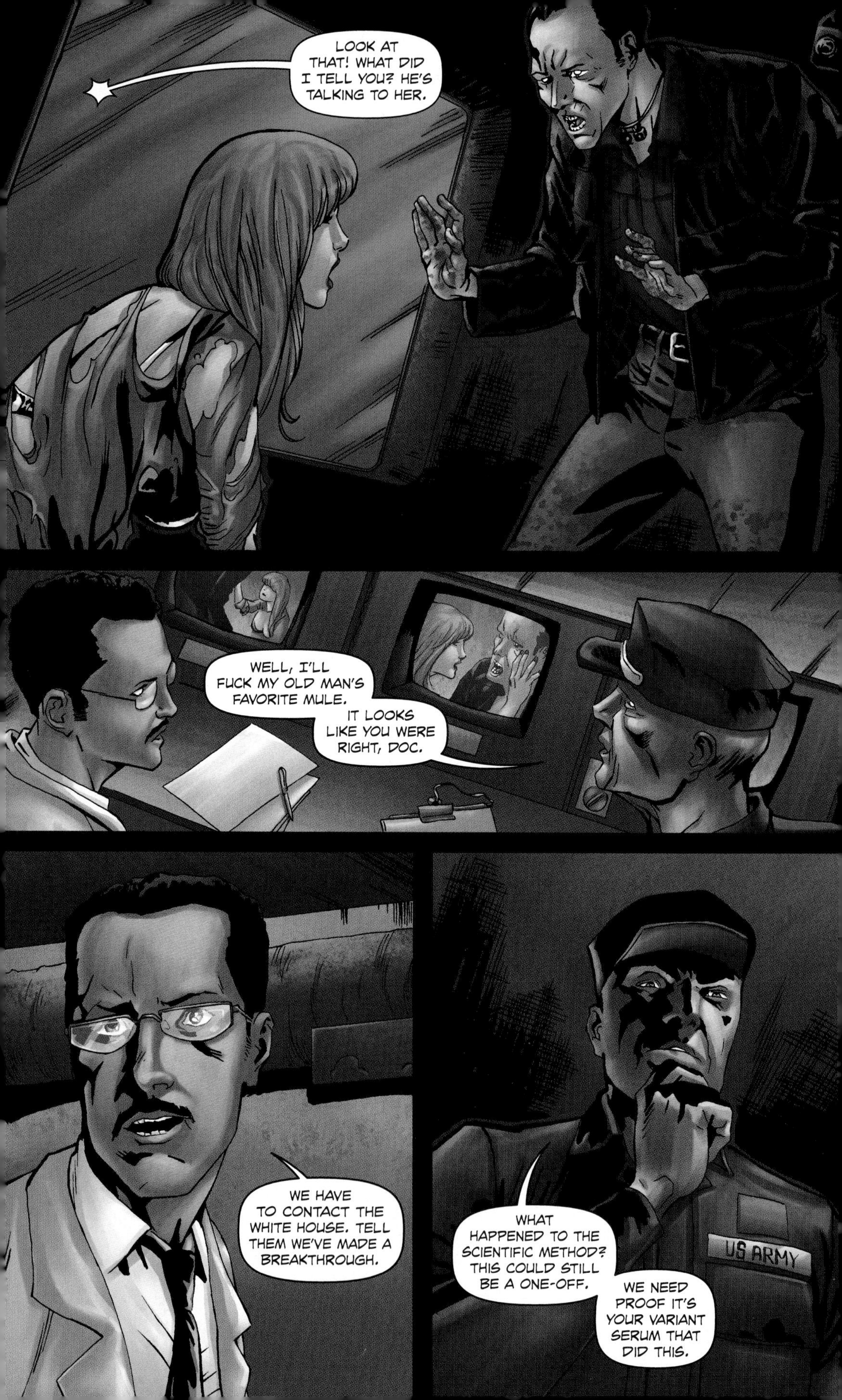
LOOK AT THAT! WHAT DID I TELL YOU? HE'S TALKING TO HER.
WELL, I'LL FUCK MY OLD MAN'S FAVORITE MULE.
IT LOOKS LIKE YOU WERE RIGHT, DOC.
WE HAVE TO CONTACT THE WHITE HOUSE. TELL THEM WE'VE MADE A BREAKTHROUGH.
WHAT HAPPENED TO THE SCIENTIFIC METHOD? THIS COULD STILL BE A ONE-OFF.
WE NEED PROOF IT'S YOUR VARIANT SERUM THAT DID THIS.
US ARMY

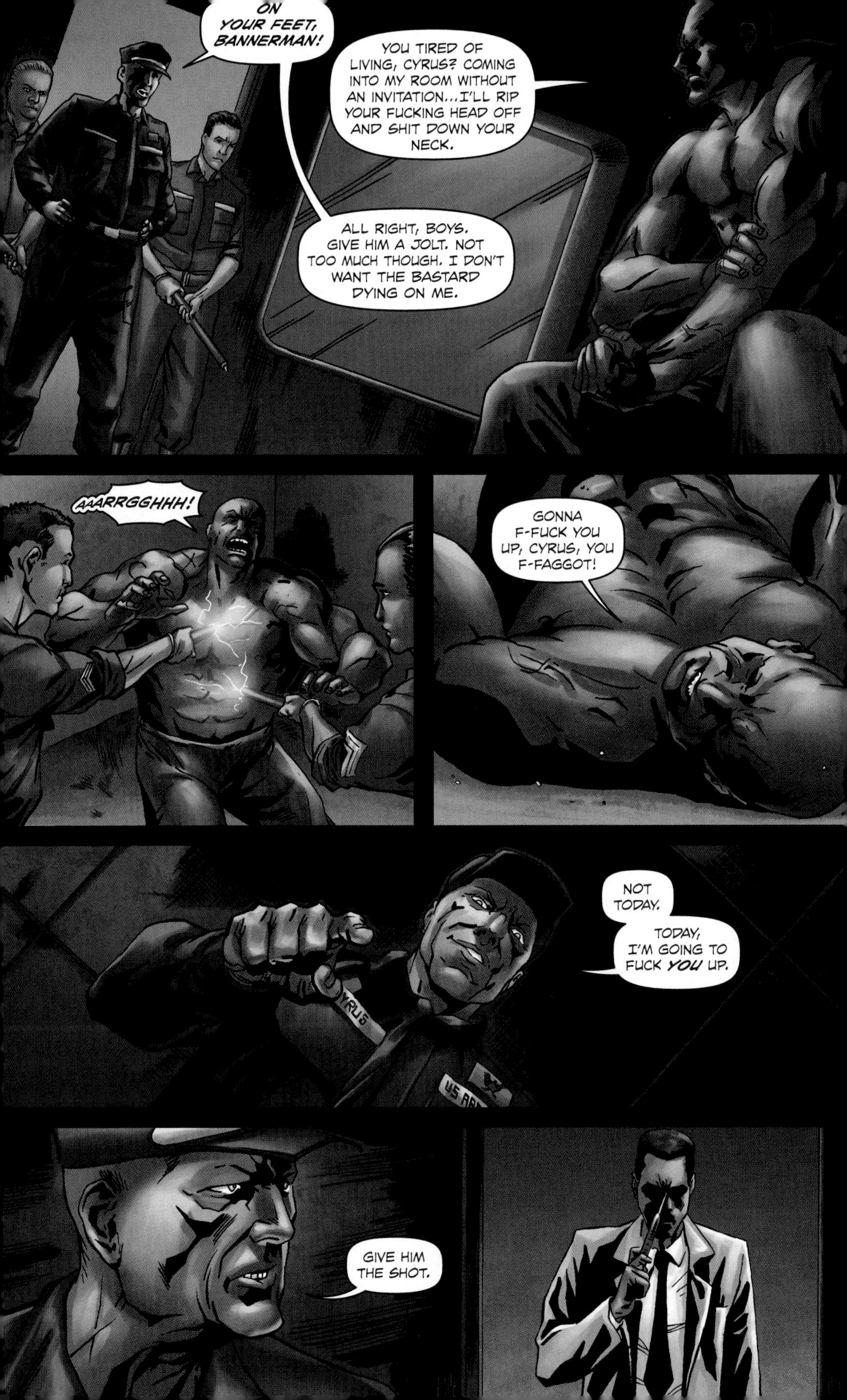
ON YOUR FEET, BANNERMAN!
YOU TIRED OF LIVING, CYRUS? COMING INTO MY ROOM WITHOUT AN INVITATION...I'LL RIP YOUR FUCKING HEAD OFF AND SHIT DOWN YOUR NECK.
ALL RIGHT, BOYS. GIVE HIM A JOLT. NOT TOO MUCH THOUGH. I DON'T WANT THE BASTARD DYING ON ME.
AAARRGGHHH!
GONNA F-FUCK YOU UP, CYRUS, YOU F-FAGGOT!
NOT TODAY.
TODAY, I'M GOING TO FUCK *YOU* UP.
GIVE HIM THE SHOT.

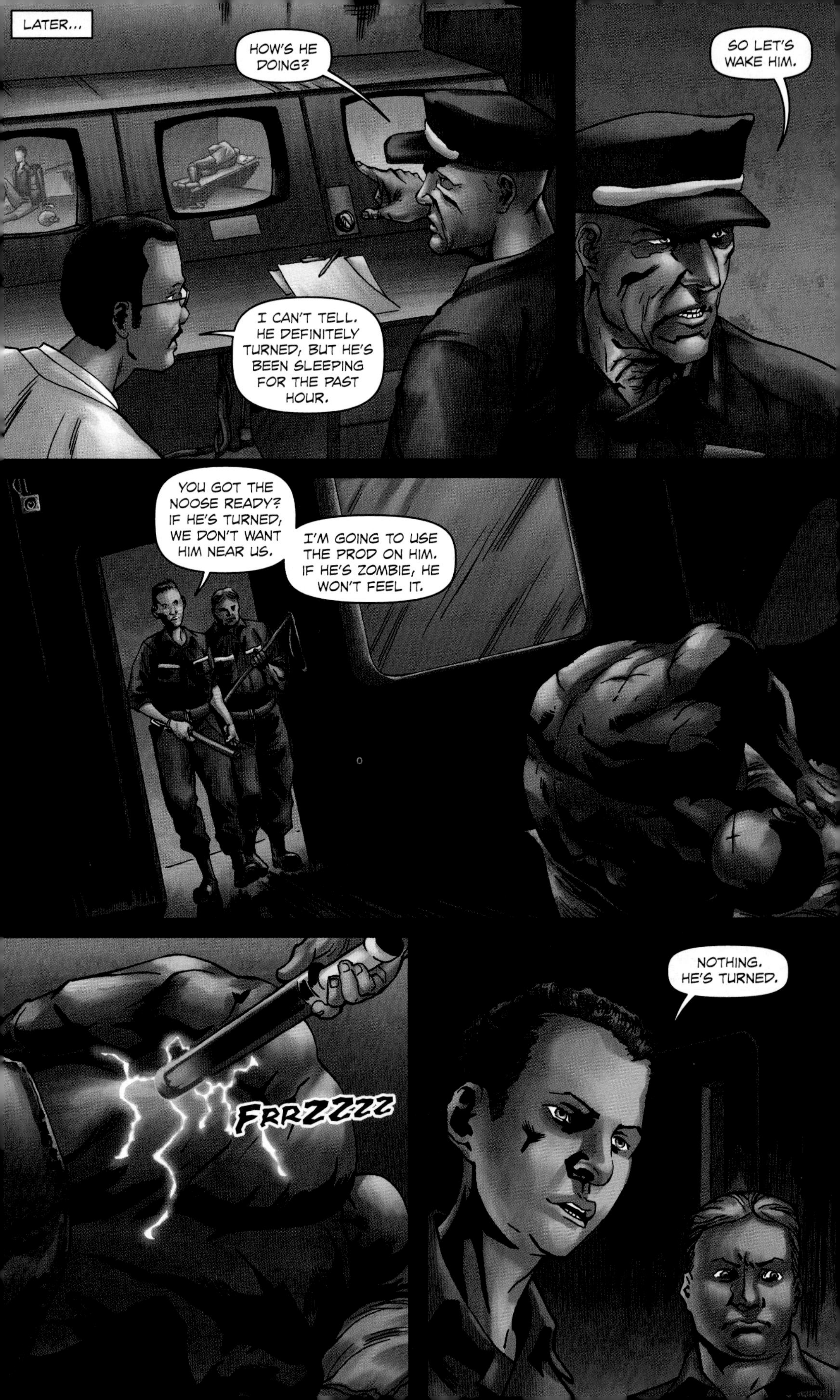
LATER...
HOW'S HE DOING?
I CAN'T TELL. HE DEFINITELY TURNED; BUT HE'S BEEN SLEEPING FOR THE PAST HOUR.
SO LET'S WAKE HIM.
YOU GOT THE NOOSE READY? IF HE'S TURNED, WE DON'T WANT HIM NEAR US.
I'M GOING TO USE THE PROD ON HIM. IF HE'S ZOMBIE, HE WON'T FEEL IT.
FRRZZZZZ
NOTHING. HE'S TURNED.

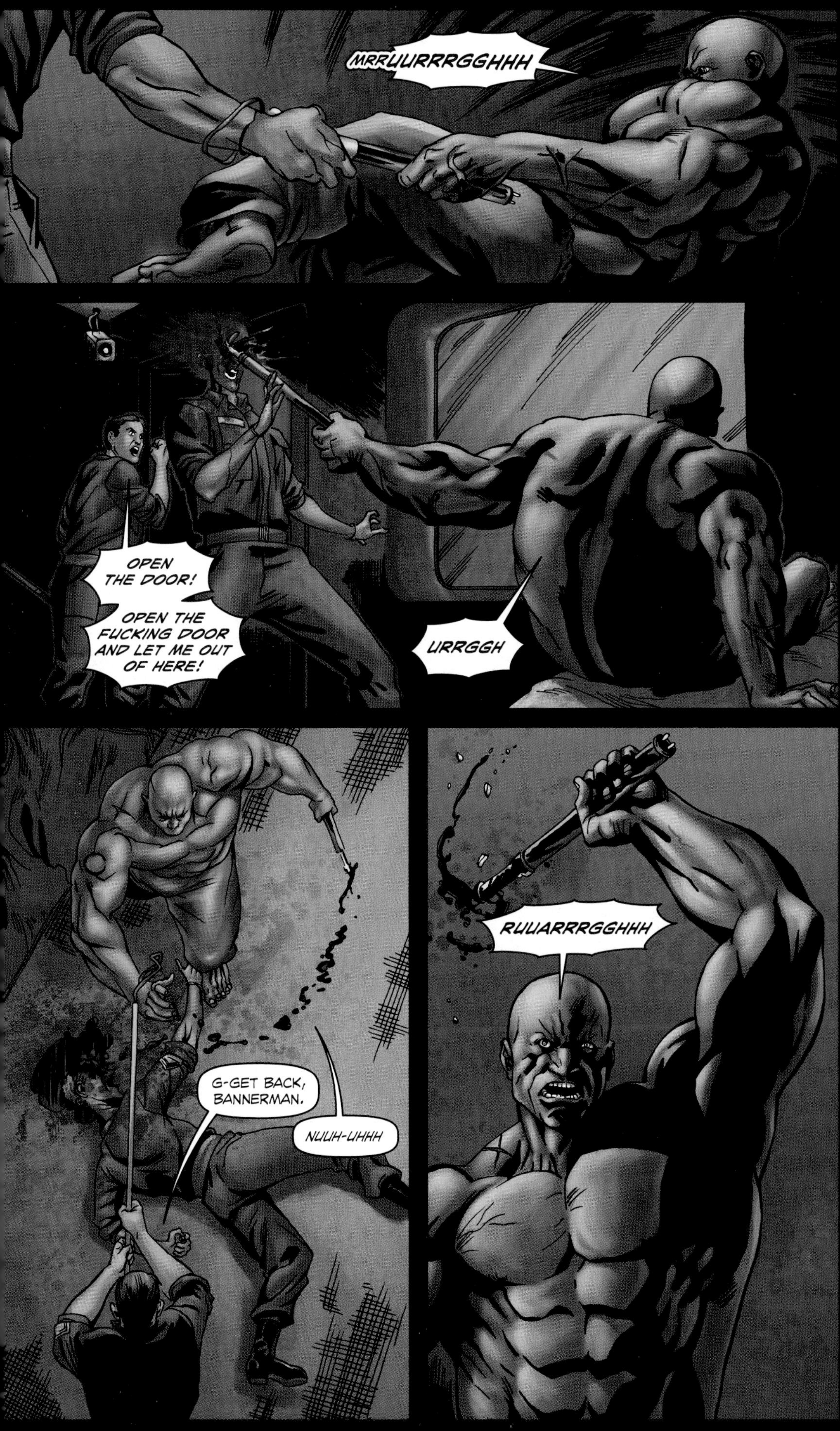
MRRUURRRGGHHH
OPEN THE DOOR!
OPEN THE FUCKING DOOR AND LET ME OUT OF HERE!
URRGGH
G-GET BACK, BANNERMAN.
NUUH-UHHH
RUUARRRGGHHH

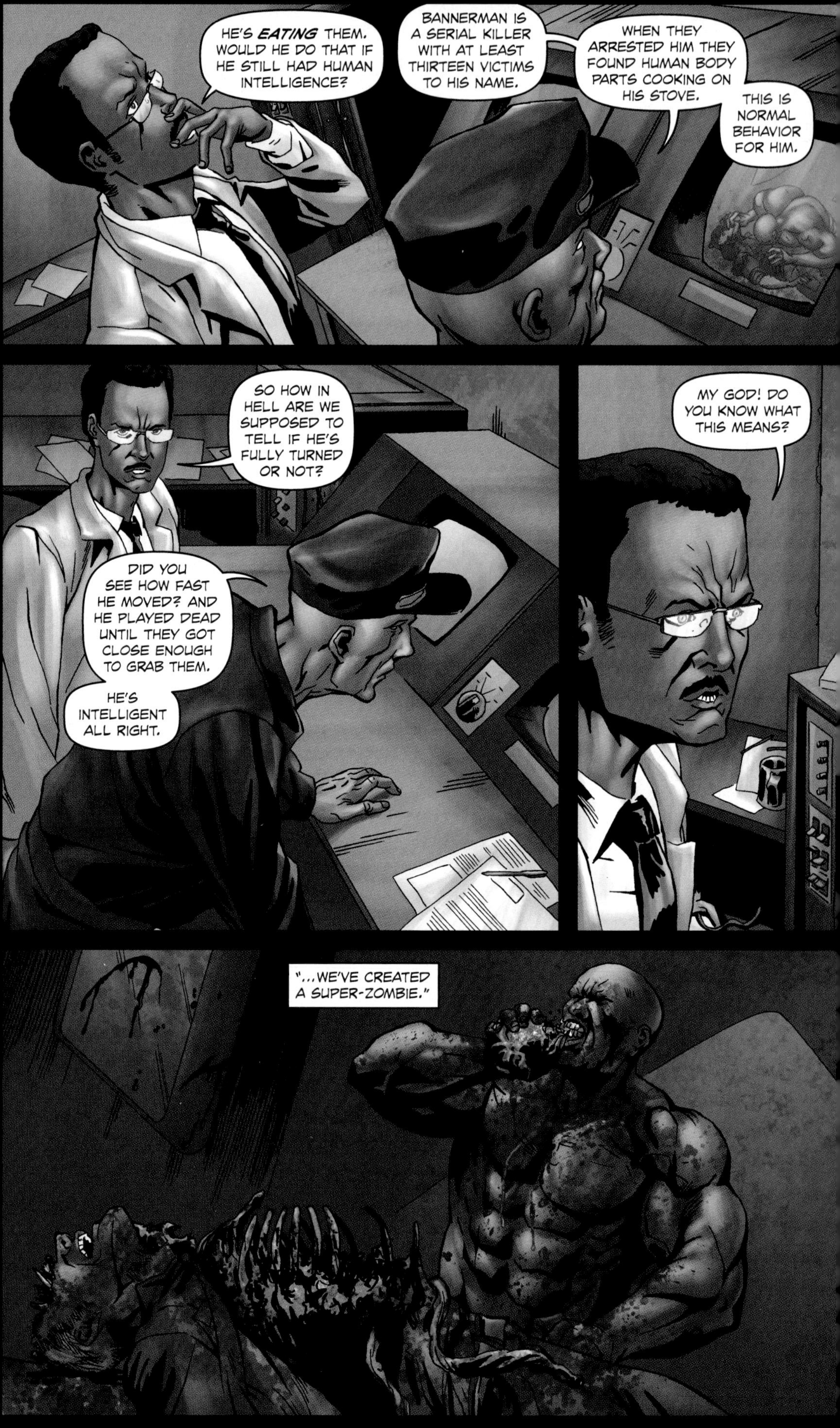

HE'S *EATING* THEM. WOULD HE DO THAT IF HE STILL HAD HUMAN INTELLIGENCE?
BANNERMAN IS A SERIAL KILLER WITH AT LEAST THIRTEEN VICTIMS TO HIS NAME.
WHEN THEY ARRESTED HIM THEY FOUND HUMAN BODY PARTS COOKING ON HIS STOVE.
THIS IS NORMAL BEHAVIOR FOR HIM.
SO HOW IN HELL ARE WE SUPPOSED TO TELL IF HE'S FULLY TURNED OR NOT?
DID YOU SEE HOW FAST HE MOVED? AND HE PLAYED DEAD UNTIL THEY GOT CLOSE ENOUGH TO GRAB THEM.
HE'S INTELLIGENT ALL RIGHT.
MY GOD! DO YOU KNOW WHAT THIS MEANS?
"...WE'VE CREATED A SUPER-ZOMBIE."

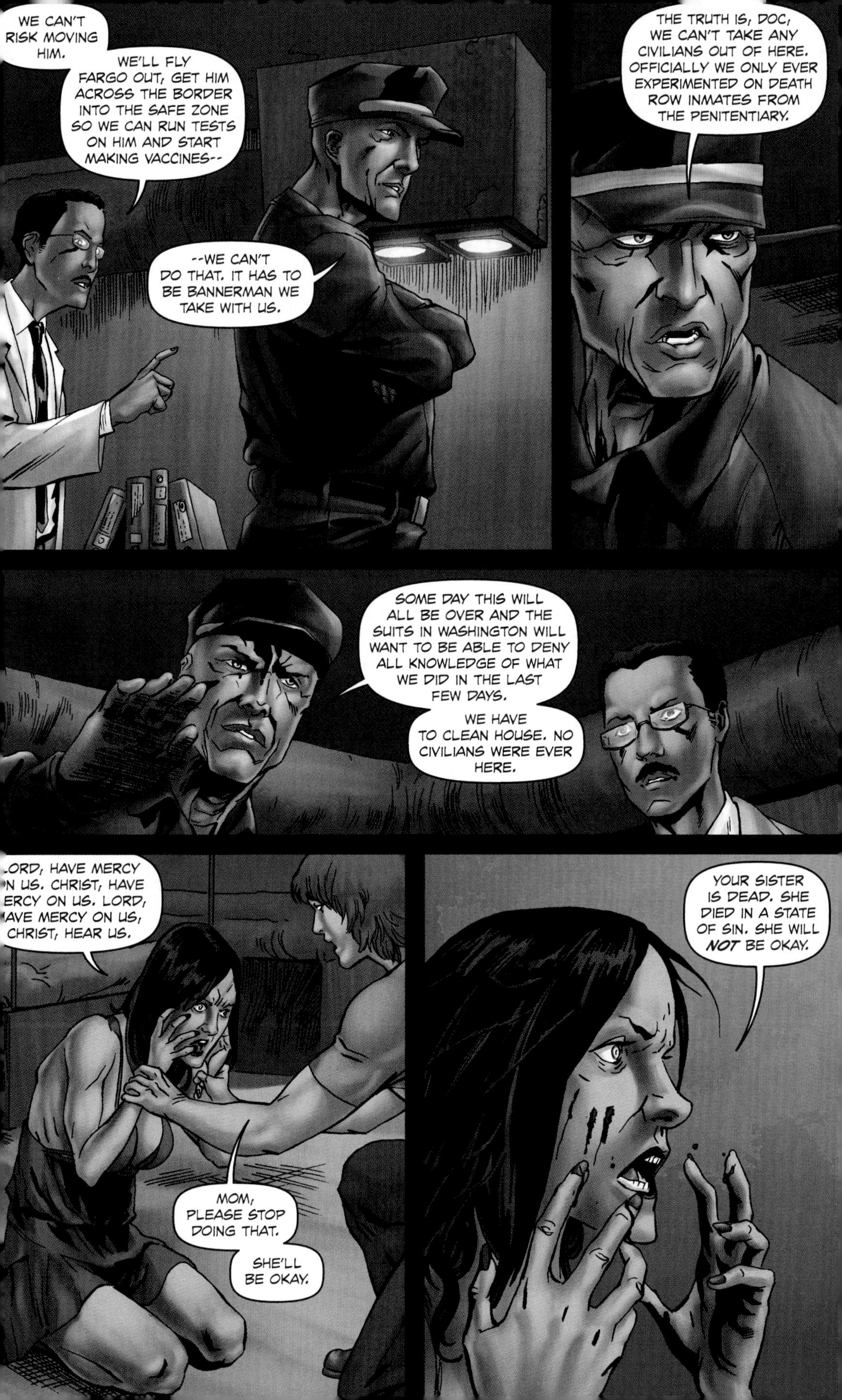
WE CAN'T RISK MOVING HIM.
WE'LL FLY FARGO OUT, GET HIM ACROSS THE BORDER INTO THE SAFE ZONE SO WE CAN RUN TESTS ON HIM AND START MAKING VACCINES--
--WE CAN'T DO THAT. IT HAS TO BE BANNERMAN WE TAKE WITH US.
THE TRUTH IS, DOC, WE CAN'T TAKE ANY CIVILIANS OUT OF HERE. OFFICIALLY WE ONLY EVER EXPERIMENTED ON DEATH ROW INMATES FROM THE PENITENTIARY.
SOME DAY THIS WILL ALL BE OVER AND THE SUITS IN WASHINGTON WILL WANT TO BE ABLE TO DENY ALL KNOWLEDGE OF WHAT WE DID IN THE LAST FEW DAYS.
WE HAVE TO CLEAN HOUSE. NO CIVILIANS WERE EVER HERE.
ORD, HAVE MERCY N US. CHRIST, HAVE ERCY ON US. LORD, AVE MERCY ON US, CHRIST, HEAR US.
MOM, PLEASE STOP DOING THAT.
SHE'LL BE OKAY.
YOUR SISTER IS DEAD. SHE DIED IN A STATE OF SIN. SHE WILL *NOT* BE OKAY.

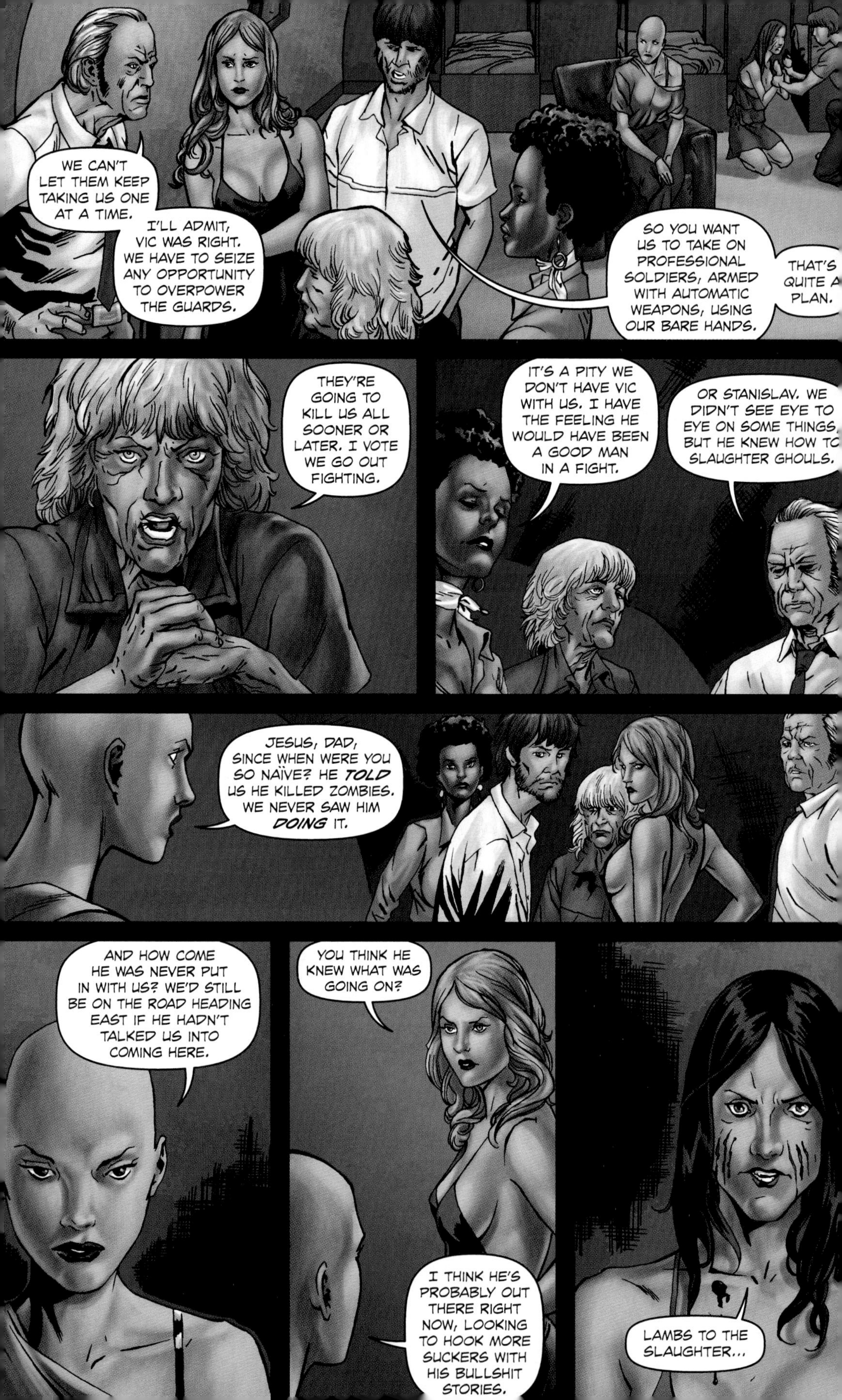
WE CAN'T LET THEM KEEP TAKING US ONE AT A TIME.
I'LL ADMIT, VIC WAS RIGHT. WE HAVE TO SEIZE ANY OPPORTUNITY TO OVERPOWER THE GUARDS.
SO YOU WANT US TO TAKE ON PROFESSIONAL SOLDIERS, ARMED WITH AUTOMATIC WEAPONS, USING OUR BARE HANDS.
THAT'S QUITE A PLAN.
THEY'RE GOING TO KILL US ALL SOONER OR LATER. I VOTE WE GO OUT FIGHTING.
IT'S A PITY WE DON'T HAVE VIC WITH US. I HAVE THE FEELING HE WOULD HAVE BEEN A GOOD MAN IN A FIGHT.
OR STANISLAV. WE DIDN'T SEE EYE TO EYE ON SOME THINGS, BUT HE KNEW HOW TO SLAUGHTER GHOULS.
JESUS, DAD, SINCE WHEN WERE YOU SO NAÏVE? HE *TOLD* US HE KILLED ZOMBIES. WE NEVER SAW HIM *DOING* IT.
AND HOW COME HE WAS NEVER PUT IN WITH US? WE'D STILL BE ON THE ROAD HEADING EAST IF HE HADN'T TALKED US INTO COMING HERE.
YOU THINK HE KNEW WHAT WAS GOING ON?
I THINK HE'S PROBABLY OUT THERE RIGHT NOW, LOOKING TO HOOK MORE SUCKERS WITH HIS BULLSHIT STORIES.
LAMBS TO THE SLAUGHTER...

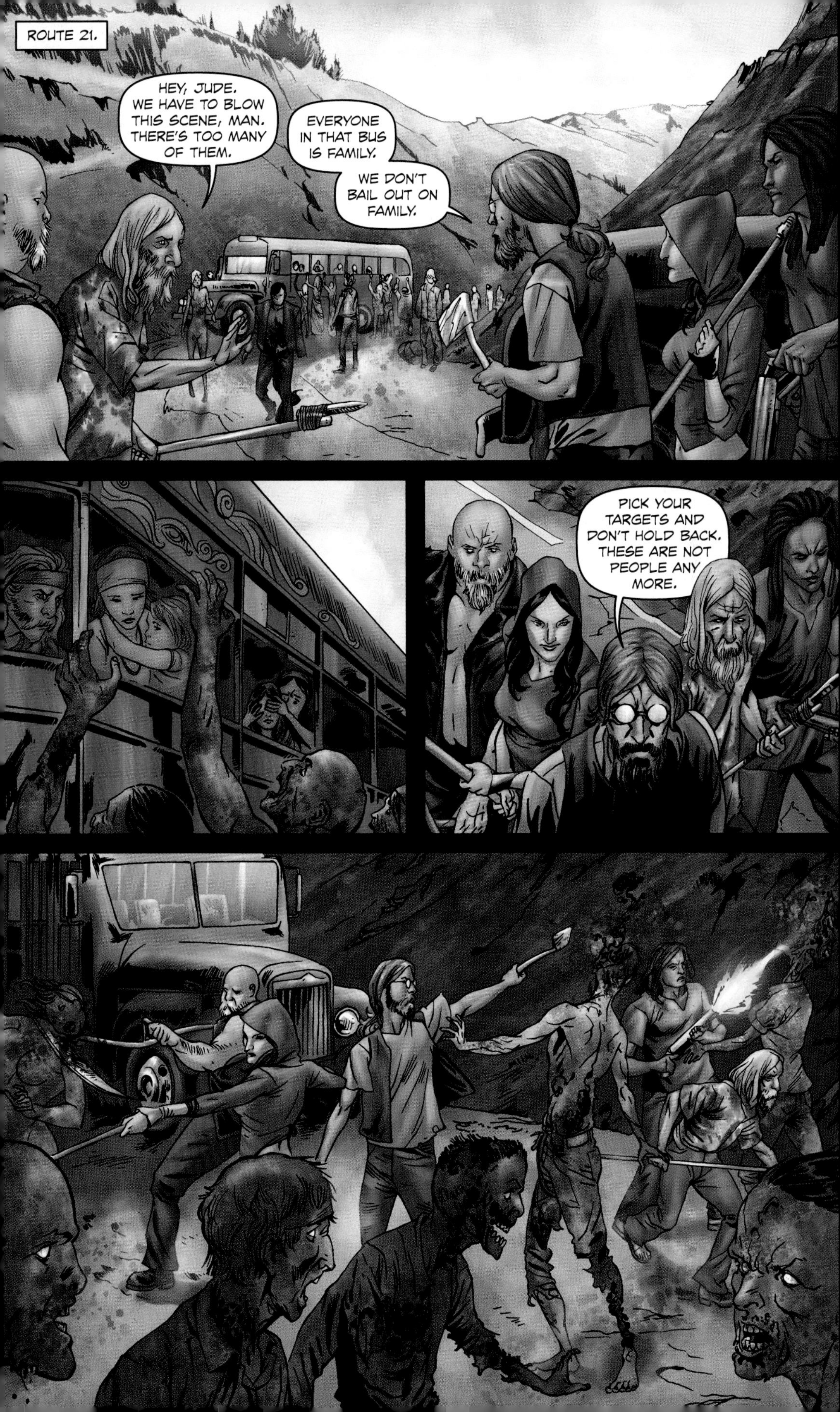
ROUTE 21.
HEY, JUDE. WE HAVE TO BLOW THIS SCENE, MAN. THERE'S TOO MANY OF THEM.
EVERYONE IN THAT BUS IS FAMILY.
WE DON'T BAIL OUT ON FAMILY.
PICK YOUR TARGETS AND DON'T HOLD BACK. THESE ARE NOT PEOPLE ANY MORE.

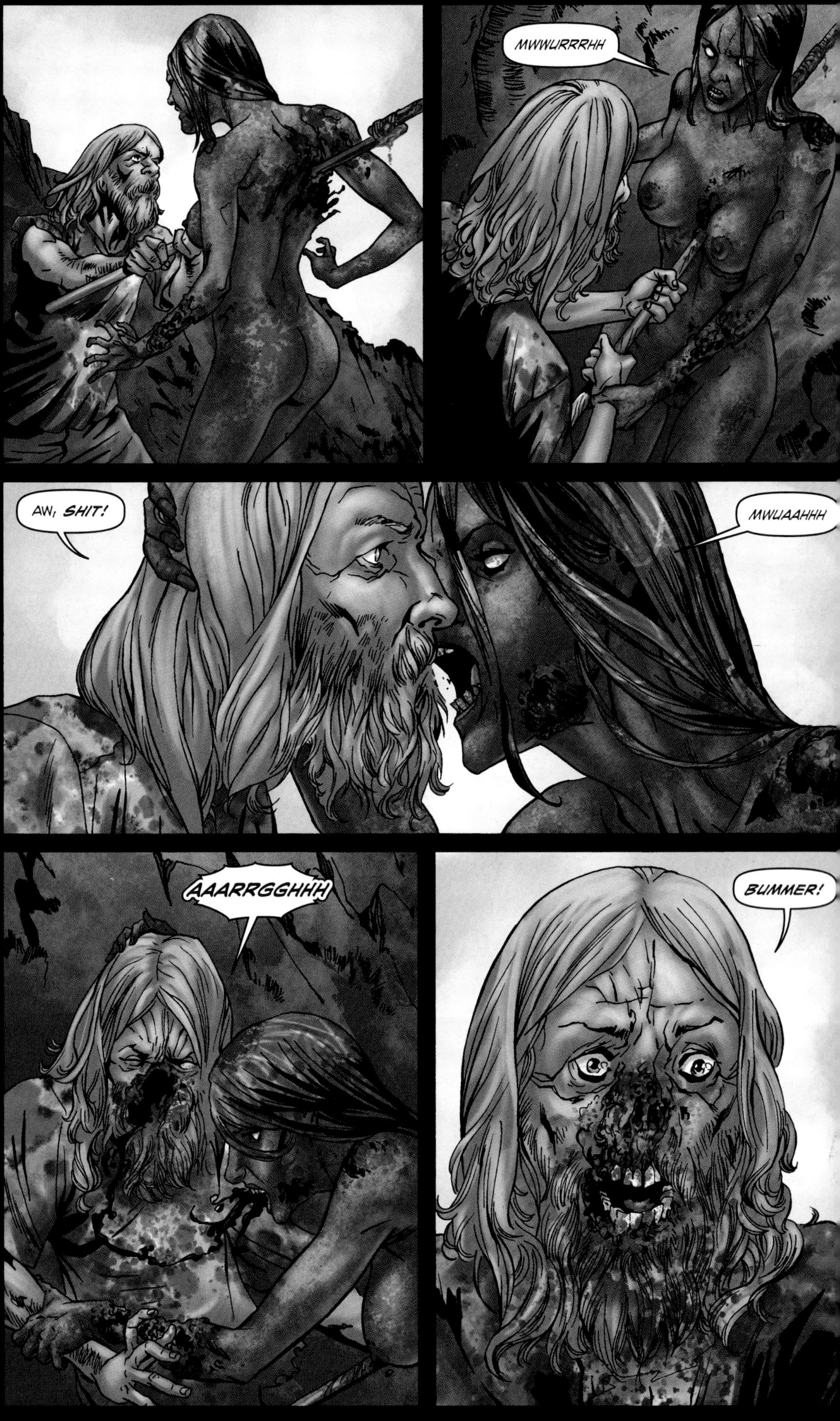
MWWURRRHH
AW, SHIT!
MWUAAHHH
AAARRGGHHH
BUMMER!

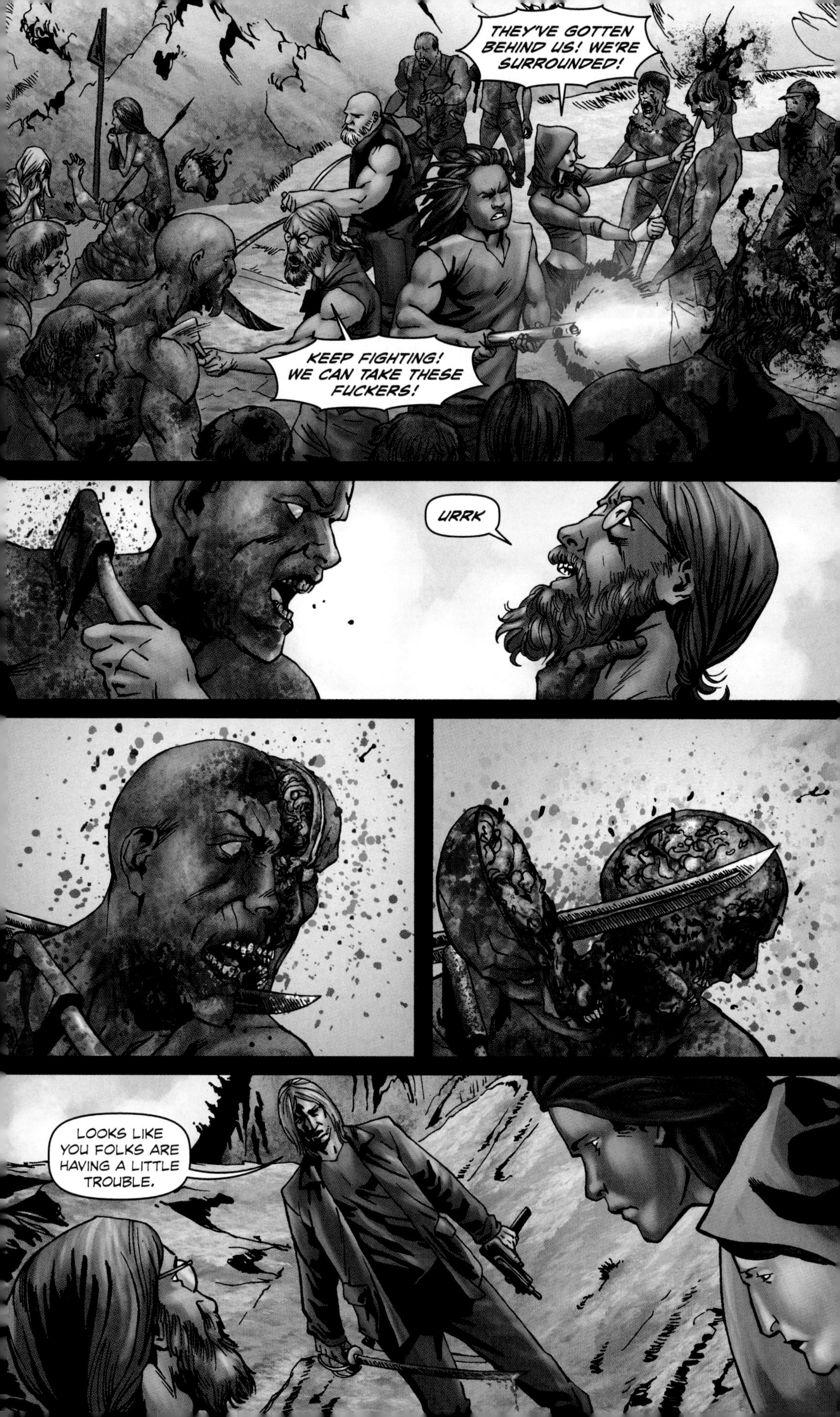
THEY'VE GOTTEN BEHIND US! WE'RE SURROUNDED!
KEEP FIGHTING! WE CAN TAKE THESE FUCKERS!
URRK
LOOKS LIKE YOU FOLKS ARE HAVING A LITTLE TROUBLE.

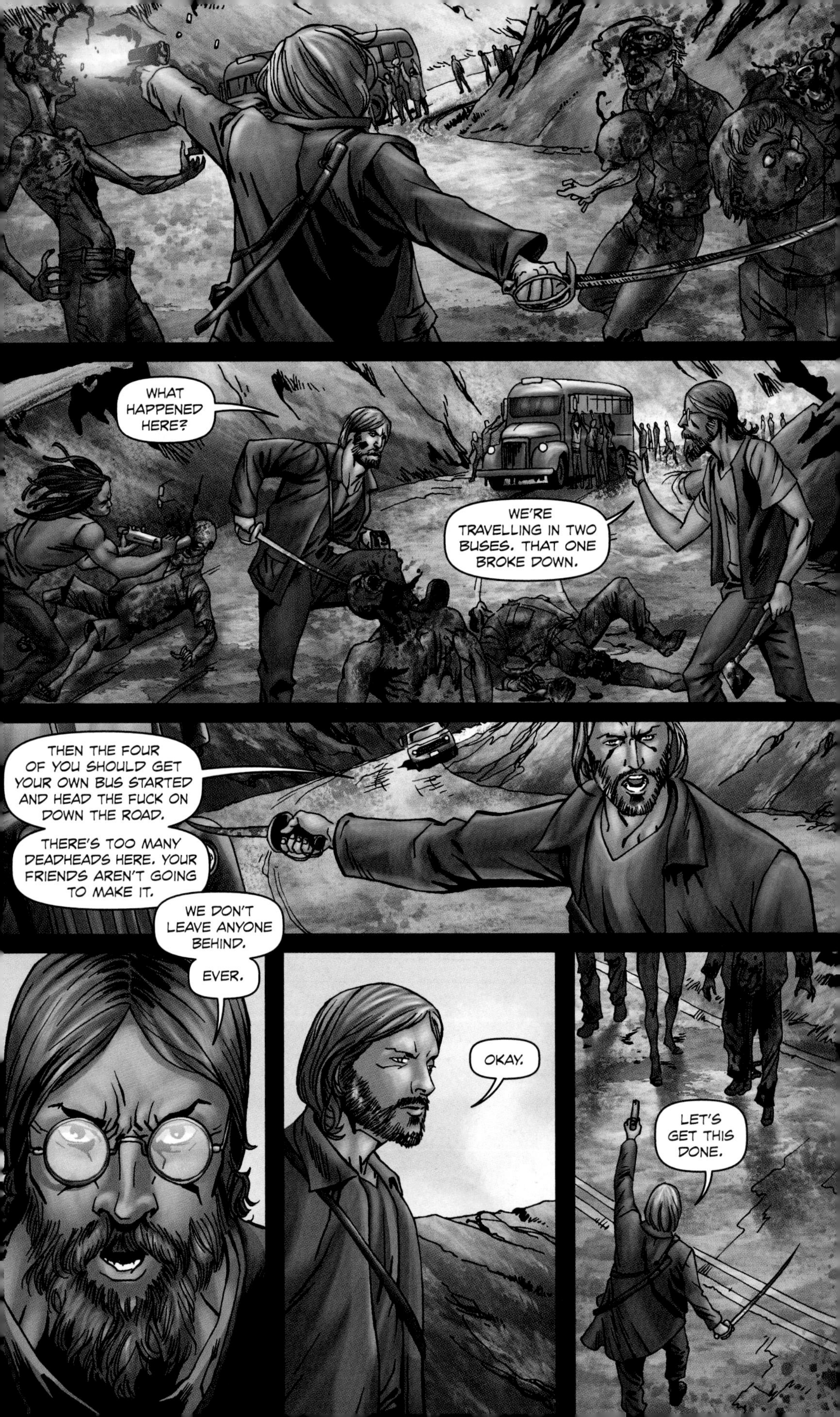
WHAT HAPPENED HERE?
WE'RE TRAVELLING IN TWO BUSES. THAT ONE BROKE DOWN.
THEN THE FOUR OF YOU SHOULD GET YOUR OWN BUS STARTED AND HEAD THE FUCK ON DOWN THE ROAD.
THERE'S TOO MANY DEADHEADS HERE. YOUR FRIENDS AREN'T GOING TO MAKE IT.
WE DON'T LEAVE ANYONE BEHIND.
EVER.
OKAY.
LET'S GET THIS DONE.

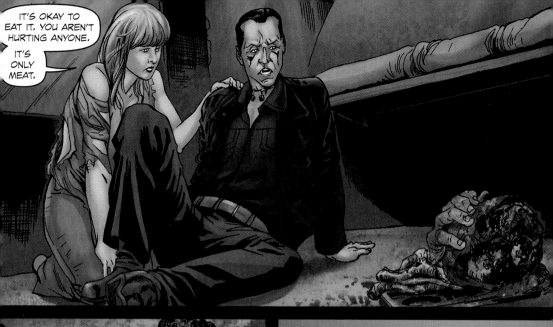

It's okay to eat it. You aren't hurting anyone.

It's only meat.

AAUUNNGHH

I don't know what they've done to you. I don't know if you're alive or dead.

I do know, if it weren't for you taking my place, they would have done it to me.

I won't leave you. We're going to get out of here together.

That's a promise.

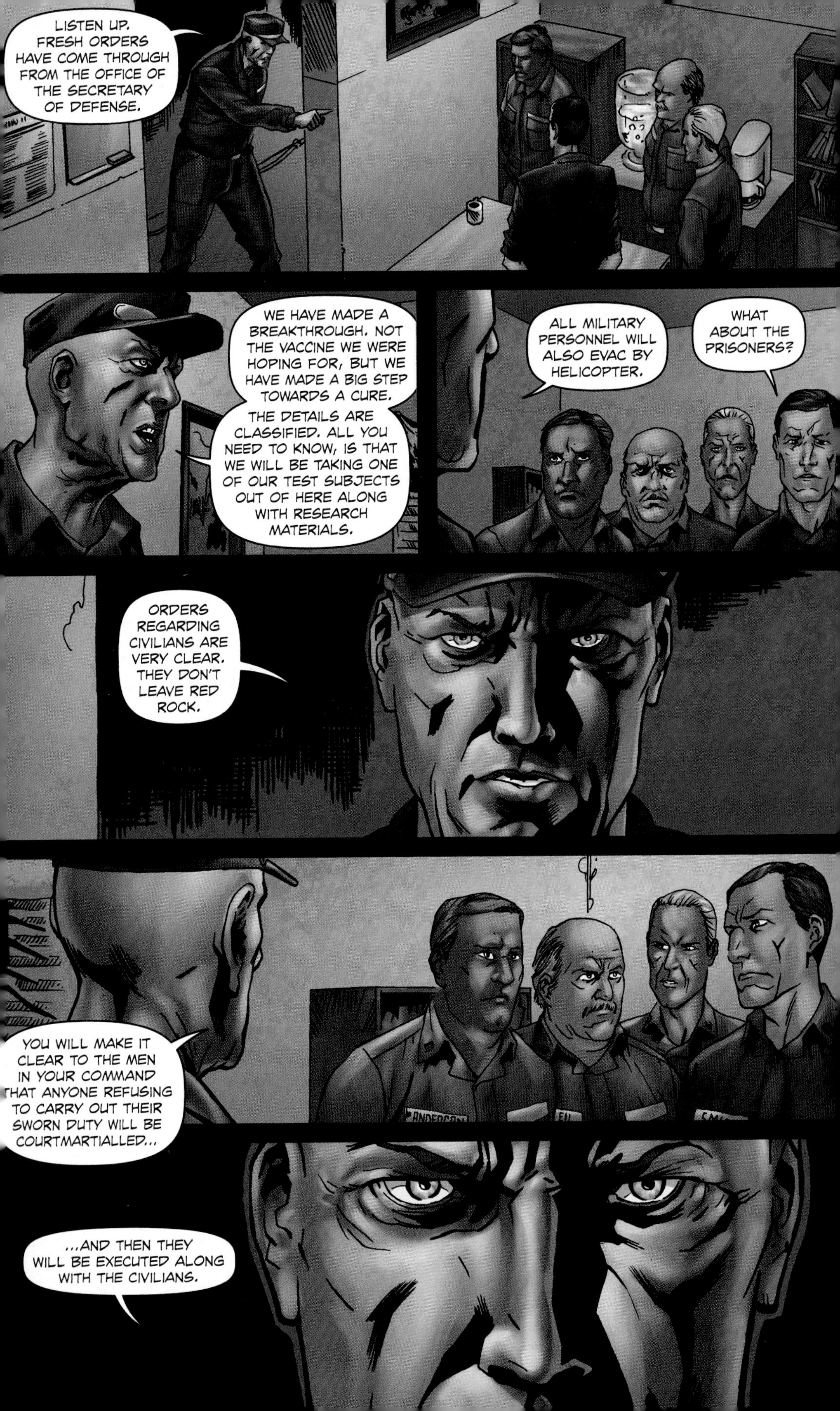

LISTEN UP. FRESH ORDERS HAVE COME THROUGH FROM THE OFFICE OF THE SECRETARY OF DEFENSE.
WE HAVE MADE A BREAKTHROUGH. NOT THE VACCINE WE WERE HOPING FOR, BUT WE HAVE MADE A BIG STEP TOWARDS A CURE.
THE DETAILS ARE CLASSIFIED. ALL YOU NEED TO KNOW, IS THAT WE WILL BE TAKING ONE OF OUR TEST SUBJECTS OUT OF HERE ALONG WITH RESEARCH MATERIALS.
ALL MILITARY PERSONNEL WILL ALSO EVAC BY HELICOPTER.
WHAT ABOUT THE PRISONERS?
ORDERS REGARDING CIVILIANS ARE VERY CLEAR. THEY DON'T LEAVE RED ROCK.
YOU WILL MAKE IT CLEAR TO THE MEN IN YOUR COMMAND THAT ANYONE REFUSING TO CARRY OUT THEIR SWORN DUTY WILL BE COURTMARTIALLED...
...AND THEN THEY WILL BE EXECUTED ALONG WITH THE CIVILIANS.

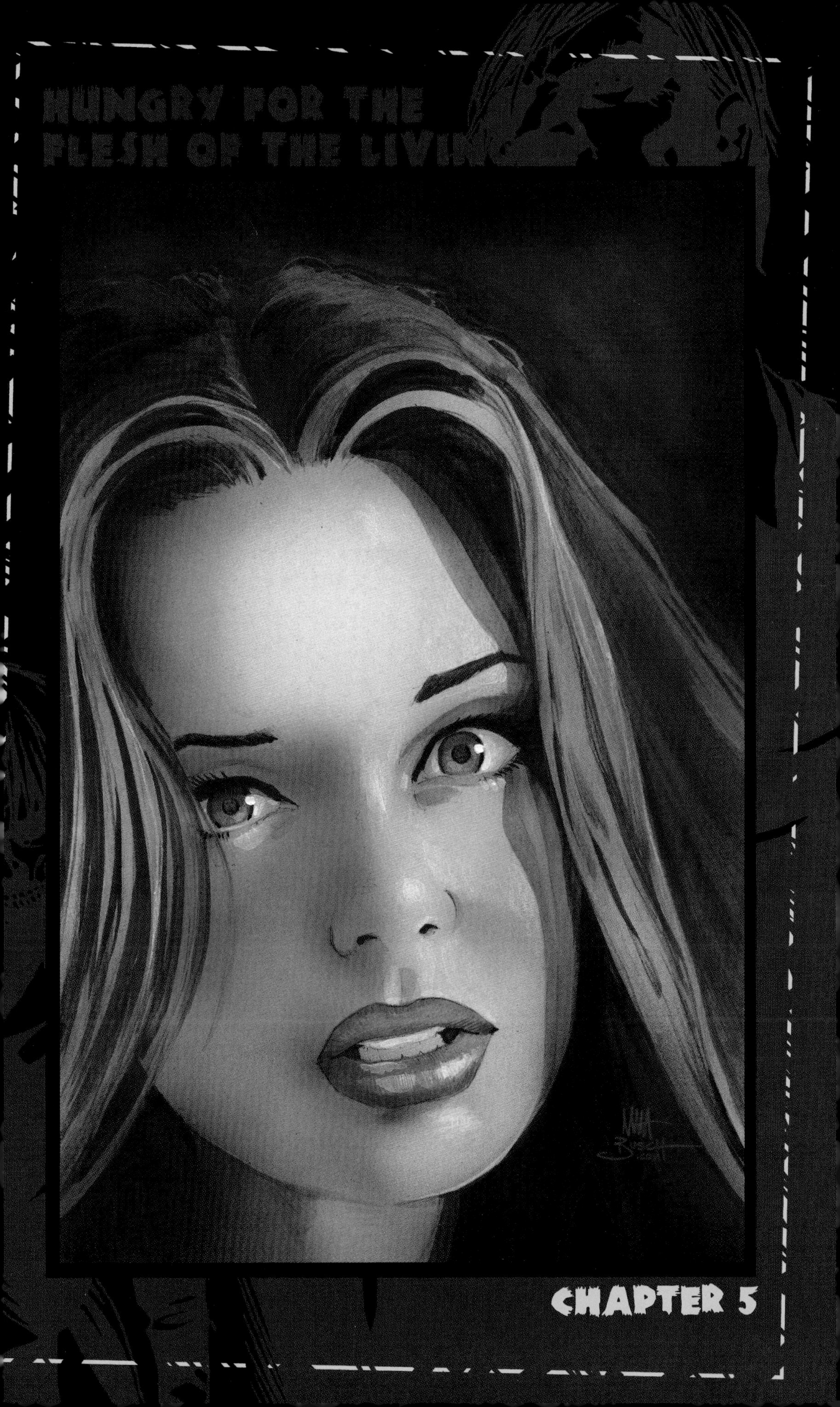
HUNGRY FOR THE
FLESH OF THE LIVING
CHAPTER 5

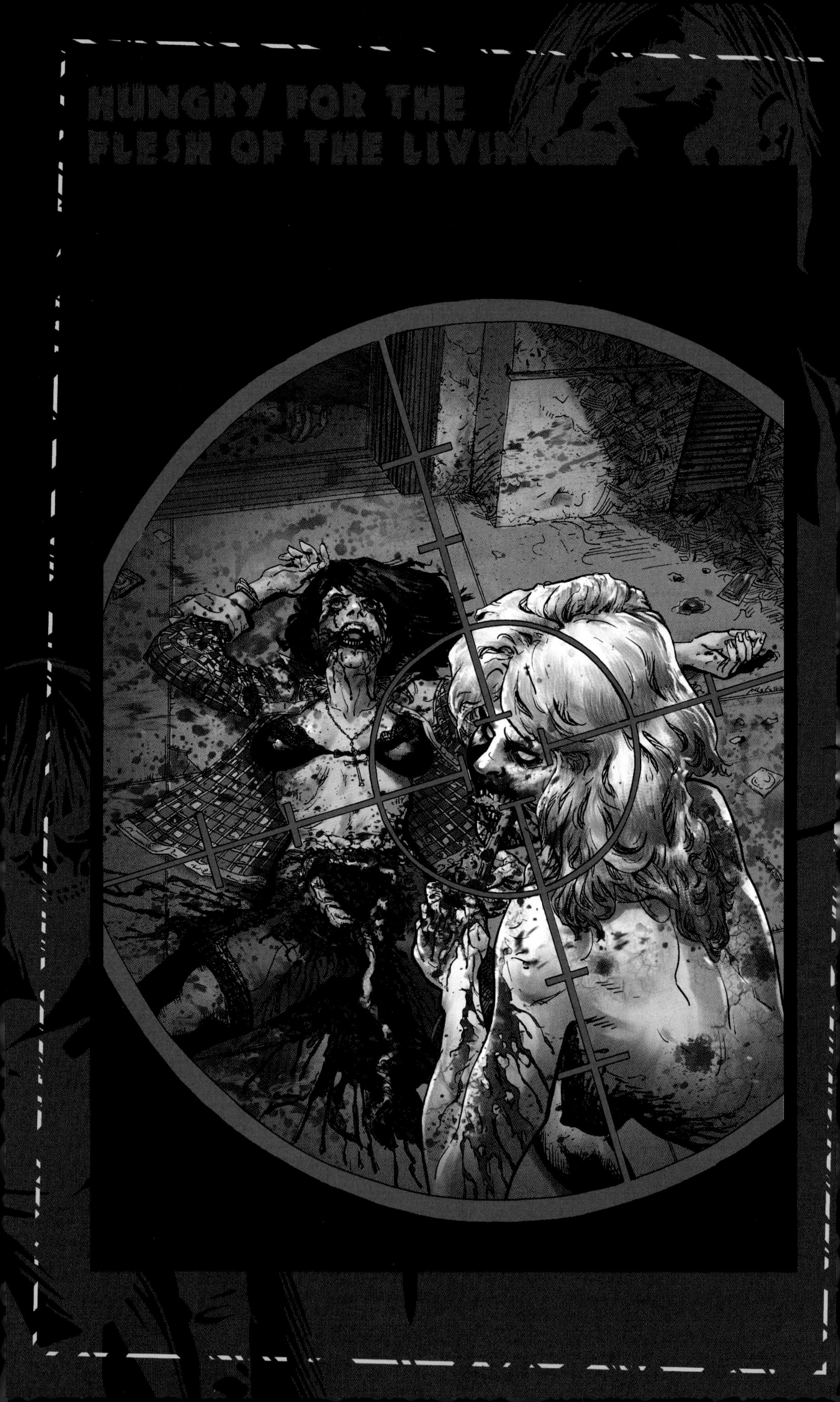
HUNGRY FOR THE
FLESH OF THE LIVIN

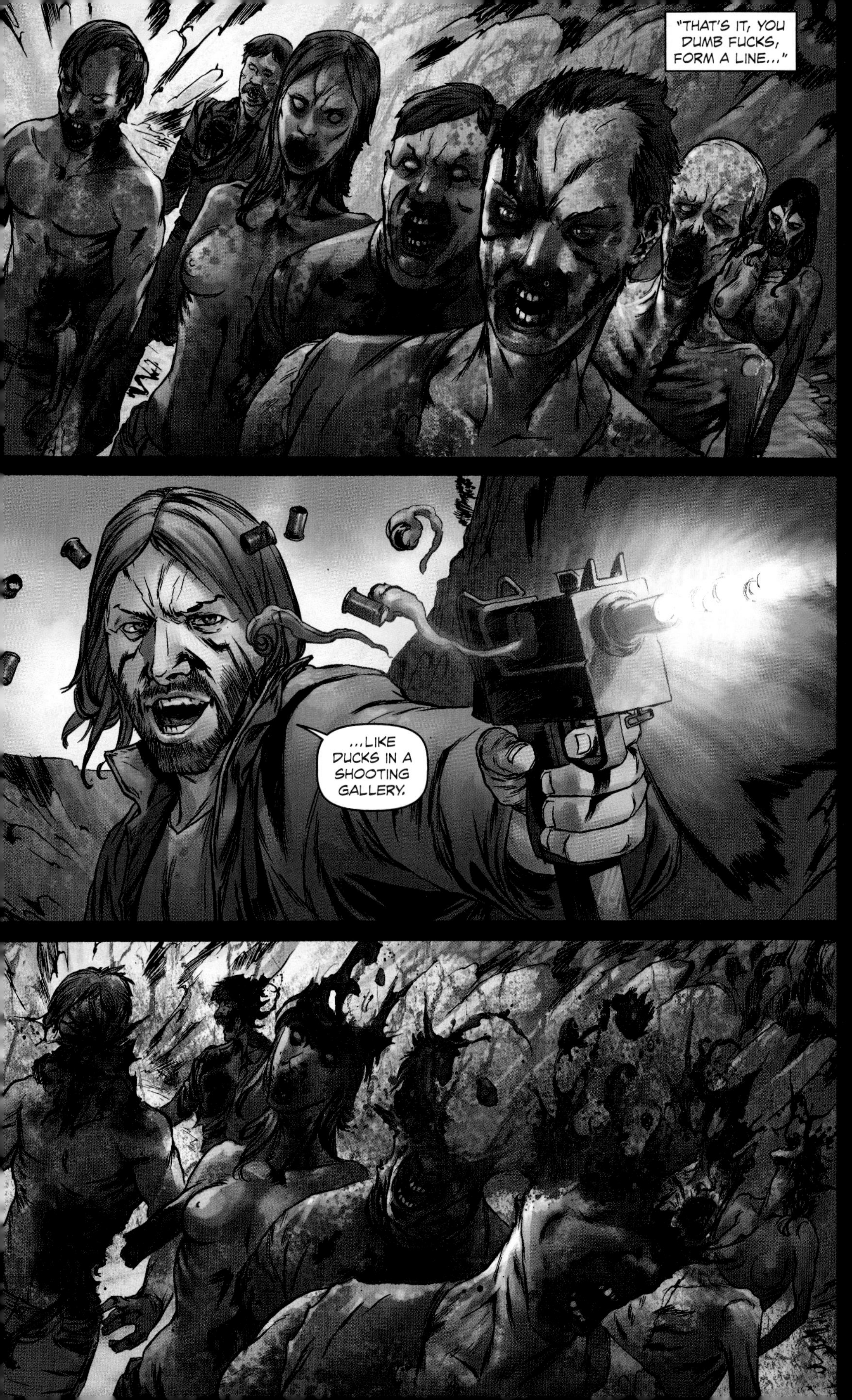
"THAT'S IT, YOU DUMB FUCKS, FORM A LINE..."
...LIKE DUCKS IN A SHOOTING GALLERY.

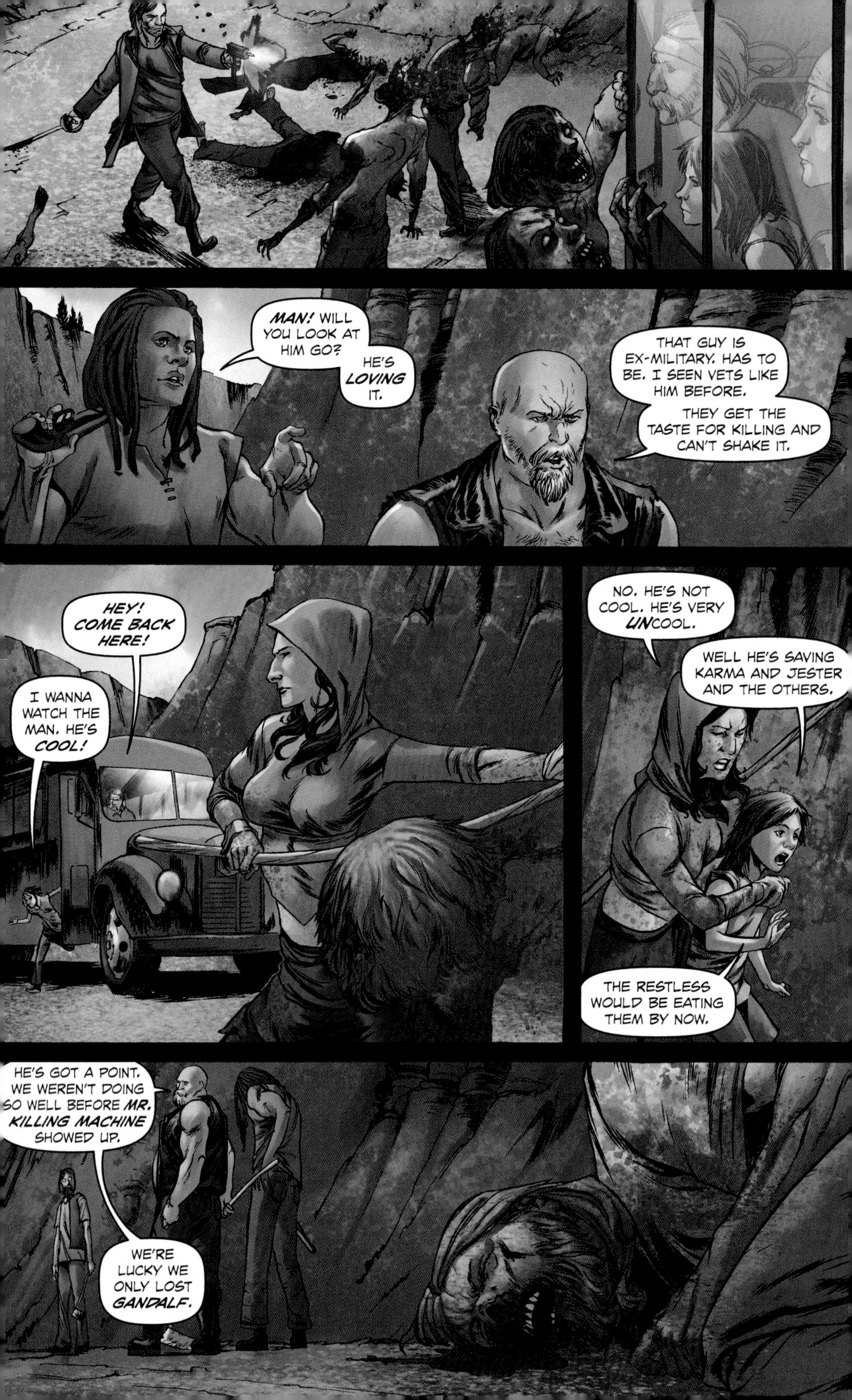
MAN! WILL YOU LOOK AT HIM GO?
HE'S LOVING IT.
THAT GUY IS EX-MILITARY. HAS TO BE. I SEEN VETS LIKE HIM BEFORE.
THEY GET THE TASTE FOR KILLING AND CAN'T SHAKE IT.
HEY! COME BACK HERE!
I WANNA WATCH THE MAN. HE'S COOL!
NO. HE'S NOT COOL. HE'S VERY UNCOOL.
WELL HE'S SAVING KARMA AND JESTER AND THE OTHERS.
THE RESTLESS WOULD BE EATING THEM BY NOW.
HE'S GOT A POINT. WE WEREN'T DOING SO WELL BEFORE MR. KILLING MACHINE SHOWED UP.
WE'RE LUCKY WE ONLY LOST GANDALF.

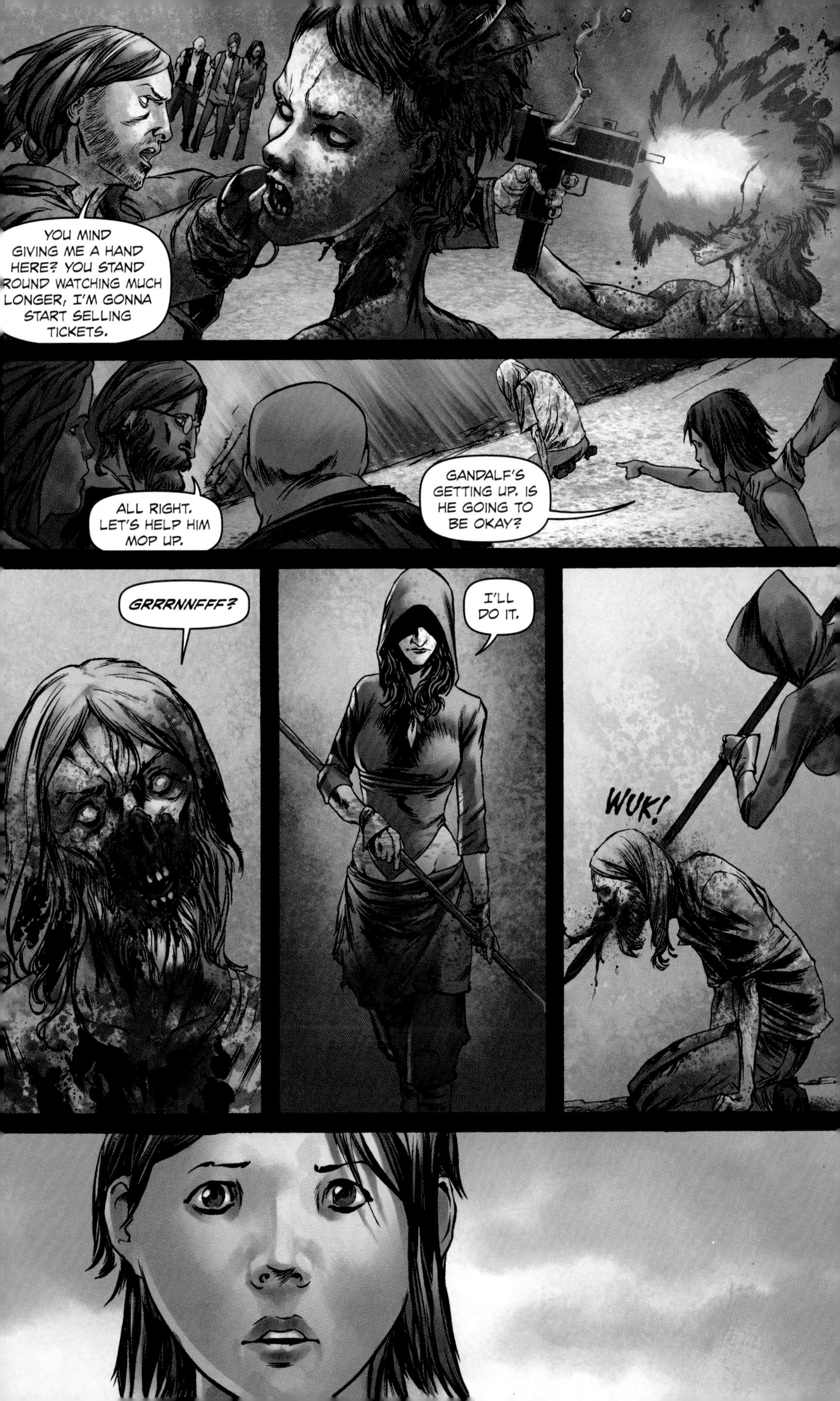
YOU MIND GIVING ME A HAND HERE? YOU STAND ROUND WATCHING MUCH LONGER, I'M GONNA START SELLING TICKETS.
ALL RIGHT. LET'S HELP HIM MOP UP.
GANDALF'S GETTING UP. IS HE GOING TO BE OKAY?
GRRRNNFFF?
I'LL DO IT.
WUK!

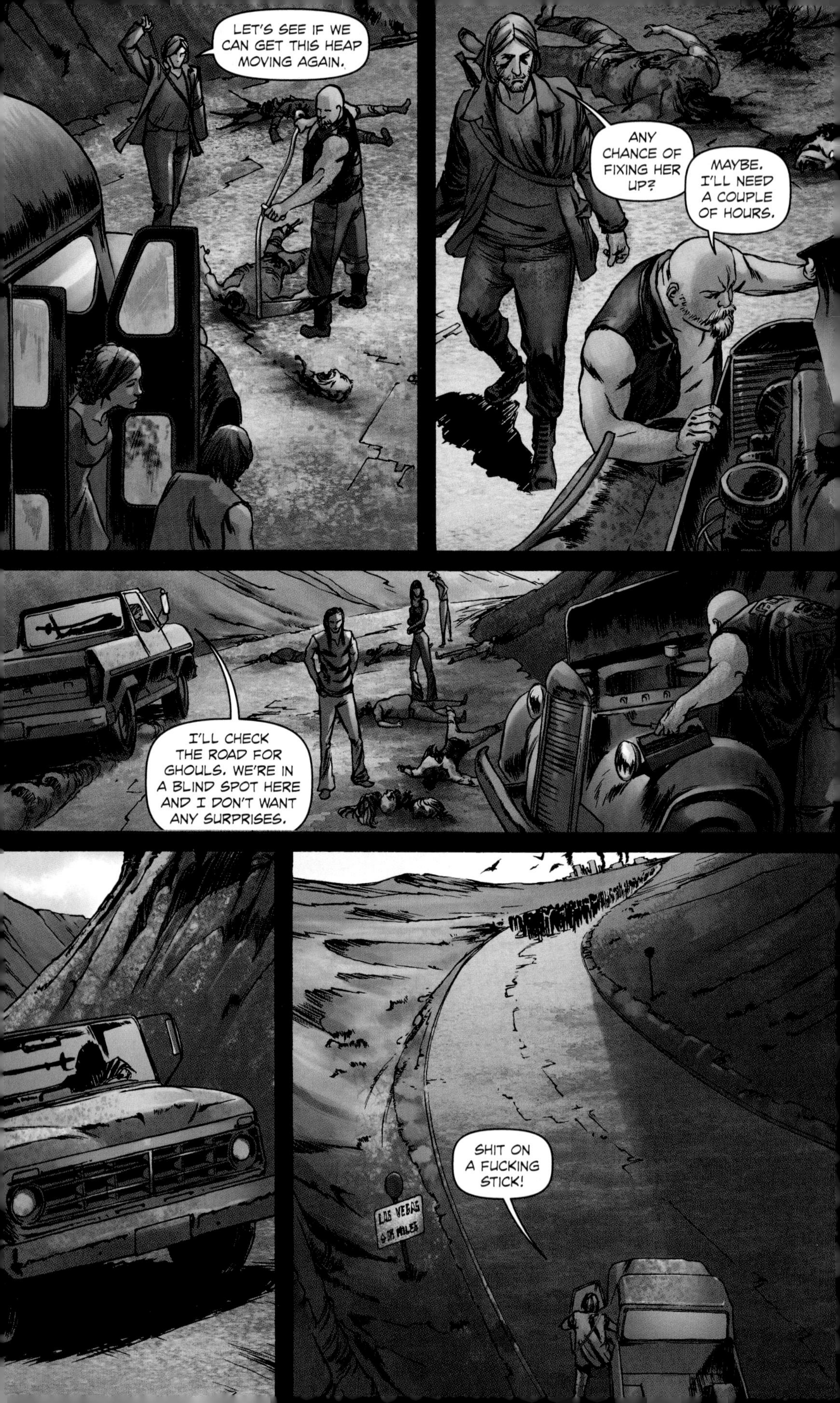
LET'S SEE IF WE CAN GET THIS HEAP MOVING AGAIN.
ANY CHANCE OF FIXING HER UP?
MAYBE. I'LL NEED A COUPLE OF HOURS.
I'LL CHECK THE ROAD FOR GHOULS. WE'RE IN A BLIND SPOT HERE AND I DON'T WANT ANY SURPRISES.
SHIT ON A FUCKING STICK!

MWUURRRGH

FORGET THE BUS! WE'RE MOVING OUT!

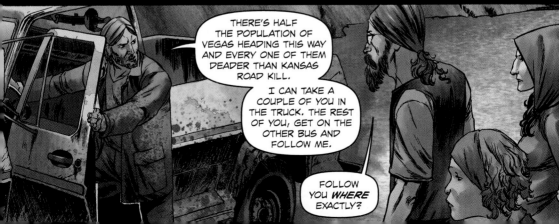

THERE'S HALF THE POPULATION OF VEGAS HEADING THIS WAY AND EVERY ONE OF THEM DEADER THAN KANSAS ROAD KILL.

I CAN TAKE A COUPLE OF YOU IN THE TRUCK. THE REST OF YOU, GET ON THE OTHER BUS AND FOLLOW ME.

FOLLOW YOU *WHERE* EXACTLY?

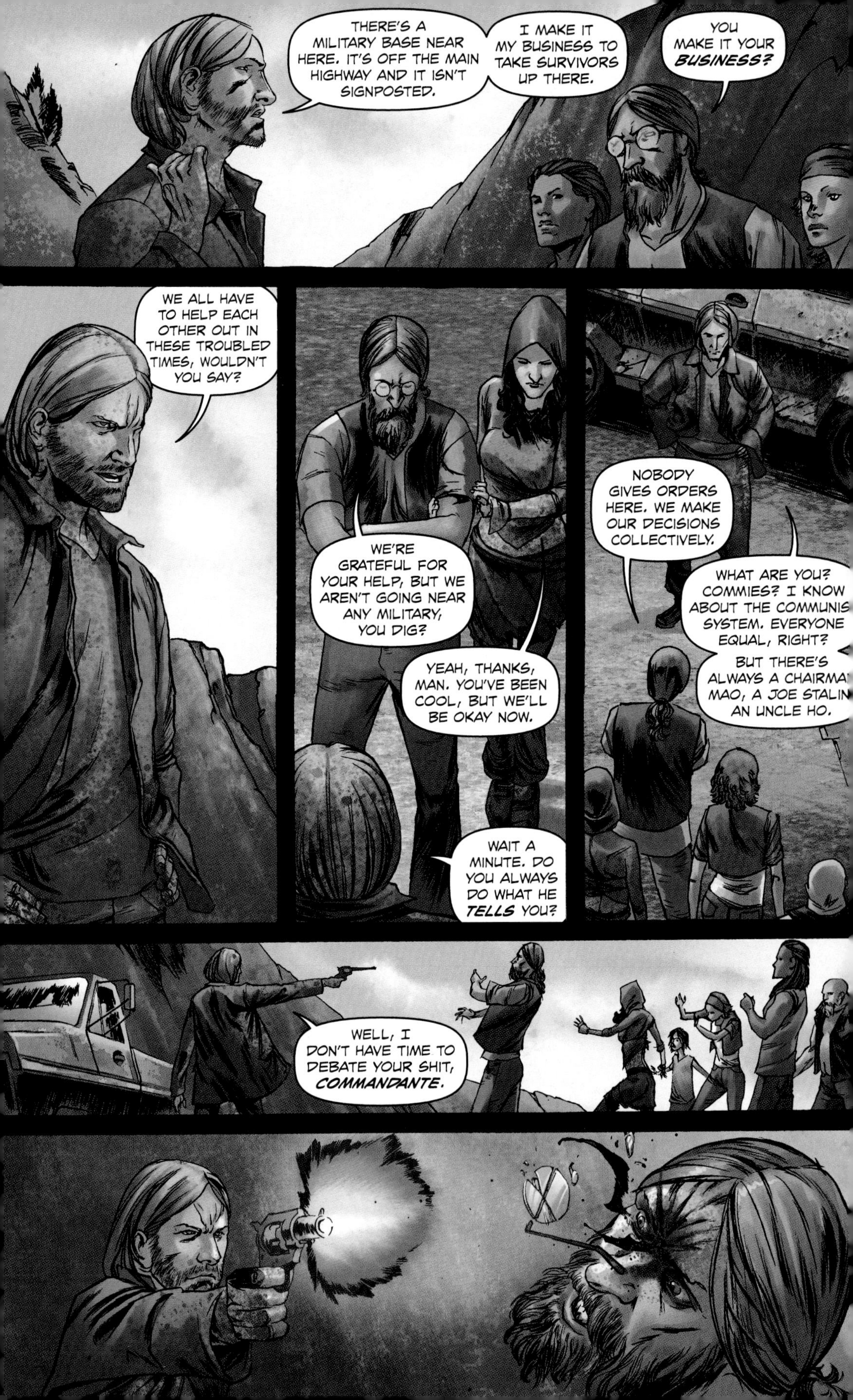
THERE'S A MILITARY BASE NEAR HERE. IT'S OFF THE MAIN HIGHWAY AND IT ISN'T SIGNPOSTED.
I MAKE IT MY BUSINESS TO TAKE SURVIVORS UP THERE.
YOU MAKE IT YOUR *BUSINESS?*
WE ALL HAVE TO HELP EACH OTHER OUT IN THESE TROUBLED TIMES, WOULDN'T YOU SAY?
WE'RE GRATEFUL FOR YOUR HELP, BUT WE AREN'T GOING NEAR ANY MILITARY, YOU DIG?
YEAH, THANKS, MAN. YOU'VE BEEN COOL, BUT WE'LL BE OKAY NOW.
WAIT A MINUTE. DO YOU ALWAYS DO WHAT HE *TELLS* YOU?
NOBODY GIVES ORDERS HERE. WE MAKE OUR DECISIONS COLLECTIVELY.
WHAT ARE YOU? COMMIES? I KNOW ABOUT THE COMMUNIS SYSTEM. EVERYONE EQUAL, RIGHT?
BUT THERE'S ALWAYS A CHAIRMA MAO, A JOE STALIN AN UNCLE HO.
WELL, I DON'T HAVE TIME TO DEBATE YOUR SHIT, *COMMANDANTE.*

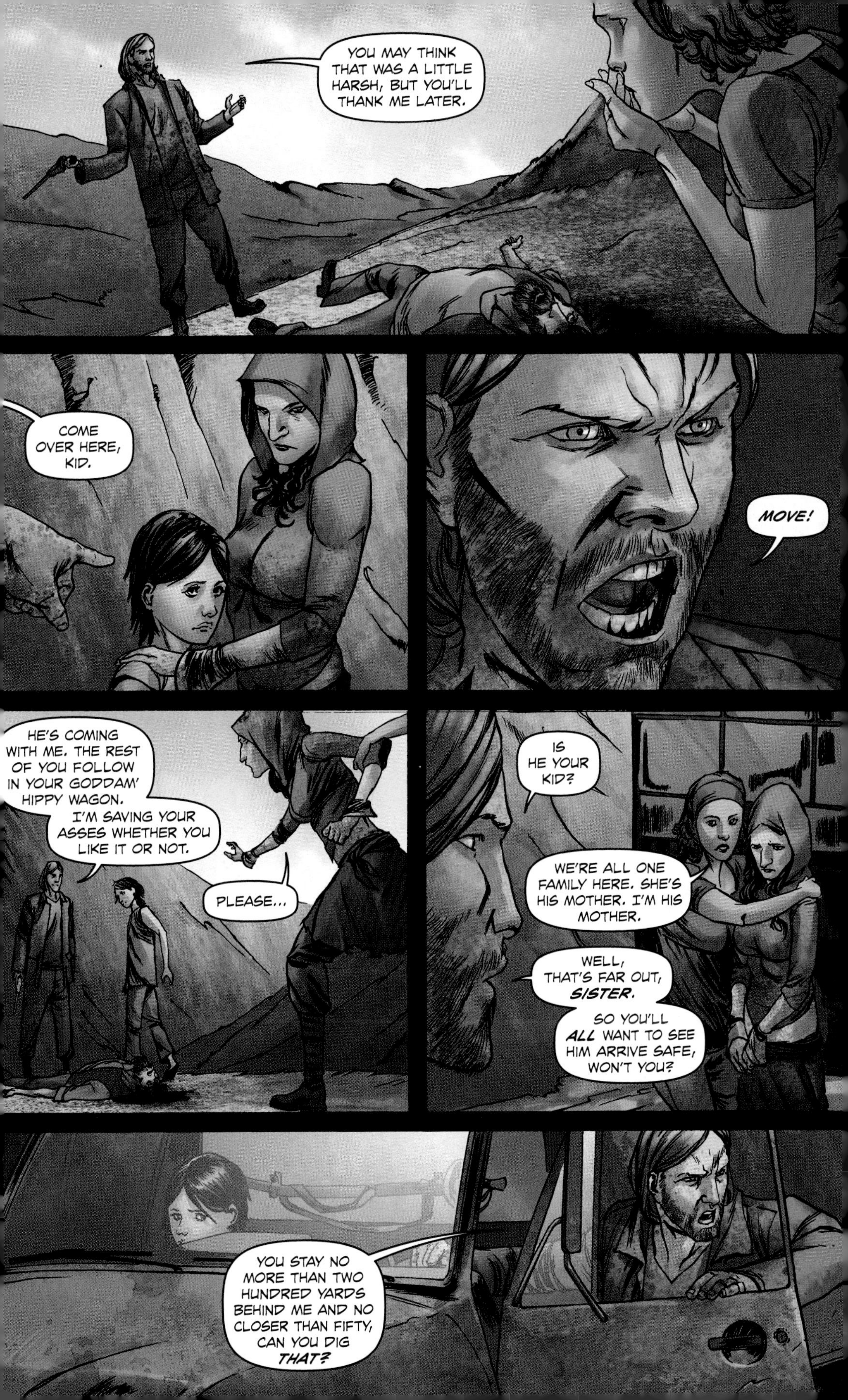
YOU MAY THINK THAT WAS A LITTLE HARSH, BUT YOU'LL THANK ME LATER.
COME OVER HERE, KID.
MOVE!
HE'S COMING WITH ME. THE REST OF YOU FOLLOW IN YOUR GODDAM' HIPPY WAGON.
I'M SAVING YOUR ASSES WHETHER YOU LIKE IT OR NOT.
PLEASE...
IS HE YOUR KID?
WE'RE ALL ONE FAMILY HERE. SHE'S HIS MOTHER. I'M HIS MOTHER.
WELL, THAT'S FAR OUT, SISTER.
SO YOU'LL ALL WANT TO SEE HIM ARRIVE SAFE, WON'T YOU?
YOU STAY NO MORE THAN TWO HUNDRED YARDS BEHIND ME AND NO CLOSER THAN FIFTY, CAN YOU DIG THAT?

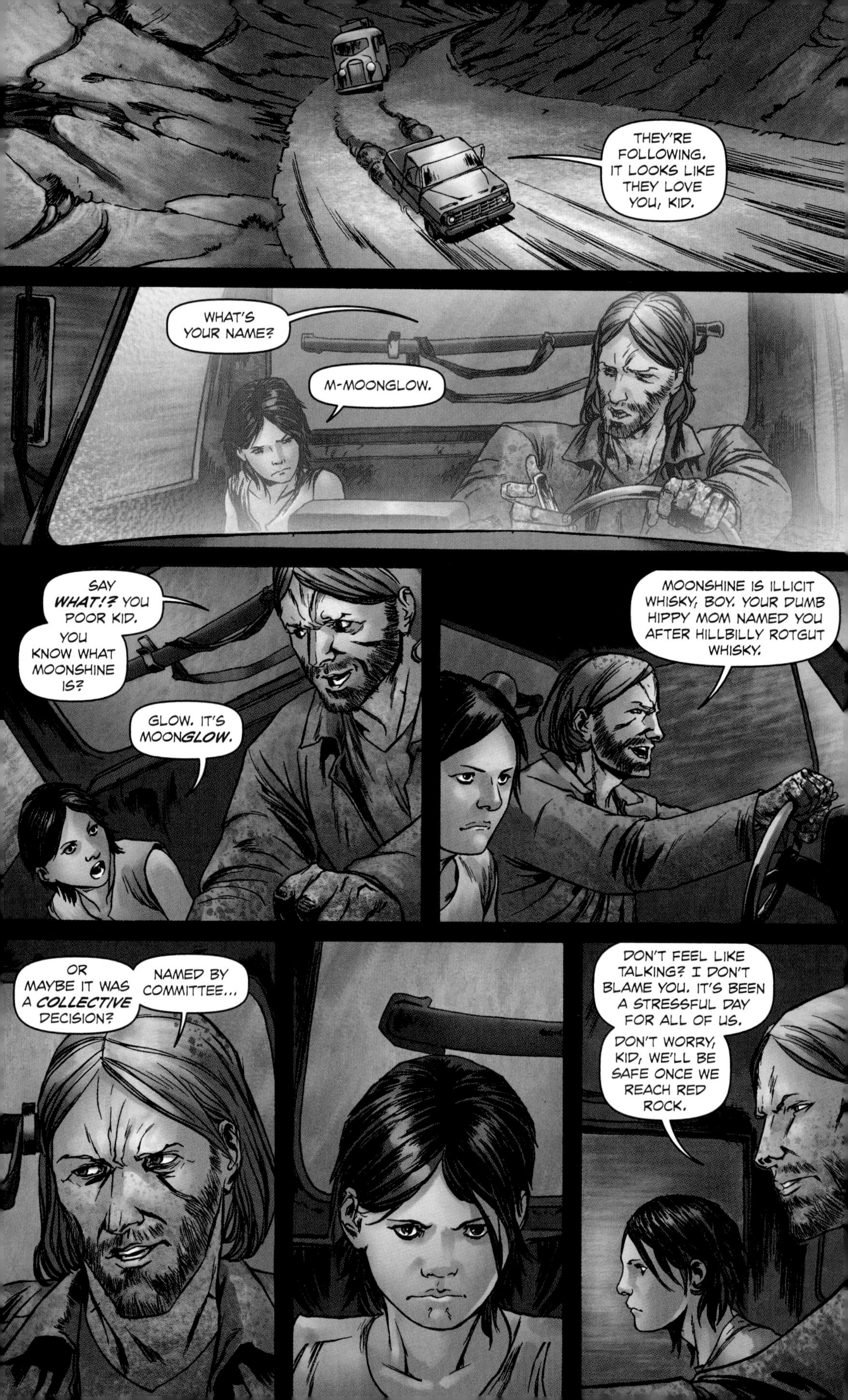
THEY'RE FOLLOWING. IT LOOKS LIKE THEY LOVE YOU, KID.
WHAT'S YOUR NAME?
M-MOONGLOW.
SAY WHAT!? YOU POOR KID.
YOU KNOW WHAT MOONSHINE IS?
GLOW. IT'S MOONGLOW.
MOONSHINE IS ILLICIT WHISKY, BOY. YOUR DUMB HIPPY MOM NAMED YOU AFTER HILLBILLY ROTGUT WHISKY.
OR MAYBE IT WAS A COLLECTIVE DECISION?
NAMED BY COMMITTEE...
DON'T FEEL LIKE TALKING? I DON'T BLAME YOU. IT'S BEEN A STRESSFUL DAY FOR ALL OF US.
DON'T WORRY, KID, WE'LL BE SAFE ONCE WE REACH RED ROCK.

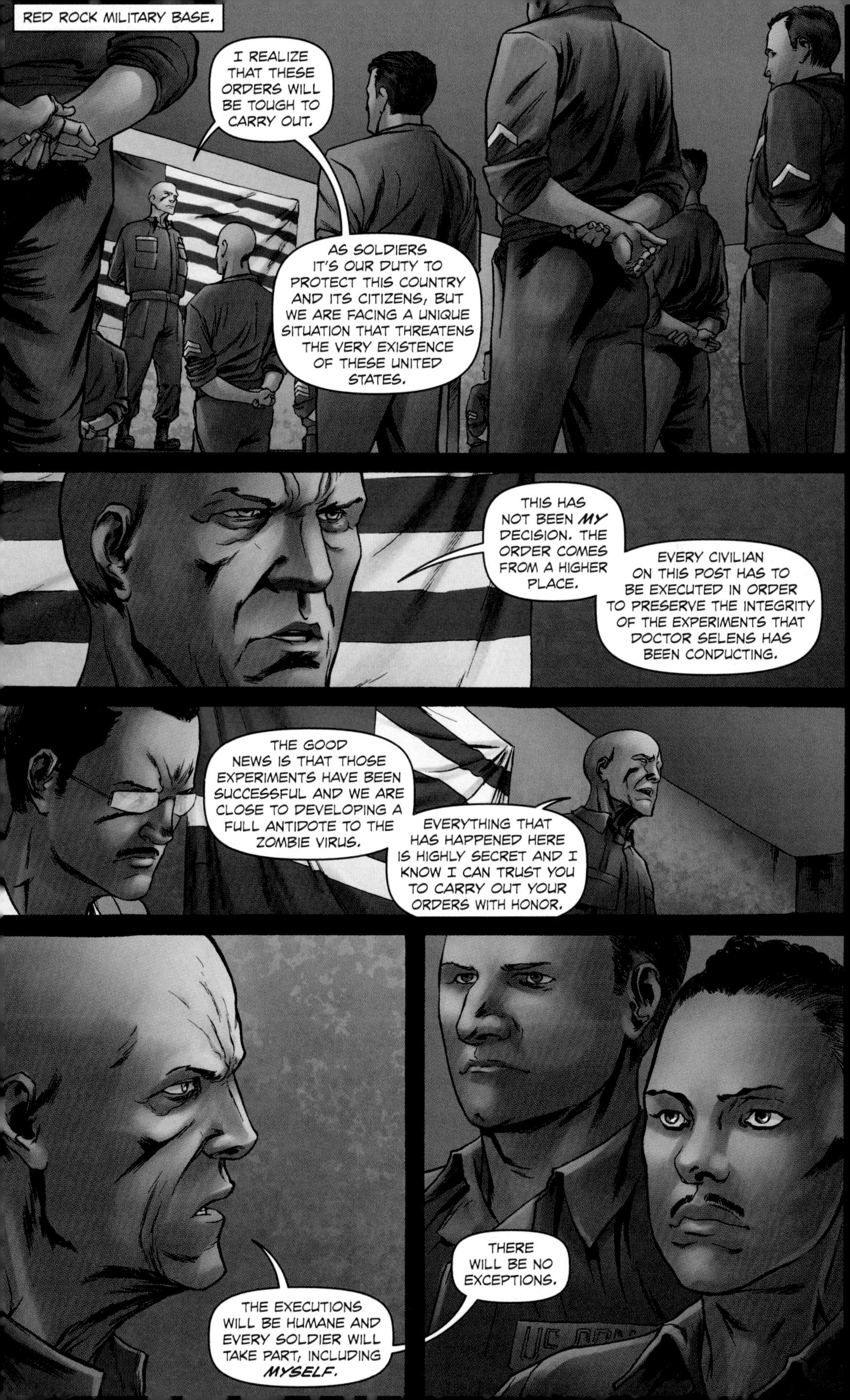
RED ROCK MILITARY BASE.
I REALIZE THAT THESE ORDERS WILL BE TOUGH TO CARRY OUT.
AS SOLDIERS IT'S OUR DUTY TO PROTECT THIS COUNTRY AND ITS CITIZENS, BUT WE ARE FACING A UNIQUE SITUATION THAT THREATENS THE VERY EXISTENCE OF THESE UNITED STATES.
THIS HAS NOT BEEN *MY* DECISION. THE ORDER COMES FROM A HIGHER PLACE.
EVERY CIVILIAN ON THIS POST HAS TO BE EXECUTED IN ORDER TO PRESERVE THE INTEGRITY OF THE EXPERIMENTS THAT DOCTOR SELENS HAS BEEN CONDUCTING.
THE GOOD NEWS IS THAT THOSE EXPERIMENTS HAVE BEEN SUCCESSFUL AND WE ARE CLOSE TO DEVELOPING A FULL ANTIDOTE TO THE ZOMBIE VIRUS.
EVERYTHING THAT HAS HAPPENED HERE IS HIGHLY SECRET AND I KNOW I CAN TRUST YOU TO CARRY OUT YOUR ORDERS WITH HONOR.
THE EXECUTIONS WILL BE HUMANE AND EVERY SOLDIER WILL TAKE PART, INCLUDING *MYSELF*.
THERE WILL BE NO EXCEPTIONS.

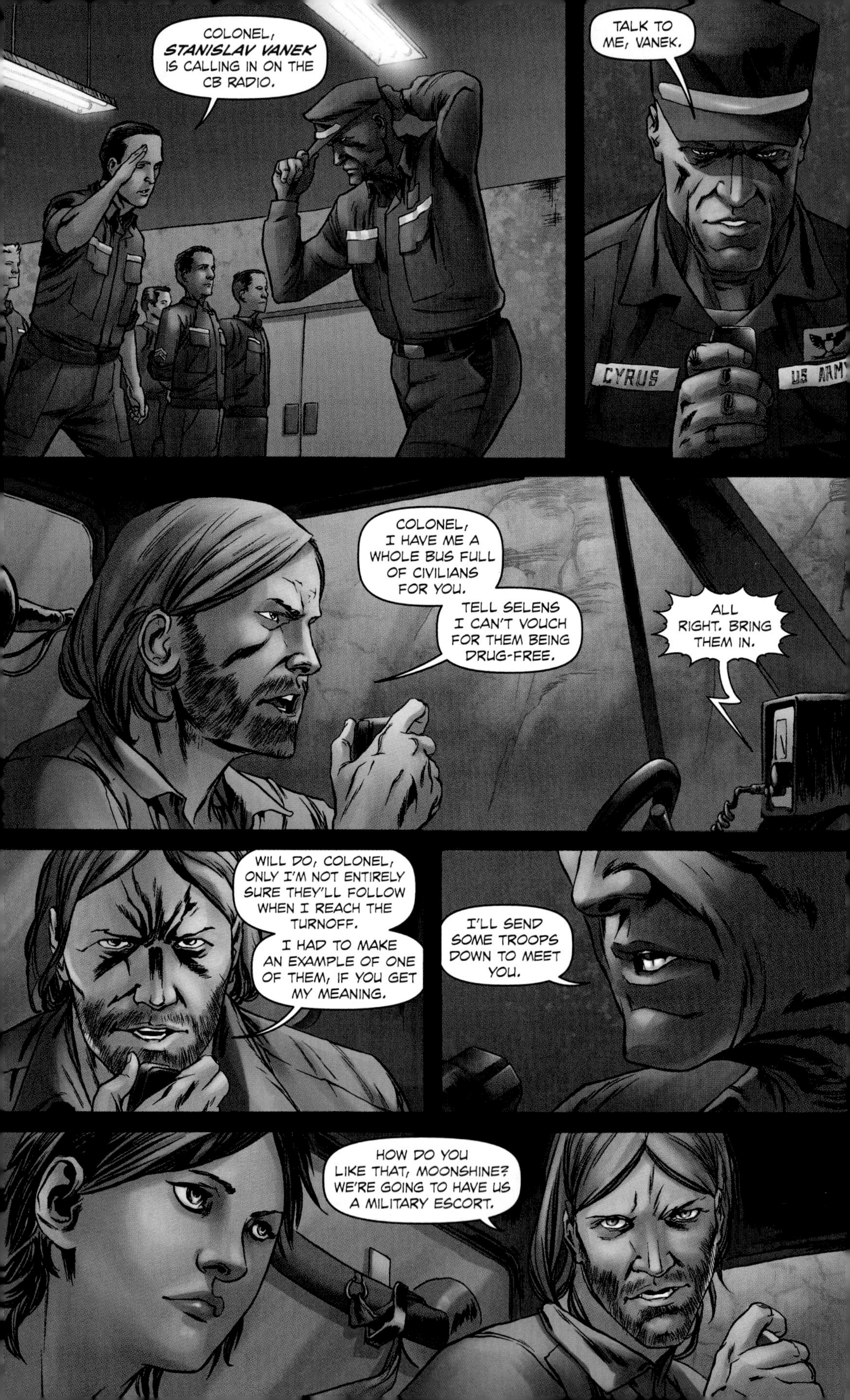
COLONEL, STANISLAV VANEK IS CALLING IN ON THE CB RADIO.
TALK TO ME, VANEK.
CYRUS
US ARMY
COLONEL, I HAVE ME A WHOLE BUS FULL OF CIVILIANS FOR YOU.
TELL SELENS I CAN'T VOUCH FOR THEM BEING DRUG-FREE.
ALL RIGHT. BRING THEM IN.
WILL DO, COLONEL, ONLY I'M NOT ENTIRELY SURE THEY'LL FOLLOW WHEN I REACH THE TURNOFF.
I HAD TO MAKE AN EXAMPLE OF ONE OF THEM, IF YOU GET MY MEANING.
I'LL SEND SOME TROOPS DOWN TO MEET YOU.
HOW DO YOU LIKE THAT, MOONSHINE? WE'RE GOING TO HAVE US A MILITARY ESCORT.

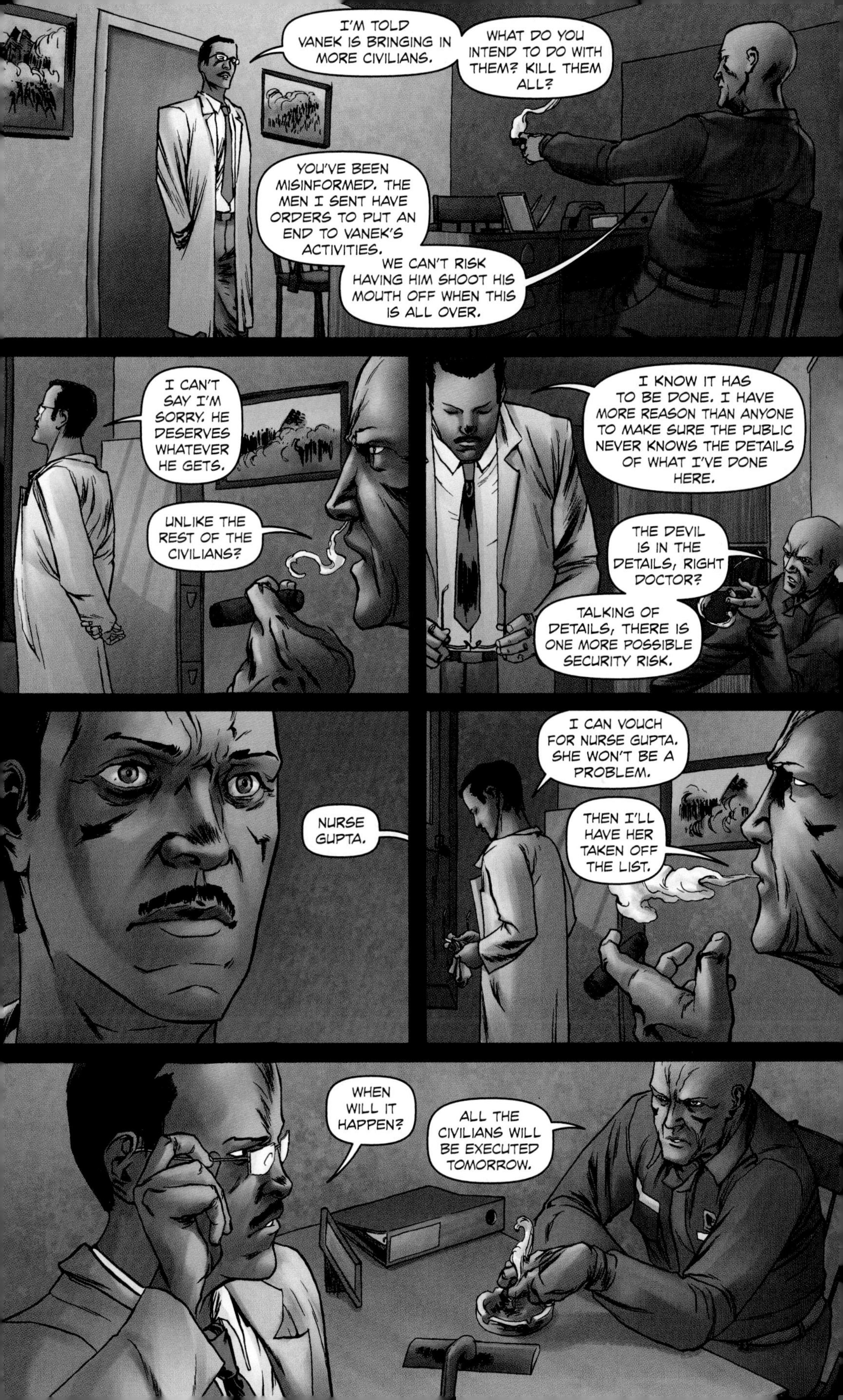

I'M TOLD VANEK IS BRINGING IN MORE CIVILIANS.
WHAT DO YOU INTEND TO DO WITH THEM? KILL THEM ALL?
YOU'VE BEEN MISINFORMED. THE MEN I SENT HAVE ORDERS TO PUT AN END TO VANEK'S ACTIVITIES.
WE CAN'T RISK HAVING HIM SHOOT HIS MOUTH OFF WHEN THIS IS ALL OVER.
I CAN'T SAY I'M SORRY. HE DESERVES WHATEVER HE GETS.
UNLIKE THE REST OF THE CIVILIANS?
I KNOW IT HAS TO BE DONE. I HAVE MORE REASON THAN ANYONE TO MAKE SURE THE PUBLIC NEVER KNOWS THE DETAILS OF WHAT I'VE DONE HERE.
THE DEVIL IS IN THE DETAILS, RIGHT DOCTOR?
TALKING OF DETAILS, THERE IS ONE MORE POSSIBLE SECURITY RISK.
NURSE GUPTA.
I CAN VOUCH FOR NURSE GUPTA. SHE WON'T BE A PROBLEM.
THEN I'LL HAVE HER TAKEN OFF THE LIST.
WHEN WILL IT HAPPEN?
ALL THE CIVILIANS WILL BE EXECUTED TOMORROW.

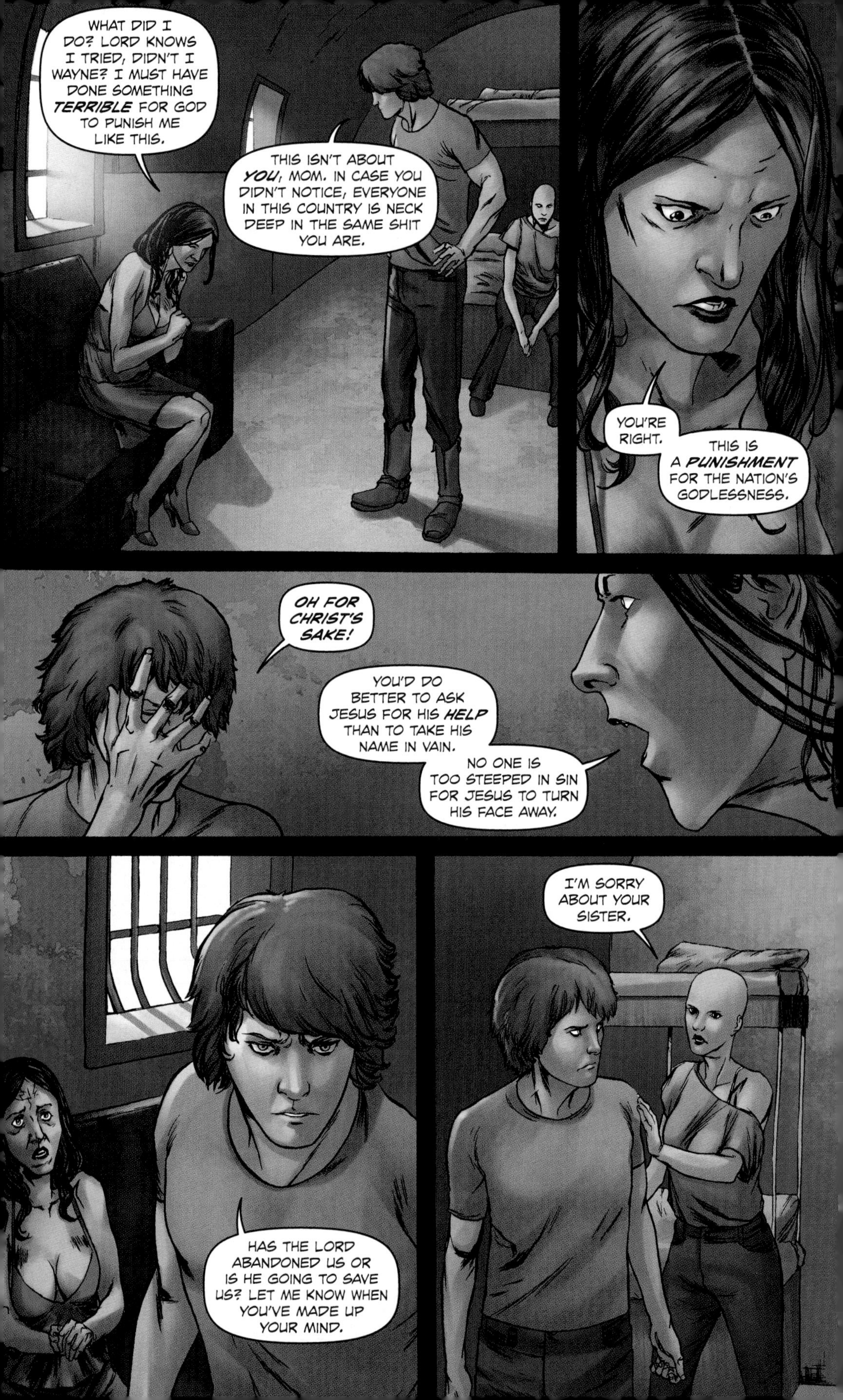

WHAT DID I DO? LORD KNOWS I TRIED, DIDN'T I WAYNE? I MUST HAVE DONE SOMETHING *TERRIBLE* FOR GOD TO PUNISH ME LIKE THIS.
THIS ISN'T ABOUT *YOU*, MOM. IN CASE YOU DIDN'T NOTICE, EVERYONE IN THIS COUNTRY IS NECK DEEP IN THE SAME SHIT YOU ARE.
YOU'RE RIGHT.
THIS IS A *PUNISHMENT* FOR THE NATION'S GODLESSNESS.
OH FOR CHRIST'S SAKE!
YOU'D DO BETTER TO ASK JESUS FOR HIS *HELP* THAN TO TAKE HIS NAME IN VAIN.
NO ONE IS TOO STEEPED IN SIN FOR JESUS TO TURN HIS FACE AWAY.
HAS THE LORD ABANDONED US OR IS HE GOING TO SAVE US? LET ME KNOW WHEN YOU'VE MADE UP YOUR MIND.
I'M SORRY ABOUT YOUR SISTER.

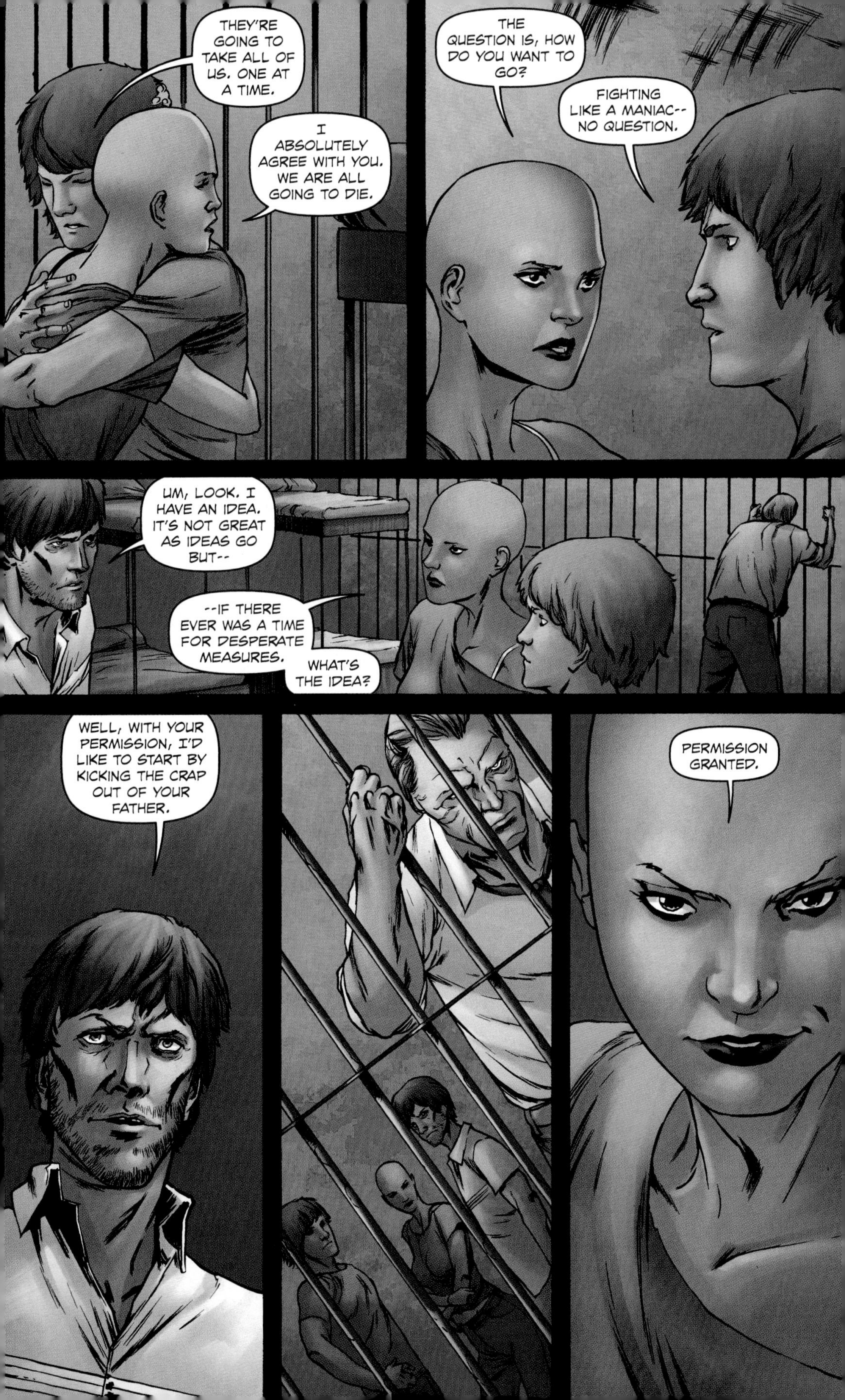
THEY'RE GOING TO TAKE ALL OF US. ONE AT A TIME.
I ABSOLUTELY AGREE WITH YOU. WE ARE ALL GOING TO DIE.
THE QUESTION IS, HOW DO YOU WANT TO GO?
FIGHTING LIKE A MANIAC-- NO QUESTION.
UM, LOOK. I HAVE AN IDEA. IT'S NOT GREAT AS IDEAS GO BUT--
--IF THERE EVER WAS A TIME FOR DESPERATE MEASURES.
WHAT'S THE IDEA?
WELL, WITH YOUR PERMISSION, I'D LIKE TO START BY KICKING THE CRAP OUT OF YOUR FATHER.
PERMISSION GRANTED.

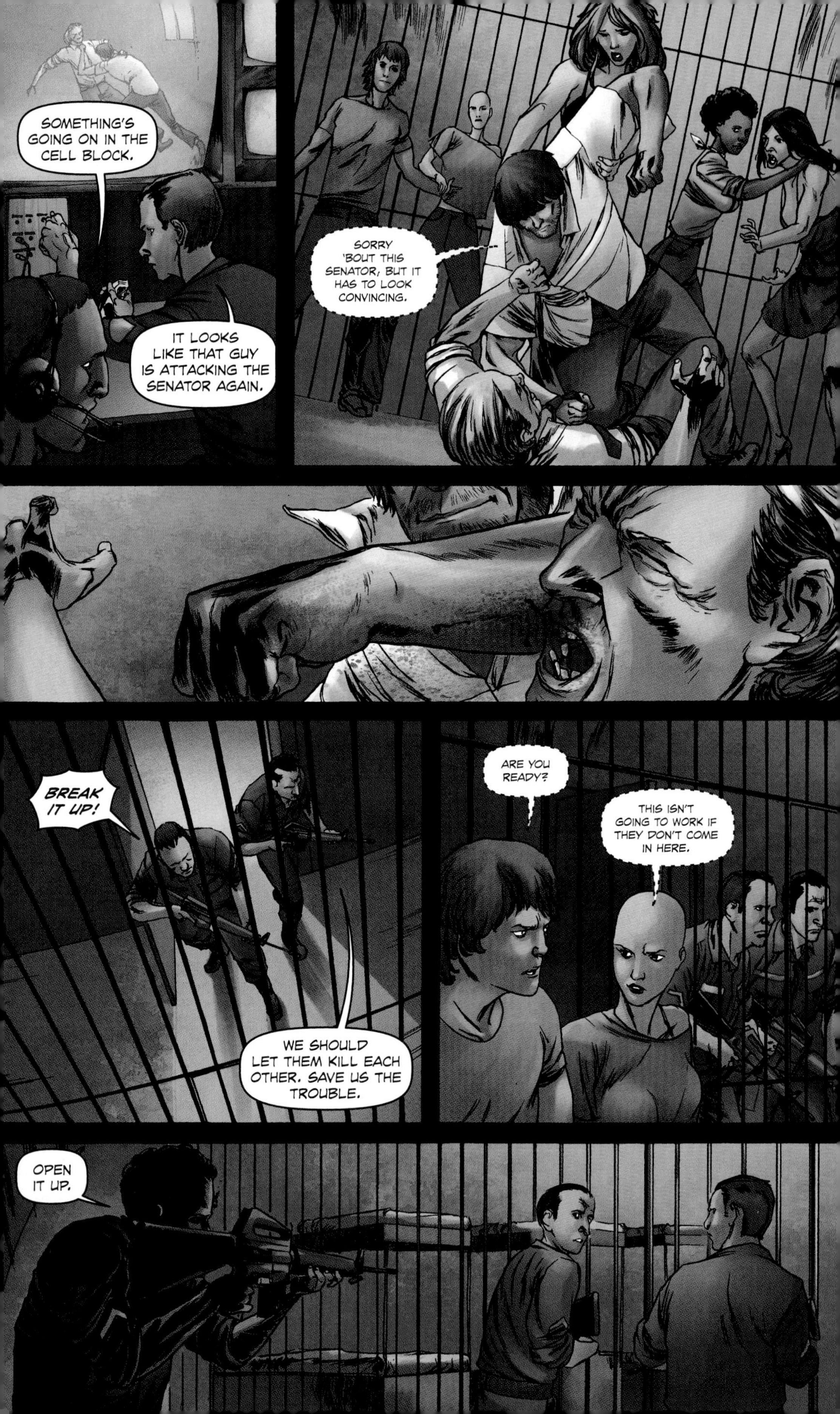
SOMETHING'S GOING ON IN THE CELL BLOCK.
IT LOOKS LIKE THAT GUY IS ATTACKING THE SENATOR AGAIN.
SORRY 'BOUT THIS SENATOR, BUT IT HAS TO LOOK CONVINCING.
BREAK IT UP!
WE SHOULD LET THEM KILL EACH OTHER. SAVE US THE TROUBLE.
ARE YOU READY?
THIS ISN'T GOING TO WORK IF THEY DON'T COME IN HERE.
OPEN IT UP.

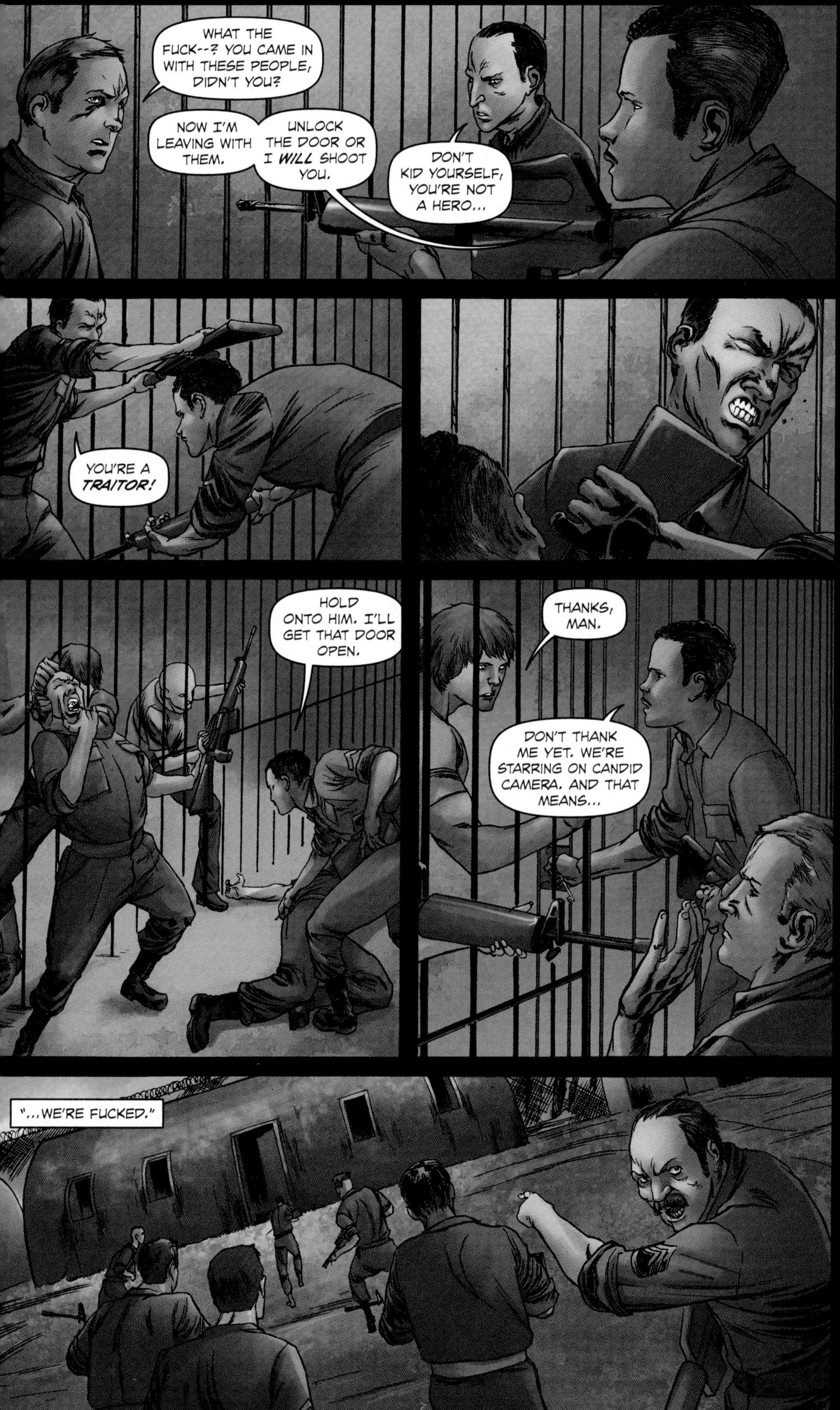
WHAT THE FUCK--? YOU CAME IN WITH THESE PEOPLE, DIDN'T YOU?
NOW I'M LEAVING WITH THEM.
UNLOCK THE DOOR OR I WILL SHOOT YOU.
DON'T KID YOURSELF, YOU'RE NOT A HERO...
YOU'RE A TRAITOR!
HOLD ONTO HIM. I'LL GET THAT DOOR OPEN.
THANKS, MAN.
DON'T THANK ME YET. WE'RE STARRING ON CANDID CAMERA. AND THAT MEANS...
"...WE'RE FUCKED."

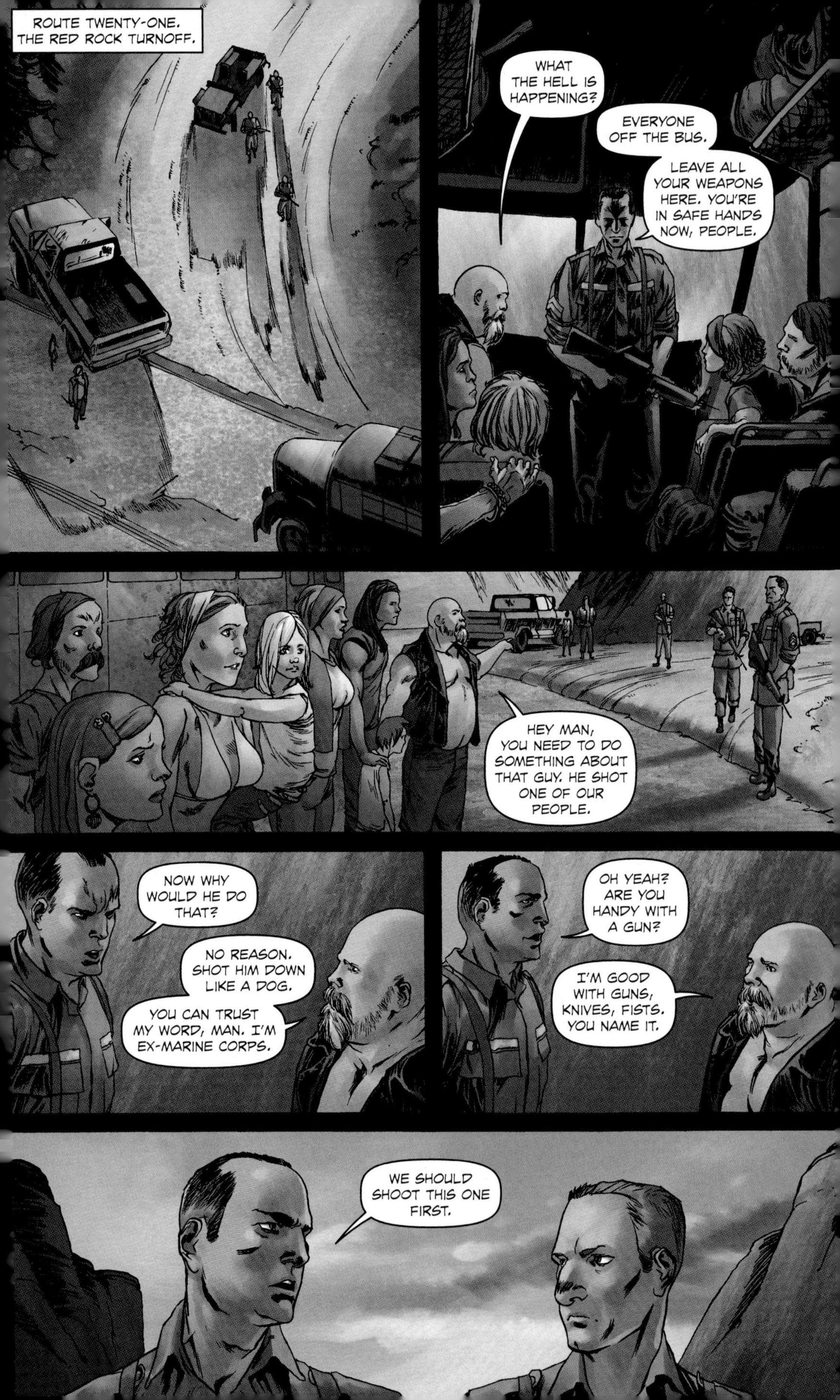
ROUTE TWENTY-ONE.
THE RED ROCK TURNOFF.
WHAT THE HELL IS HAPPENING?
EVERYONE OFF THE BUS.
LEAVE ALL YOUR WEAPONS HERE. YOU'RE IN SAFE HANDS NOW, PEOPLE.
HEY MAN, YOU NEED TO DO SOMETHING ABOUT THAT GUY. HE SHOT ONE OF OUR PEOPLE.
NOW WHY WOULD HE DO THAT?
NO REASON. SHOT HIM DOWN LIKE A DOG.
YOU CAN TRUST MY WORD, MAN. I'M EX-MARINE CORPS.
OH YEAH? ARE YOU HANDY WITH A GUN?
I'M GOOD WITH GUNS, KNIVES, FISTS. YOU NAME IT.
WE SHOULD SHOOT THIS ONE FIRST.

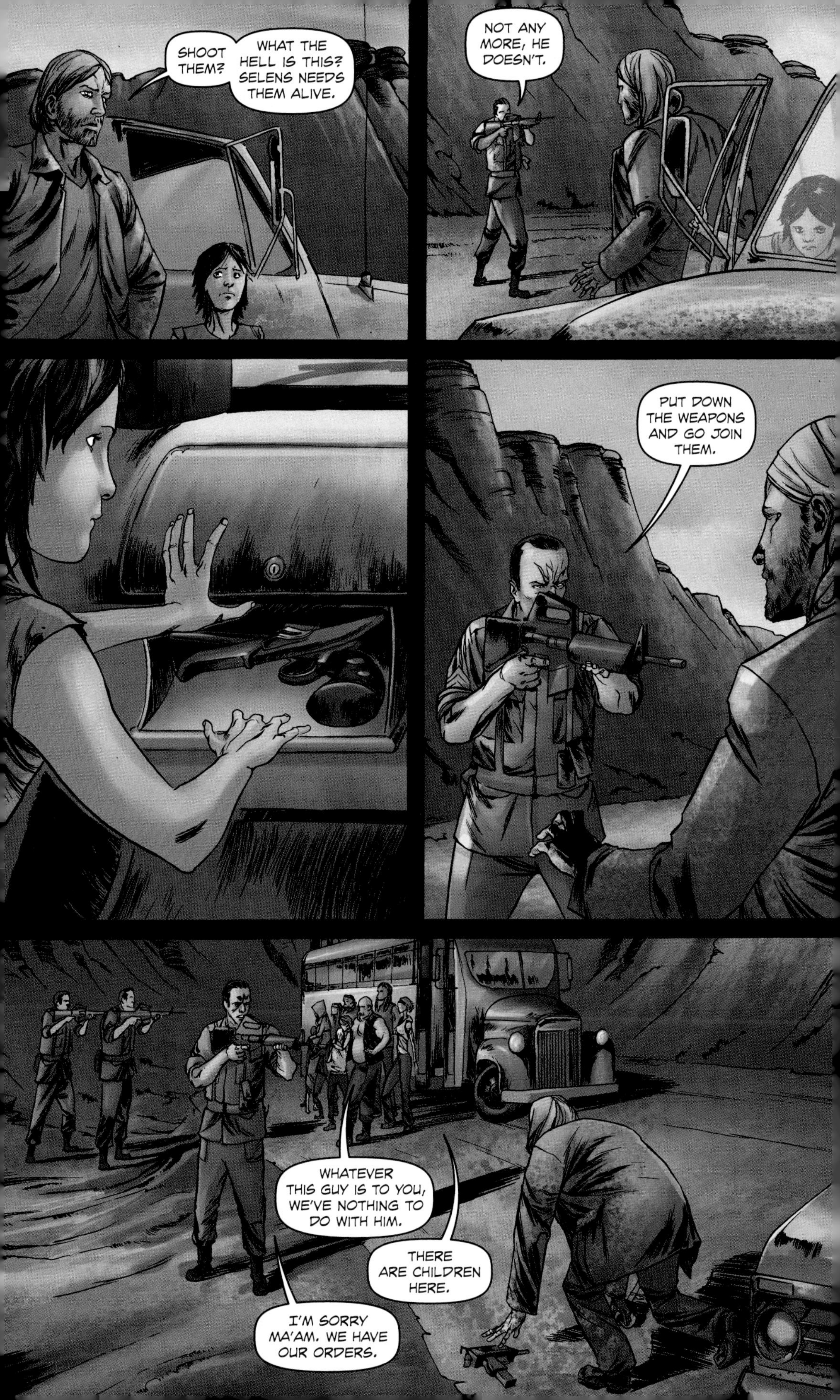

SHOOT THEM?
WHAT THE HELL IS THIS? SELENS NEEDS THEM ALIVE.
NOT ANY MORE, HE DOESN'T.
PUT DOWN THE WEAPONS AND GO JOIN THEM.
WHATEVER THIS GUY IS TO YOU, WE'VE NOTHING TO DO WITH HIM.
THERE ARE CHILDREN HERE.
I'M SORRY MA'AM. WE HAVE OUR ORDERS.

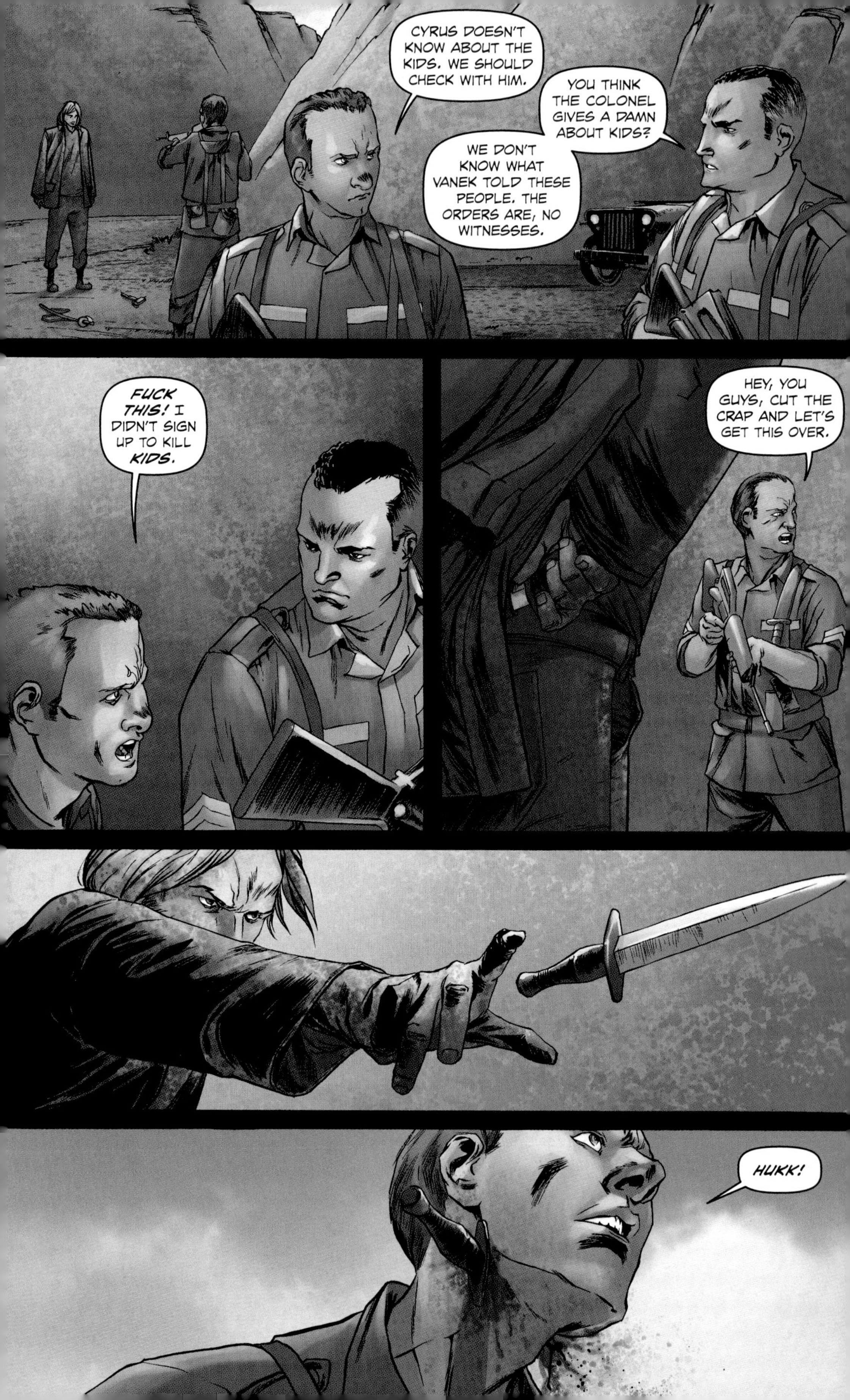
CYRUS DOESN'T KNOW ABOUT THE KIDS. WE SHOULD CHECK WITH HIM.
YOU THINK THE COLONEL GIVES A DAMN ABOUT KIDS?
WE DON'T KNOW WHAT VANEK TOLD THESE PEOPLE. THE ORDERS ARE, NO WITNESSES.
FUCK THIS! I DIDN'T SIGN UP TO KILL KIDS.
HEY, YOU GUYS, CUT THE CRAP AND LET'S GET THIS OVER.
HUKK!

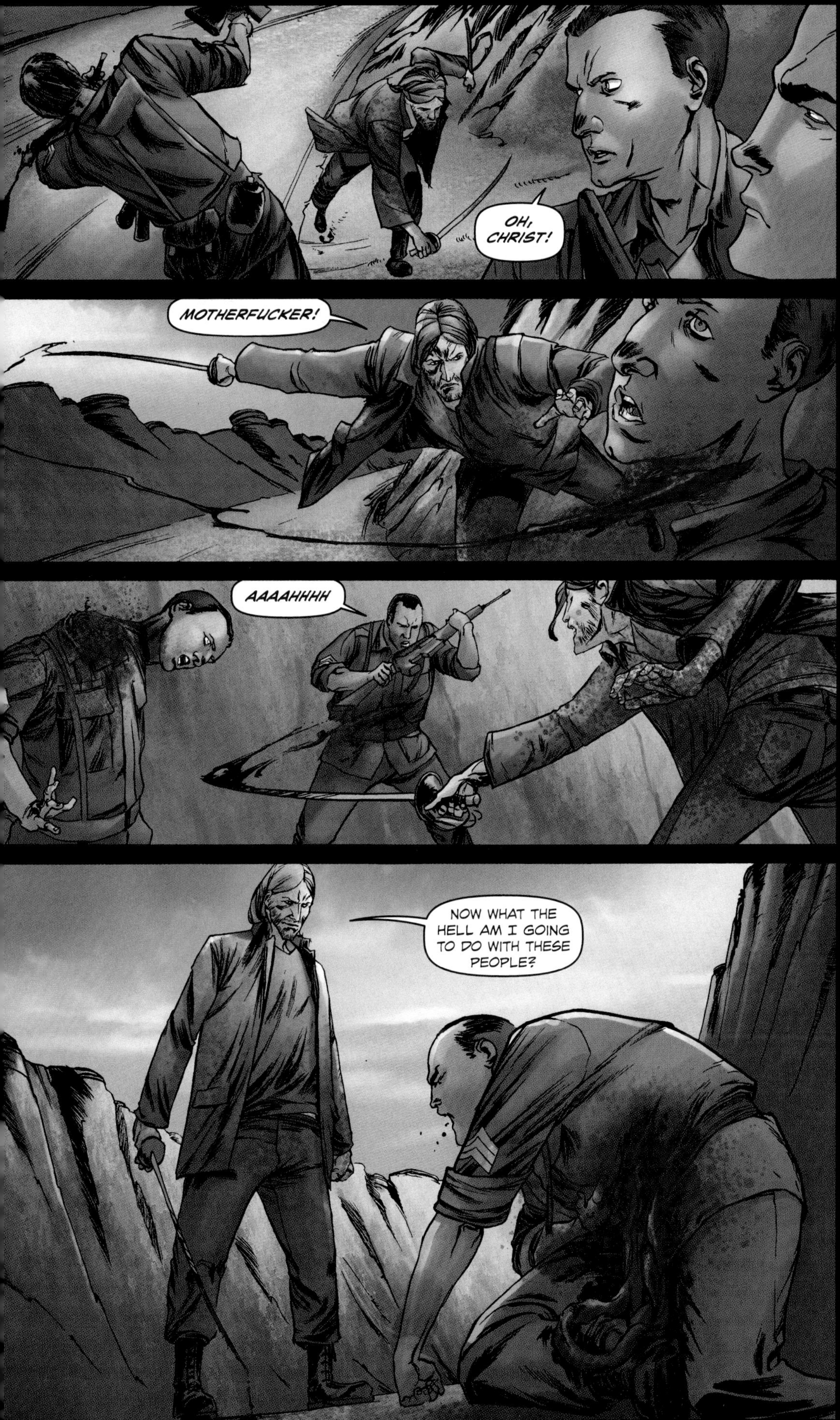
OH, CHRIST!
MOTHERFUCKER!
AAAAHHHH
NOW WHAT THE HELL AM I GOING TO DO WITH THESE PEOPLE?

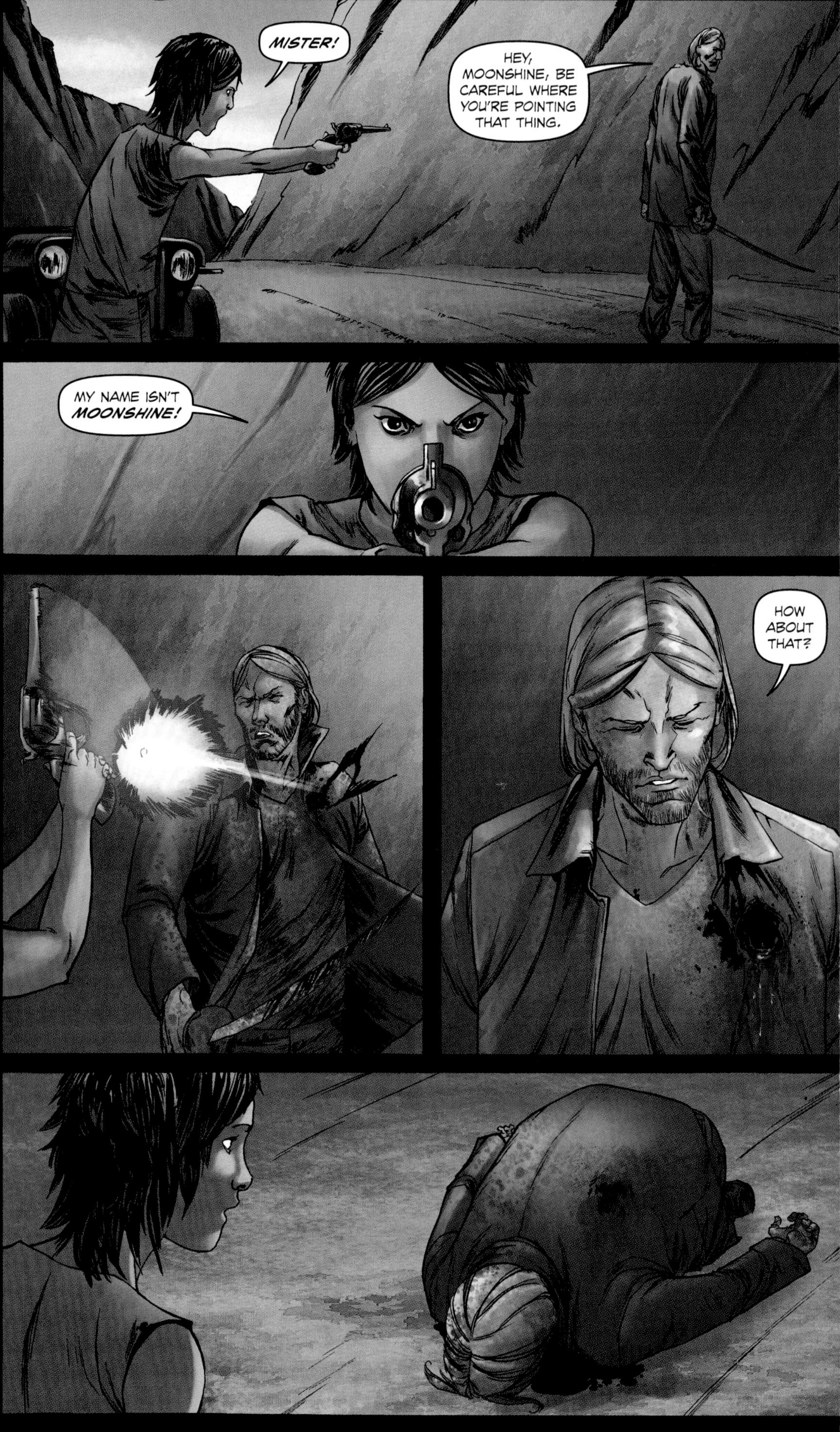
MISTER!
HEY, MOONSHINE, BE CAREFUL WHERE YOU'RE POINTING THAT THING.
MY NAME ISN'T MOONSHINE!
HOW ABOUT THAT?

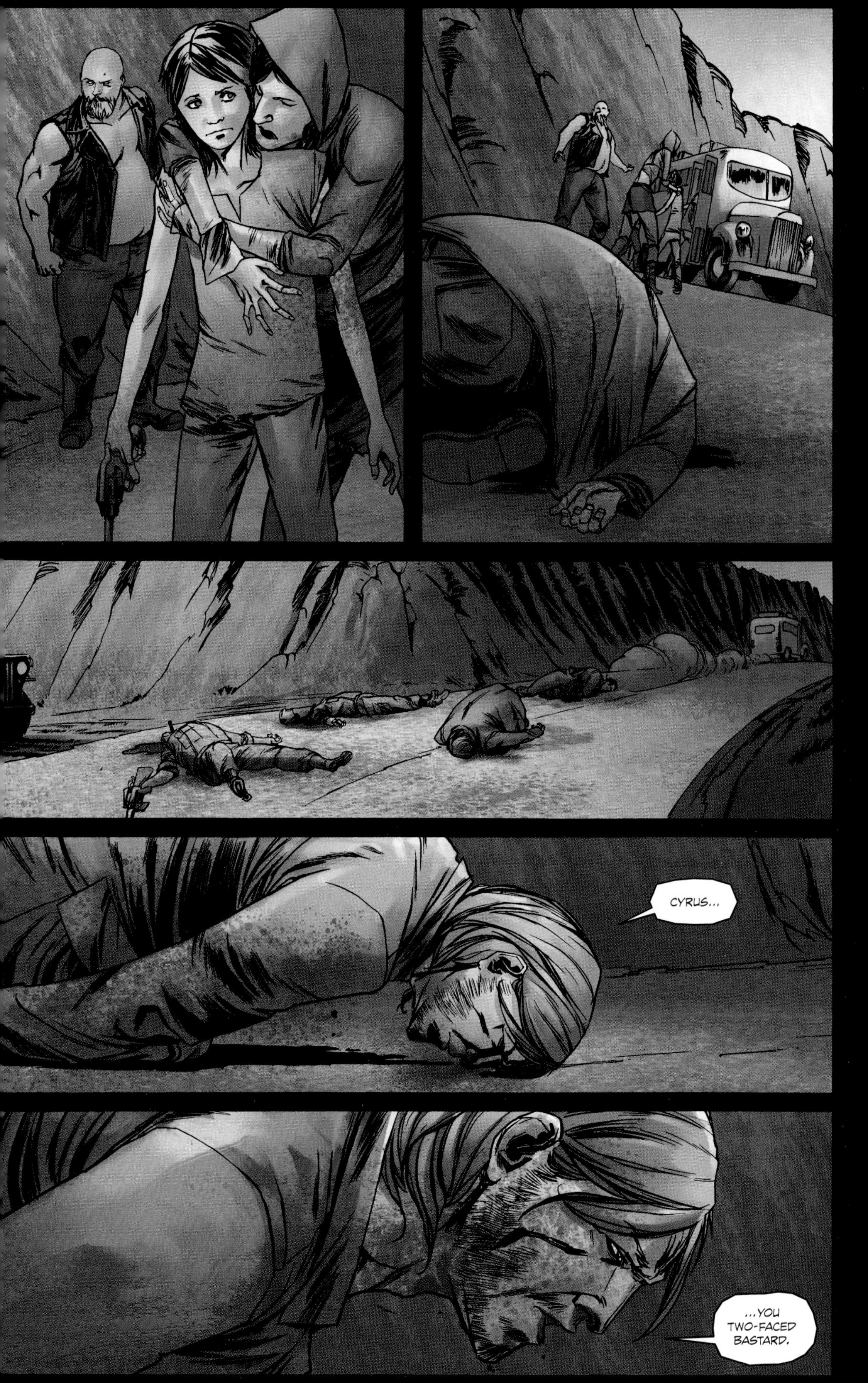
CYRUS...
...YOU TWO-FACED BASTARD.

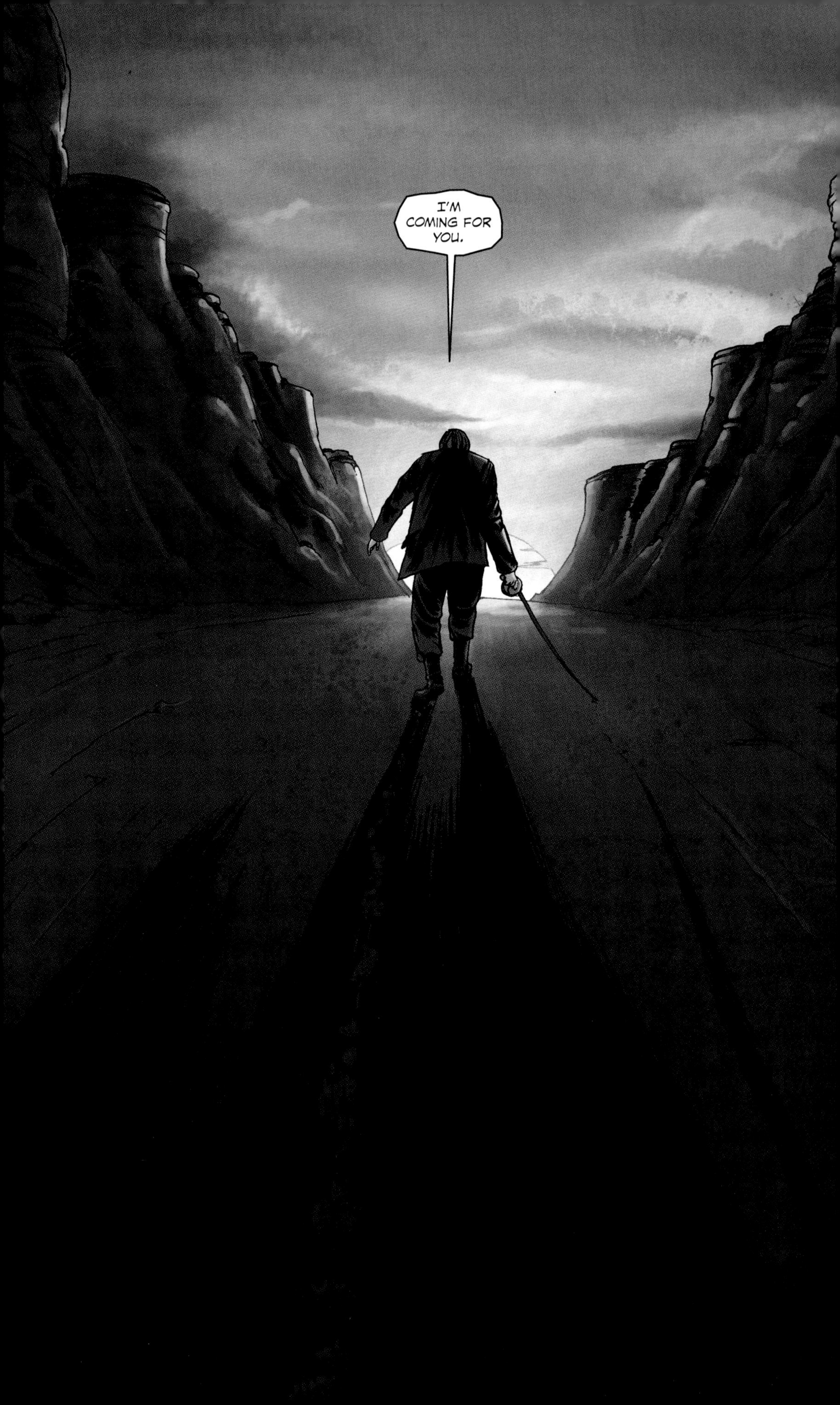
I'M COMING FOR YOU.

HUNGRY FOR THE FLESH OF THE LIVING

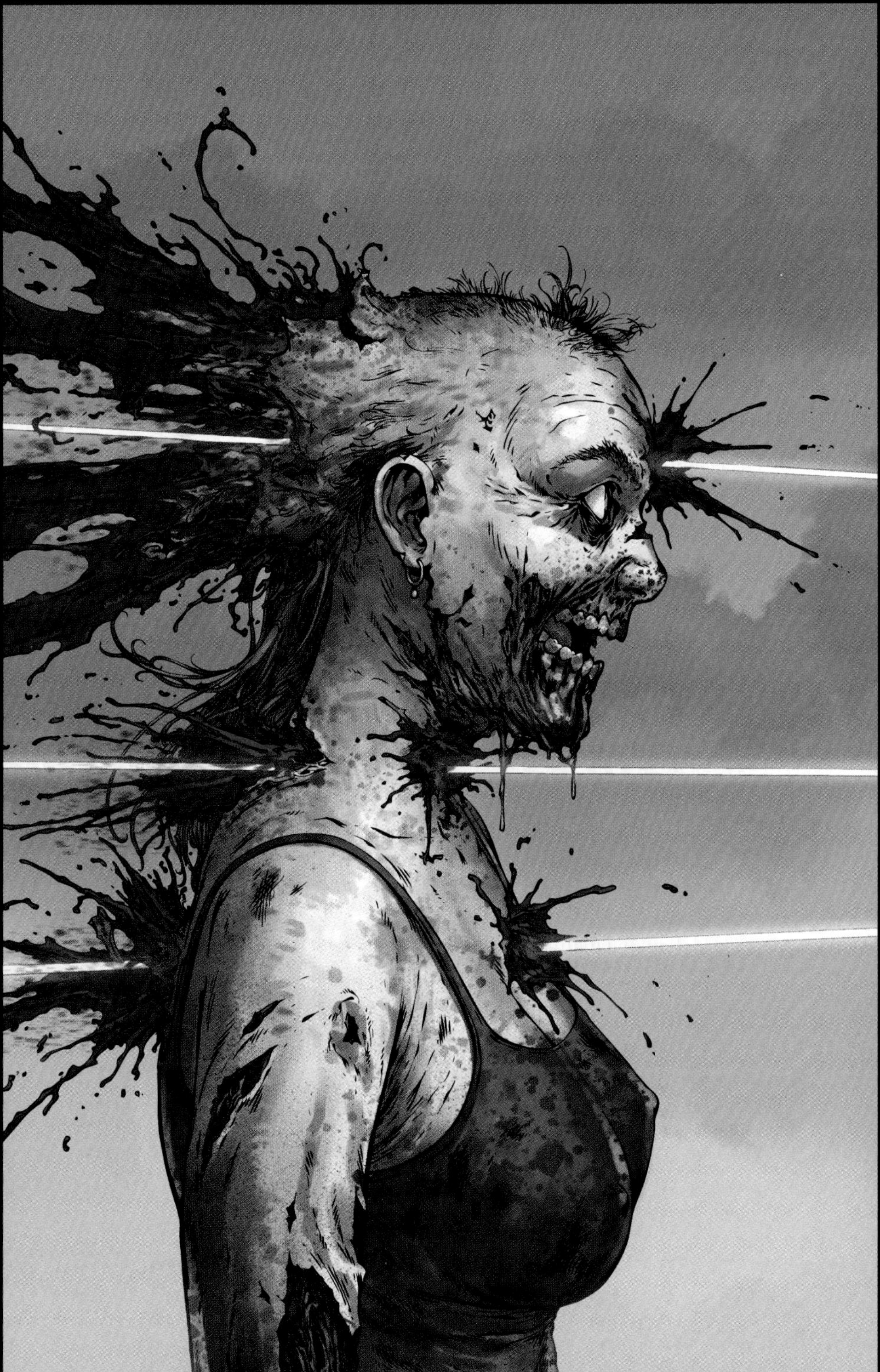

CHAPTER 6

HUNGRY FOR THE FLESH OF THE LIVING

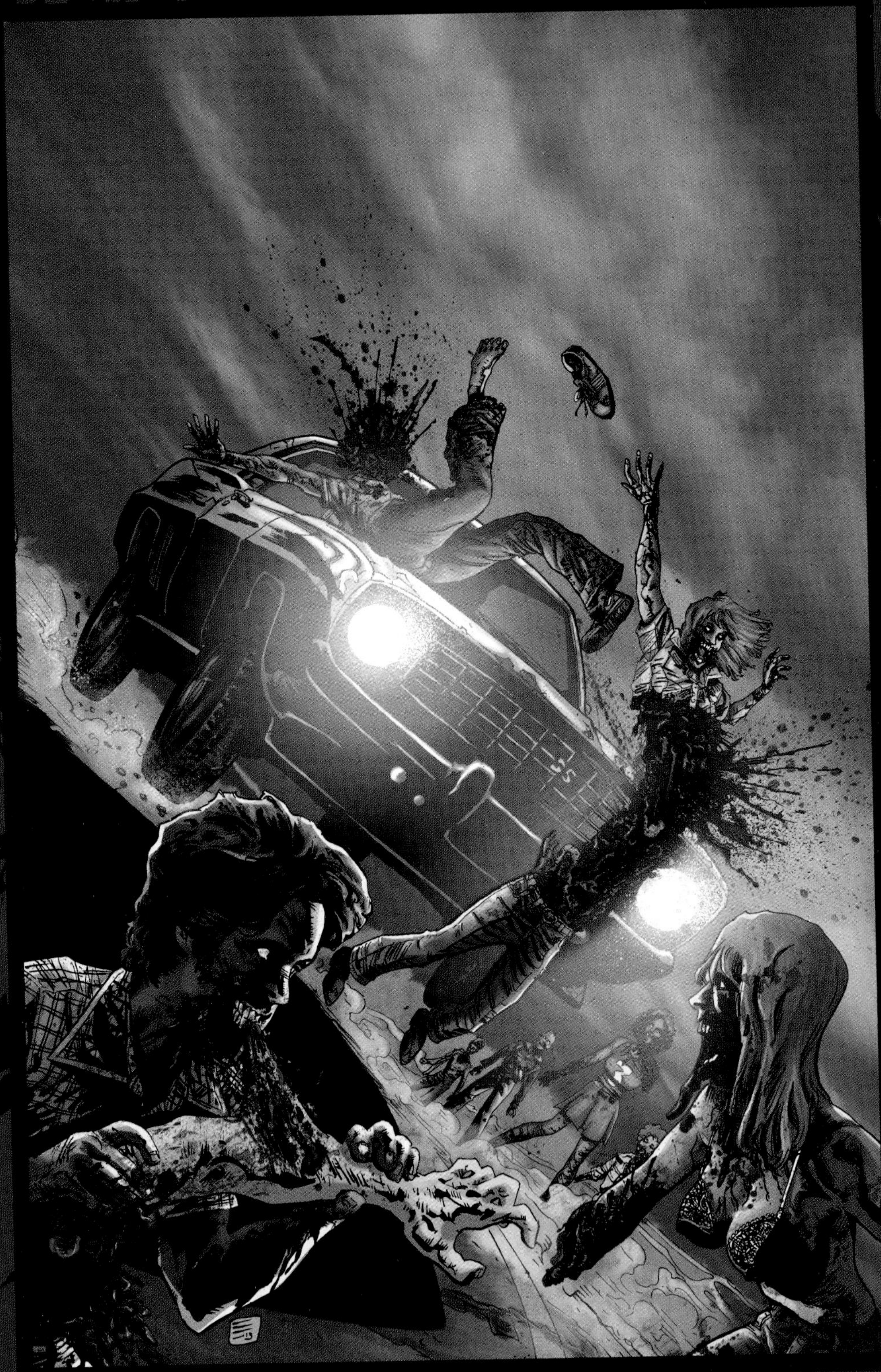

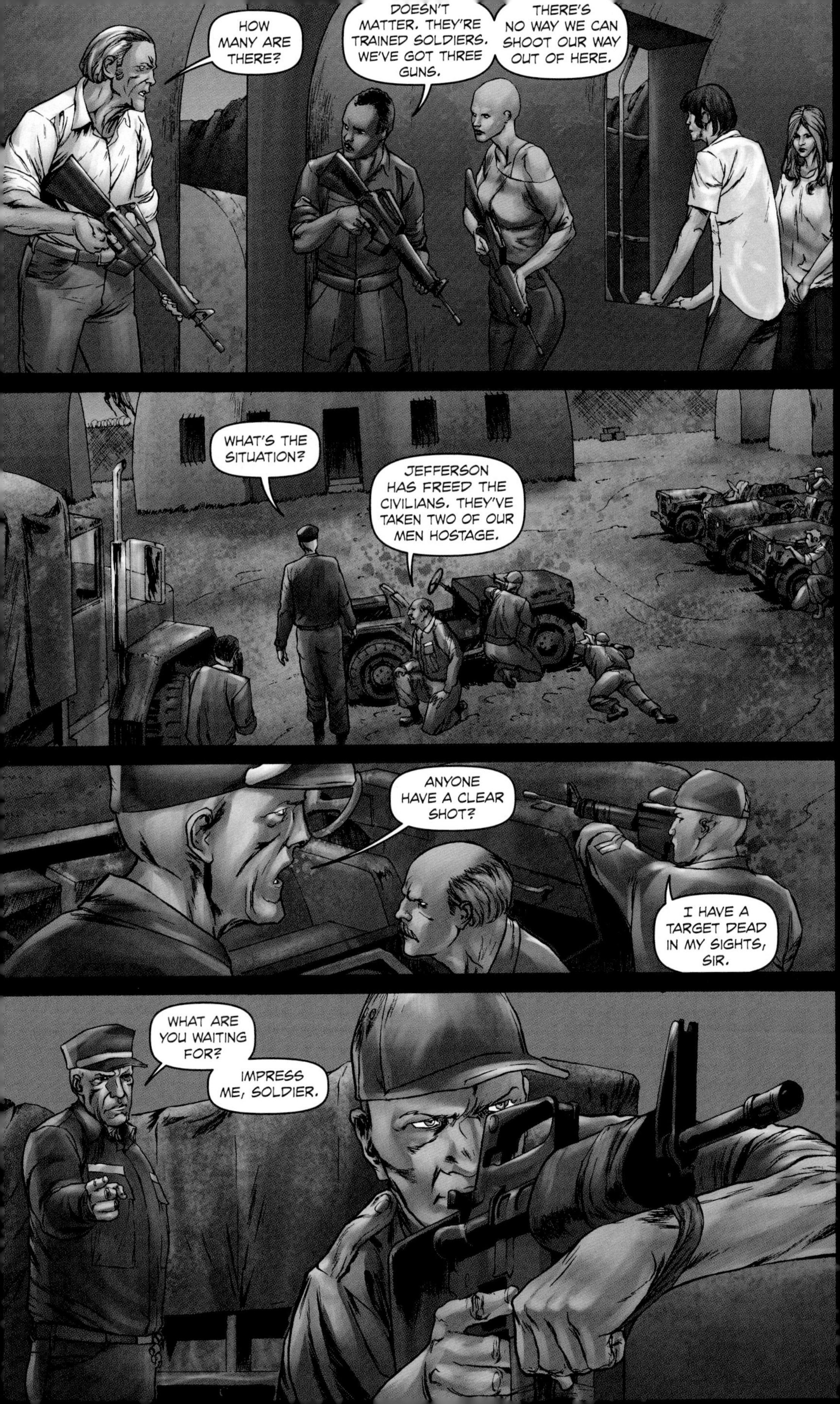
HOW MANY ARE THERE?
DOESN'T MATTER. THEY'RE TRAINED SOLDIERS. WE'VE GOT THREE GUNS.
THERE'S NO WAY WE CAN SHOOT OUR WAY OUT OF HERE.
WHAT'S THE SITUATION?
JEFFERSON HAS FREED THE CIVILIANS. THEY'VE TAKEN TWO OF OUR MEN HOSTAGE.
ANYONE HAVE A CLEAR SHOT?
I HAVE A TARGET DEAD IN MY SIGHTS, SIR.
WHAT ARE YOU WAITING FOR?
IMPRESS ME, SOLDIER.

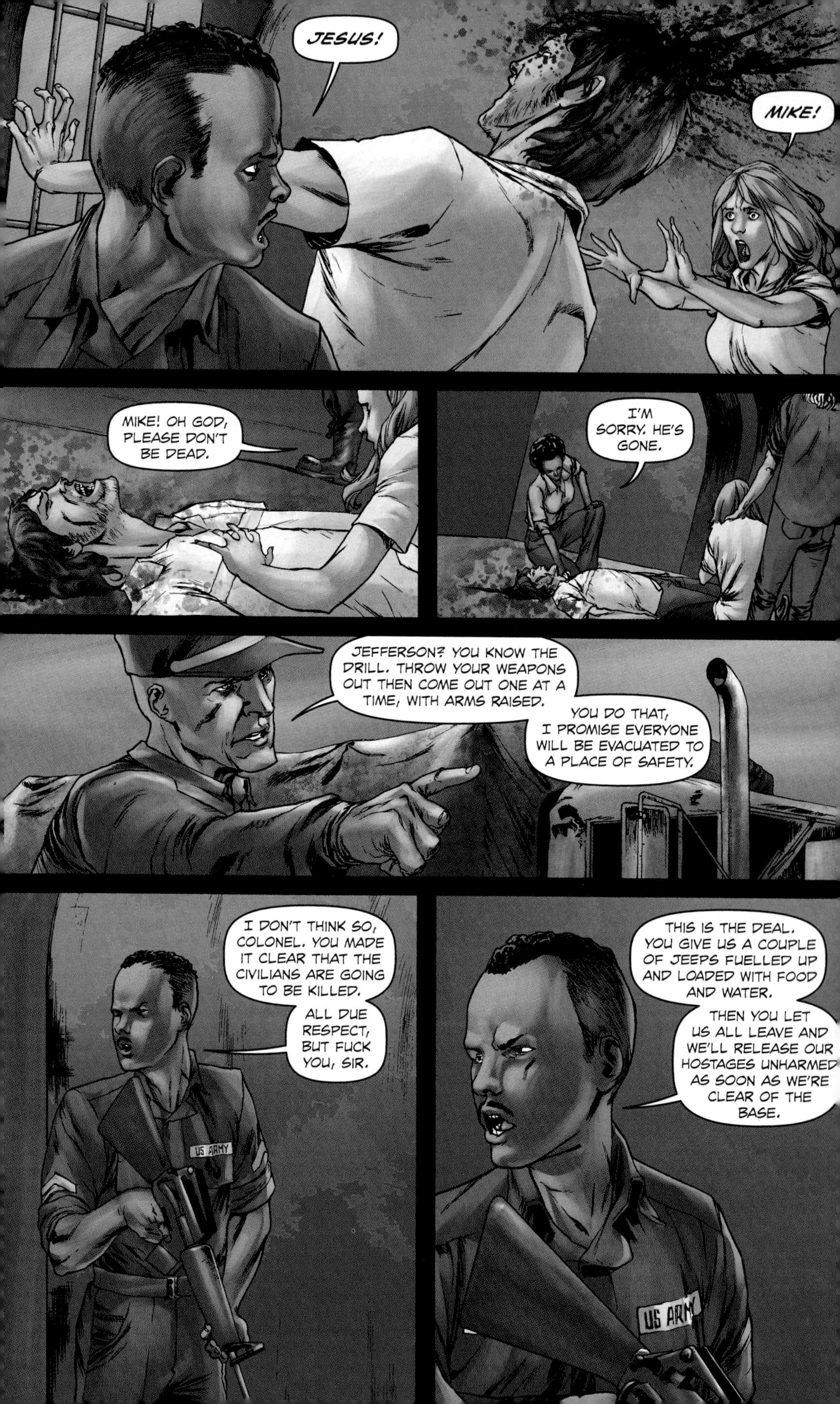
JESUS!
MIKE!
MIKE! OH GOD, PLEASE DON'T BE DEAD.
I'M SORRY. HE'S GONE.
JEFFERSON? YOU KNOW THE DRILL. THROW YOUR WEAPONS OUT THEN COME OUT ONE AT A TIME, WITH ARMS RAISED.
YOU DO THAT, I PROMISE EVERYONE WILL BE EVACUATED TO A PLACE OF SAFETY.
I DON'T THINK SO, COLONEL. YOU MADE IT CLEAR THAT THE CIVILIANS ARE GOING TO BE KILLED.
ALL DUE RESPECT, BUT FUCK YOU, SIR.
US ARMY
THIS IS THE DEAL. YOU GIVE US A COUPLE OF JEEPS FUELLED UP AND LOADED WITH FOOD AND WATER.
THEN YOU LET US ALL LEAVE AND WE'LL RELEASE OUR HOSTAGES UNHARMED AS SOON AS WE'RE CLEAR OF THE BASE.
US ARMY

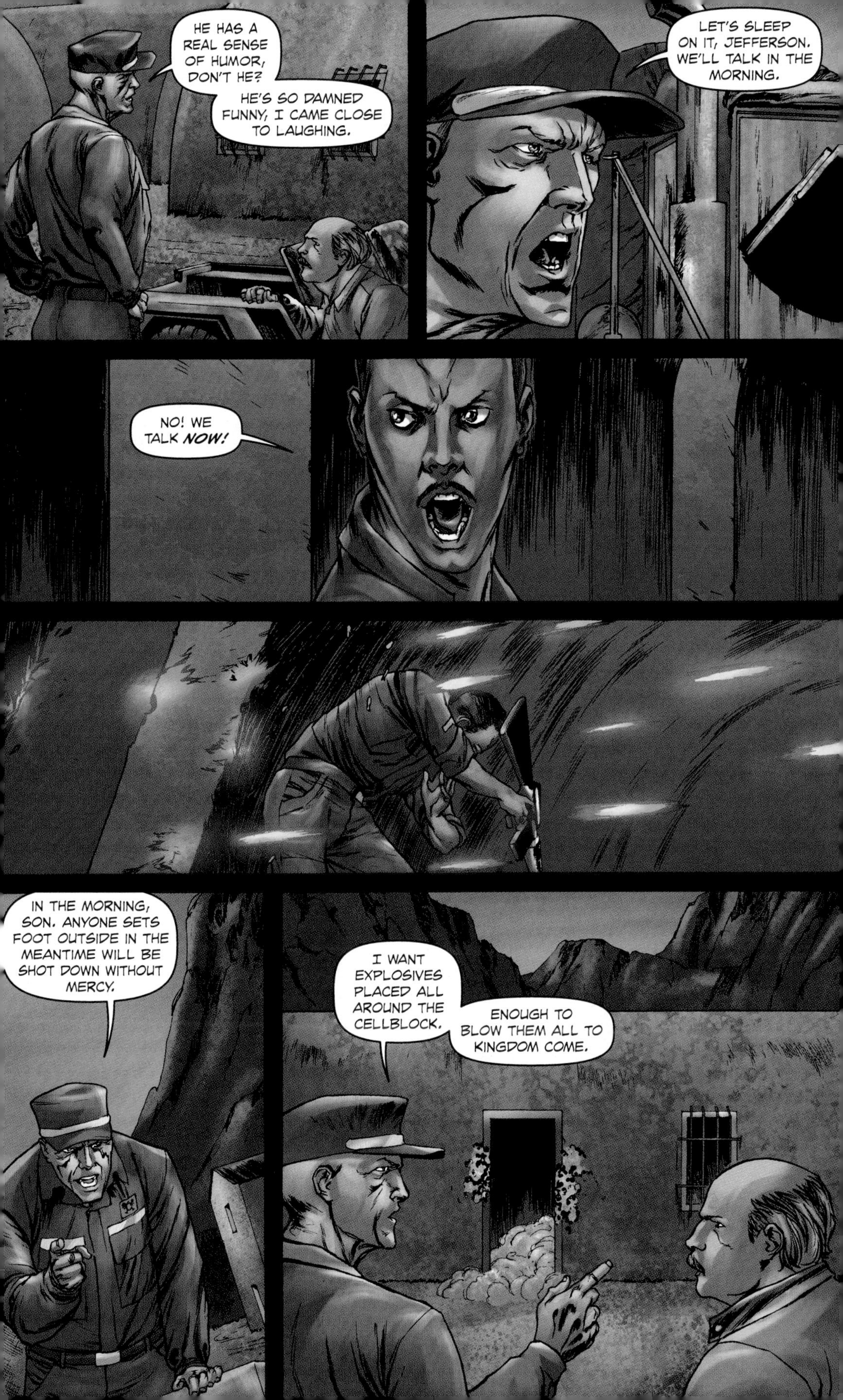
HE HAS A REAL SENSE OF HUMOR, DON'T HE?
HE'S SO DAMNED FUNNY, I CAME CLOSE TO LAUGHING.
LET'S SLEEP ON IT, JEFFERSON. WE'LL TALK IN THE MORNING.
NO! WE TALK *NOW!*
IN THE MORNING, SON. ANYONE SETS FOOT OUTSIDE IN THE MEANTIME WILL BE SHOT DOWN WITHOUT MERCY.
I WANT EXPLOSIVES PLACED ALL AROUND THE CELLBLOCK.
ENOUGH TO BLOW THEM ALL TO KINGDOM COME.

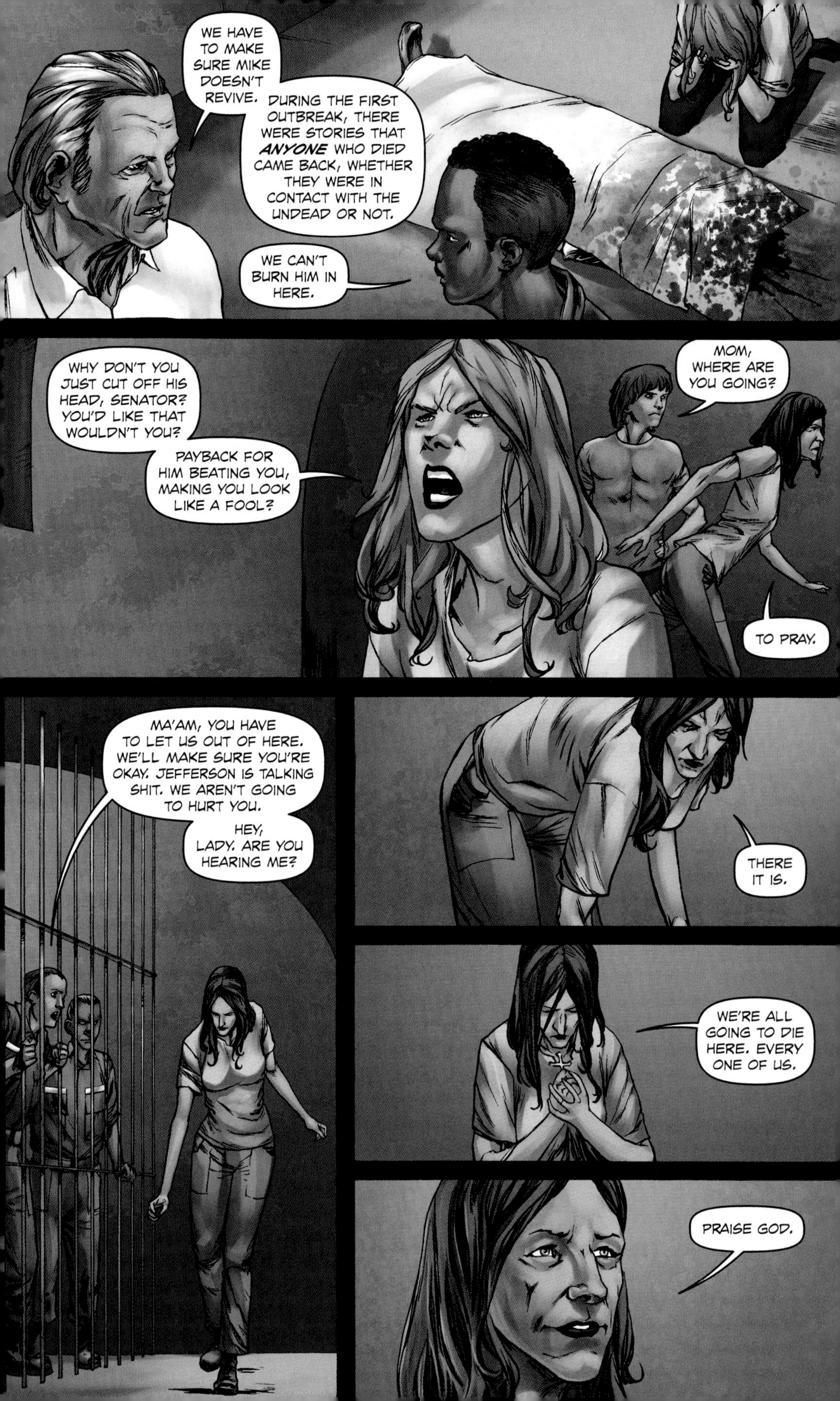
WE HAVE TO MAKE SURE MIKE DOESN'T REVIVE.
DURING THE FIRST OUTBREAK, THERE WERE STORIES THAT ANYONE WHO DIED CAME BACK, WHETHER THEY WERE IN CONTACT WITH THE UNDEAD OR NOT.
WE CAN'T BURN HIM IN HERE.
WHY DON'T YOU JUST CUT OFF HIS HEAD, SENATOR? YOU'D LIKE THAT WOULDN'T YOU?
PAYBACK FOR HIM BEATING YOU, MAKING YOU LOOK LIKE A FOOL?
MOM, WHERE ARE YOU GOING?
TO PRAY.
MA'AM, YOU HAVE TO LET US OUT OF HERE. WE'LL MAKE SURE YOU'RE OKAY. JEFFERSON IS TALKING SHIT. WE AREN'T GOING TO HURT YOU.
HEY, LADY. ARE YOU HEARING ME?
THERE IT IS.
WE'RE ALL GOING TO DIE HERE. EVERY ONE OF US.
PRAISE GOD.

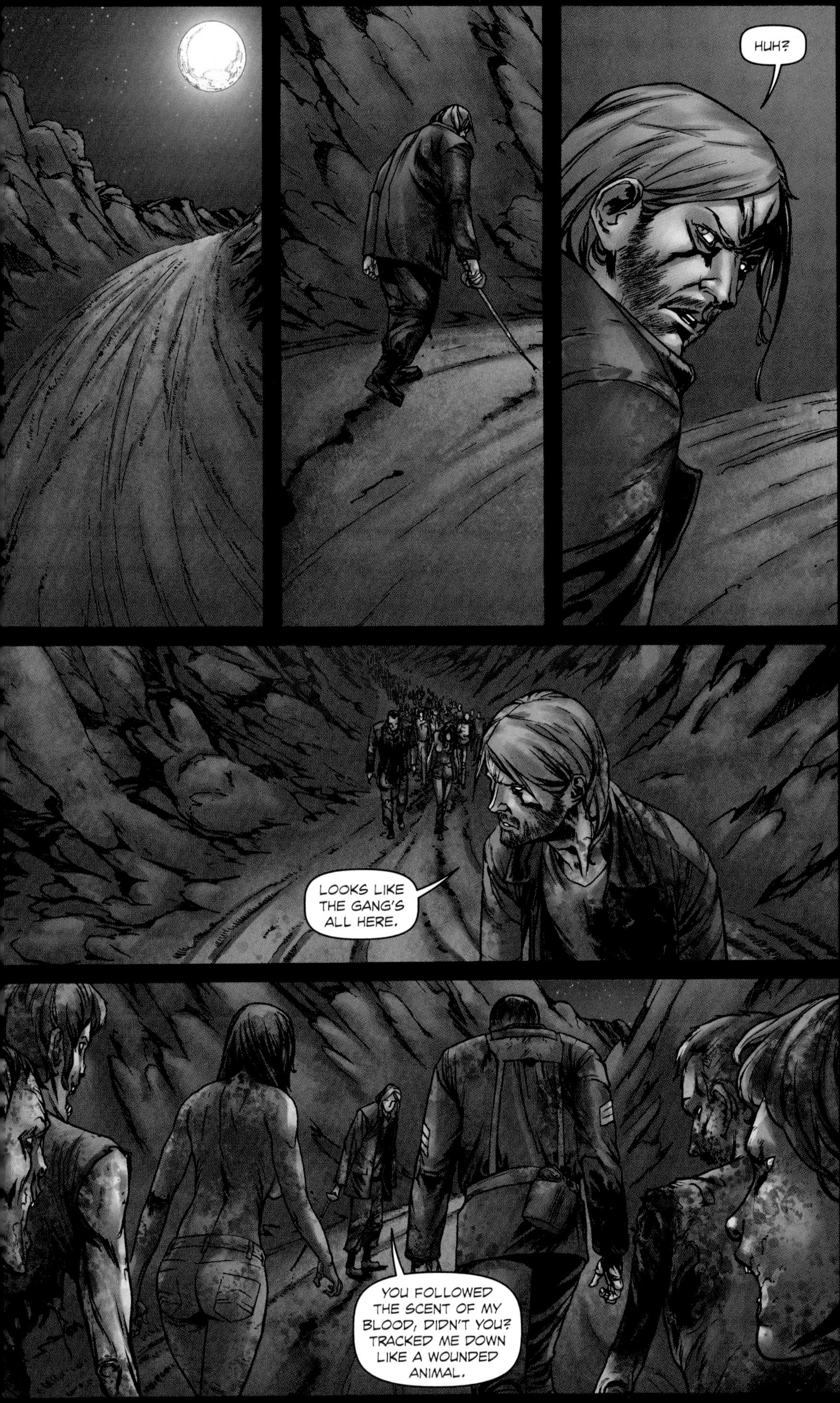
HUH?
LOOKS LIKE THE GANG'S ALL HERE.
YOU FOLLOWED THE SCENT OF MY BLOOD, DIDN'T YOU? TRACKED ME DOWN LIKE A WOUNDED ANIMAL.

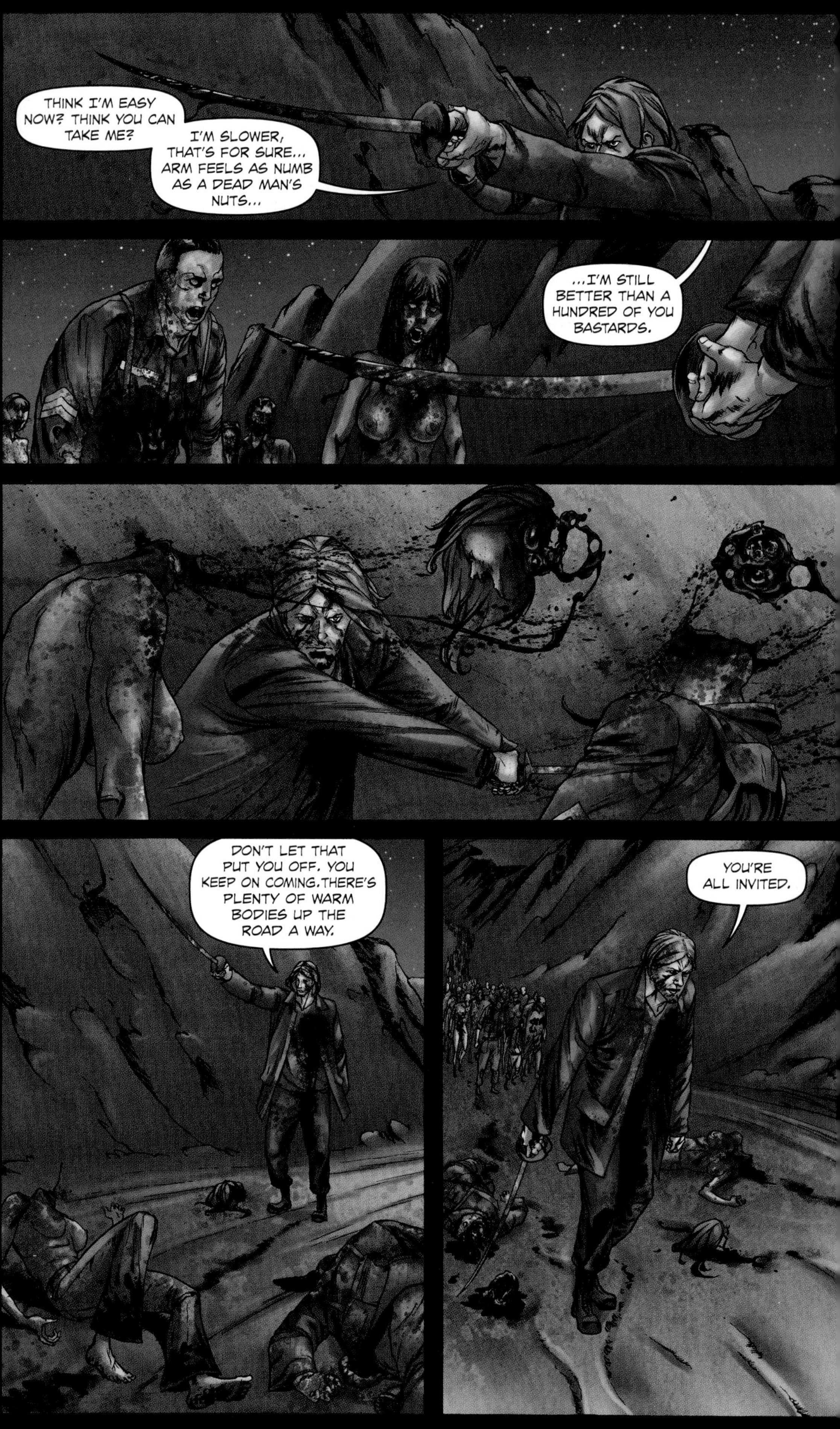
THINK I'M EASY NOW? THINK YOU CAN TAKE ME?
I'M SLOWER, THAT'S FOR SURE... ARM FEELS AS NUMB AS A DEAD MAN'S NUTS...
...I'M STILL BETTER THAN A HUNDRED OF YOU BASTARDS.
DON'T LET THAT PUT YOU OFF. YOU KEEP ON COMING. THERE'S PLENTY OF WARM BODIES UP THE ROAD A WAY.
YOU'RE ALL INVITED.

SUNRISE.

TAKE IT EASY WITH HIM. WE DON'T WANT HIM WAKING UP.

DON'T WORRY. NOTHING'S GOING TO WAKE HIM.

ARE YOU SURE ABOUT THAT?

HE'S GOT ENOUGH HORSE TRANQUILIZER IN HIM TO KEEP HIM UNDER FOR A WEEK.

YOU KNOW HOW IMPORTANT THIS MAN IS?

YES, SIR. THE FUTURE OF THIS COUNTRY DEPENDS ON THE SAFE DELIVERY OF THE PRISONER TO THE EASTERN ZONE.

DR SELENS AND I WILL FOLLOW WITHIN THE HOUR. IF WE DON'T RENDEZVOUS AT THE FIRST FUEL STOP WITHIN FIVE HOURS FROM NOW, YOU CONTINUE ON WITH THE PRISONER.

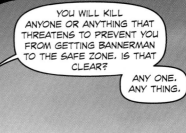

YOU WILL KILL ANYONE OR ANYTHING THAT THREATENS TO PREVENT YOU FROM GETTING BANNERMAN TO THE SAFE ZONE. IS THAT CLEAR?

ANY ONE. ANY THING.

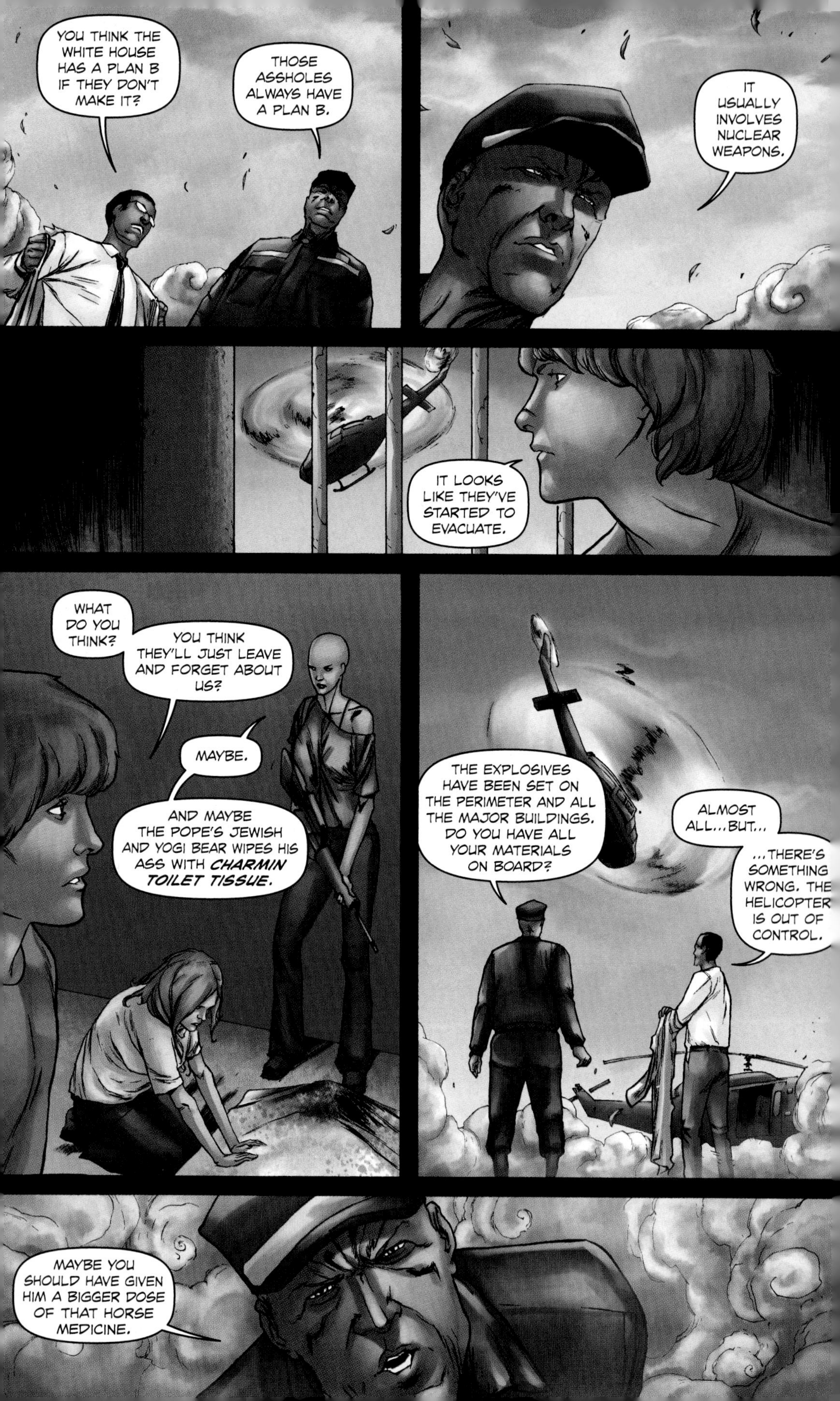
YOU THINK THE WHITE HOUSE HAS A PLAN B IF THEY DON'T MAKE IT?
THOSE ASSHOLES ALWAYS HAVE A PLAN B.
IT USUALLY INVOLVES NUCLEAR WEAPONS.
IT LOOKS LIKE THEY'VE STARTED TO EVACUATE.
WHAT DO YOU THINK?
YOU THINK THEY'LL JUST LEAVE AND FORGET ABOUT US?
MAYBE.
AND MAYBE THE POPE'S JEWISH AND YOGI BEAR WIPES HIS ASS WITH *CHARMIN TOILET TISSUE*.
THE EXPLOSIVES HAVE BEEN SET ON THE PERIMETER AND ALL THE MAJOR BUILDINGS. DO YOU HAVE ALL YOUR MATERIALS ON BOARD?
ALMOST ALL...BUT...
...THERE'S SOMETHING WRONG. THE HELICOPTER IS OUT OF CONTROL.
MAYBE YOU SHOULD HAVE GIVEN HIM A BIGGER DOSE OF THAT HORSE MEDICINE.

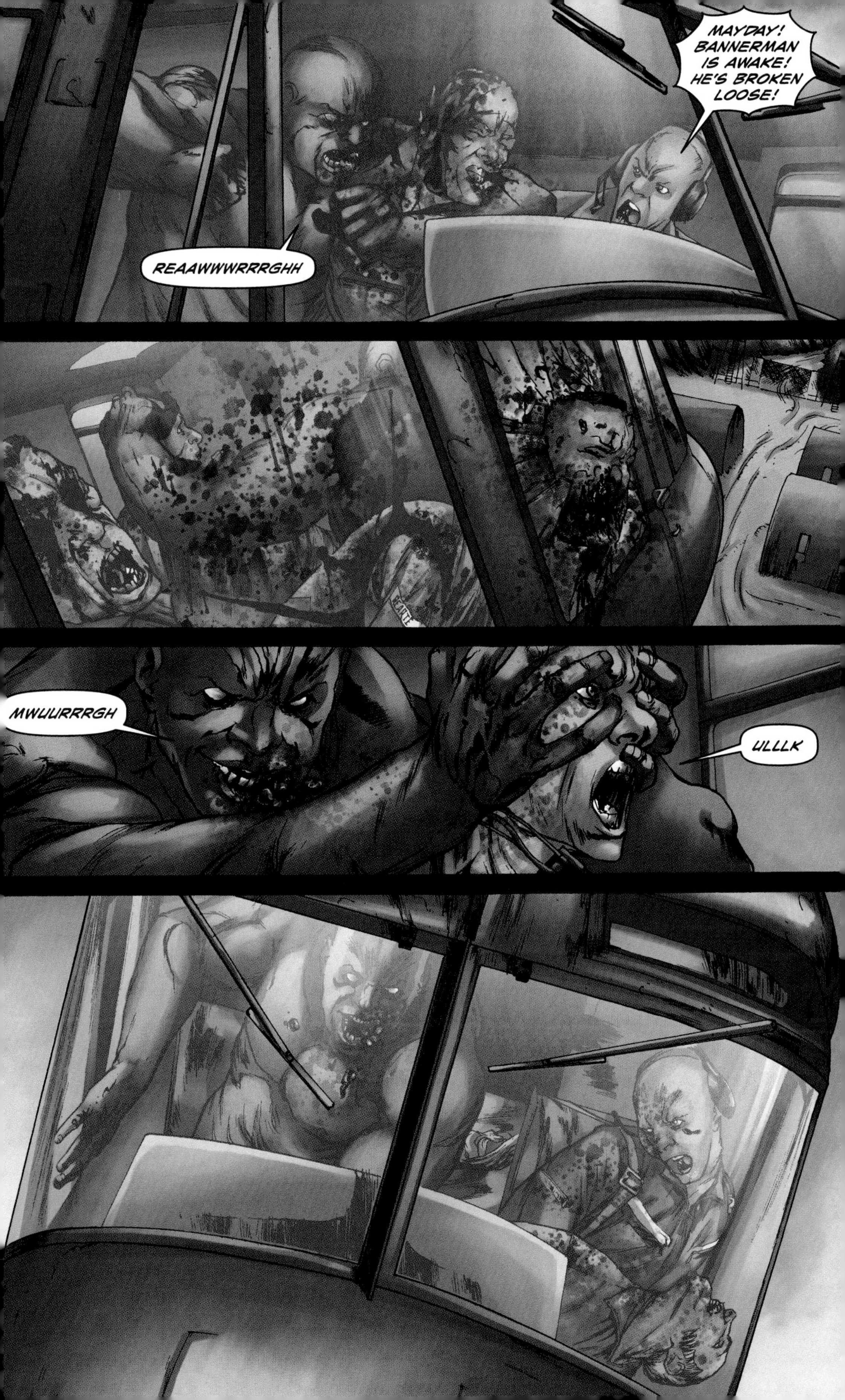
MAYDAY! BANNERMAN IS AWAKE! HE'S BROKEN LOOSE!
REAAWWWRRRGHH
MWUURRRGH
ULLLK

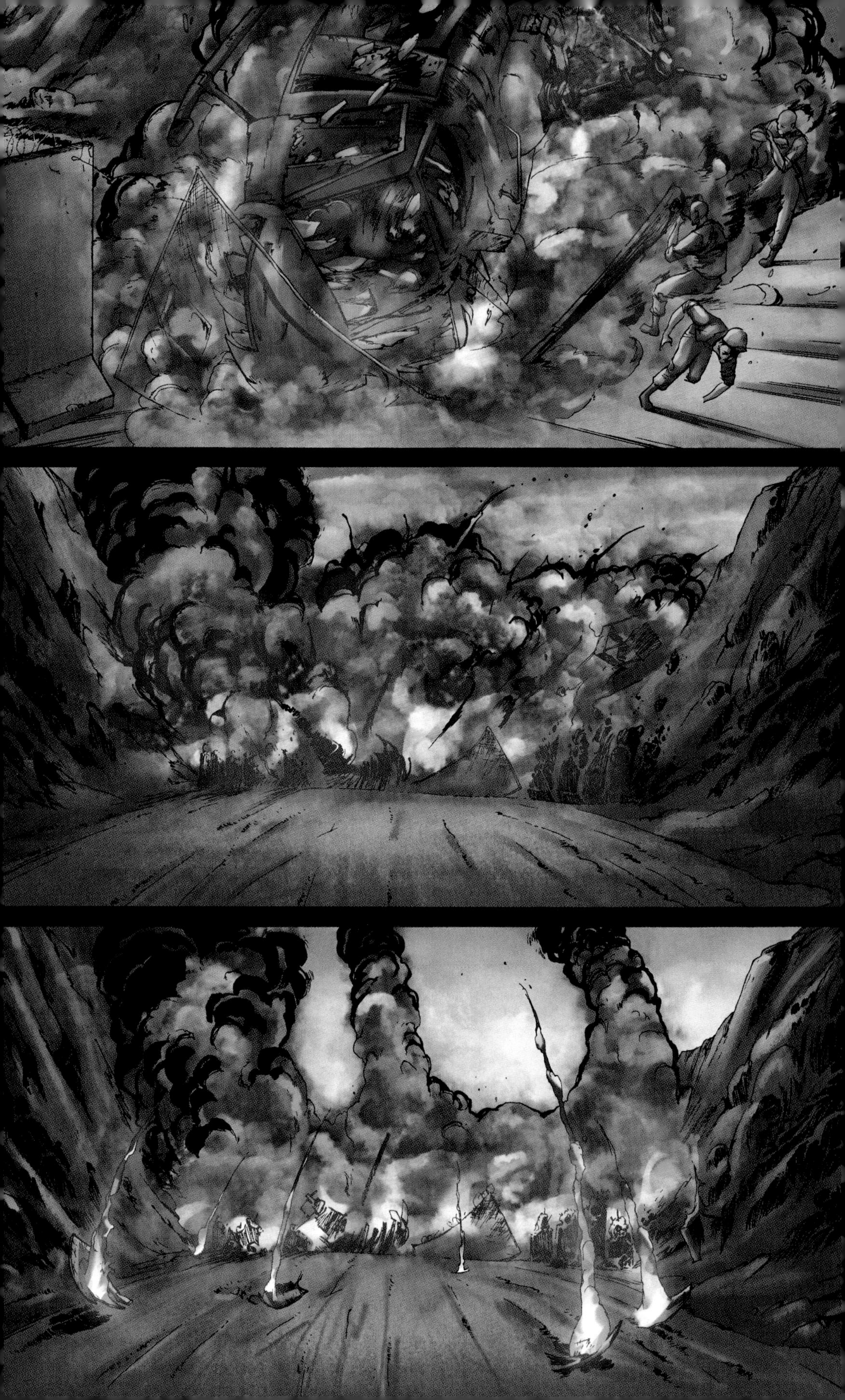

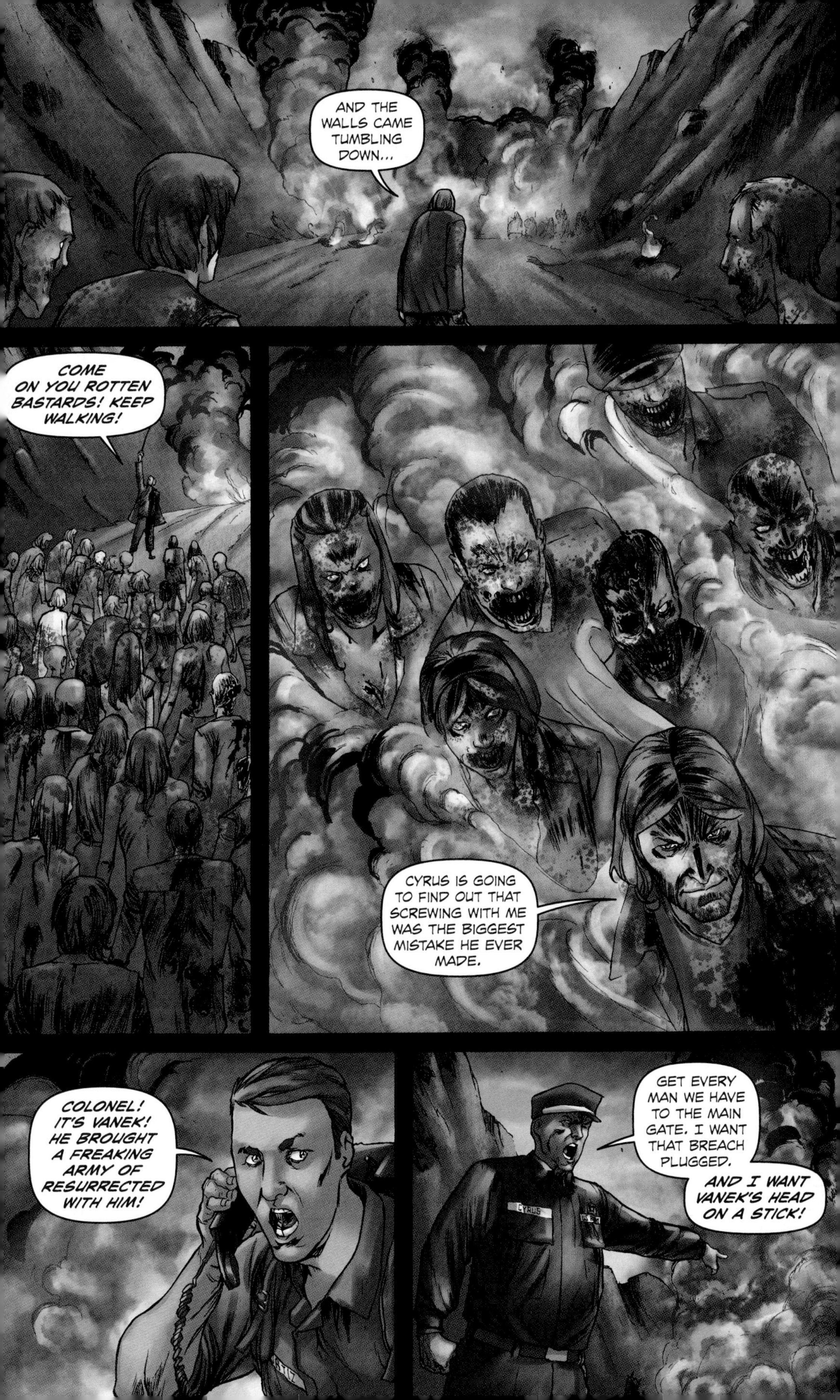
AND THE WALLS CAME TUMBLING DOWN...
COME ON YOU ROTTEN BASTARDS! KEEP WALKING!
CYRUS IS GOING TO FIND OUT THAT SCREWING WITH ME WAS THE BIGGEST MISTAKE HE EVER MADE.
COLONEL! IT'S VANEK! HE BROUGHT A FREAKING ARMY OF RESURRECTED WITH HIM!
GET EVERY MAN WE HAVE TO THE MAIN GATE. I WANT THAT BREACH PLUGGED.
AND I WANT VANEK'S HEAD ON A STICK!
CYRUS

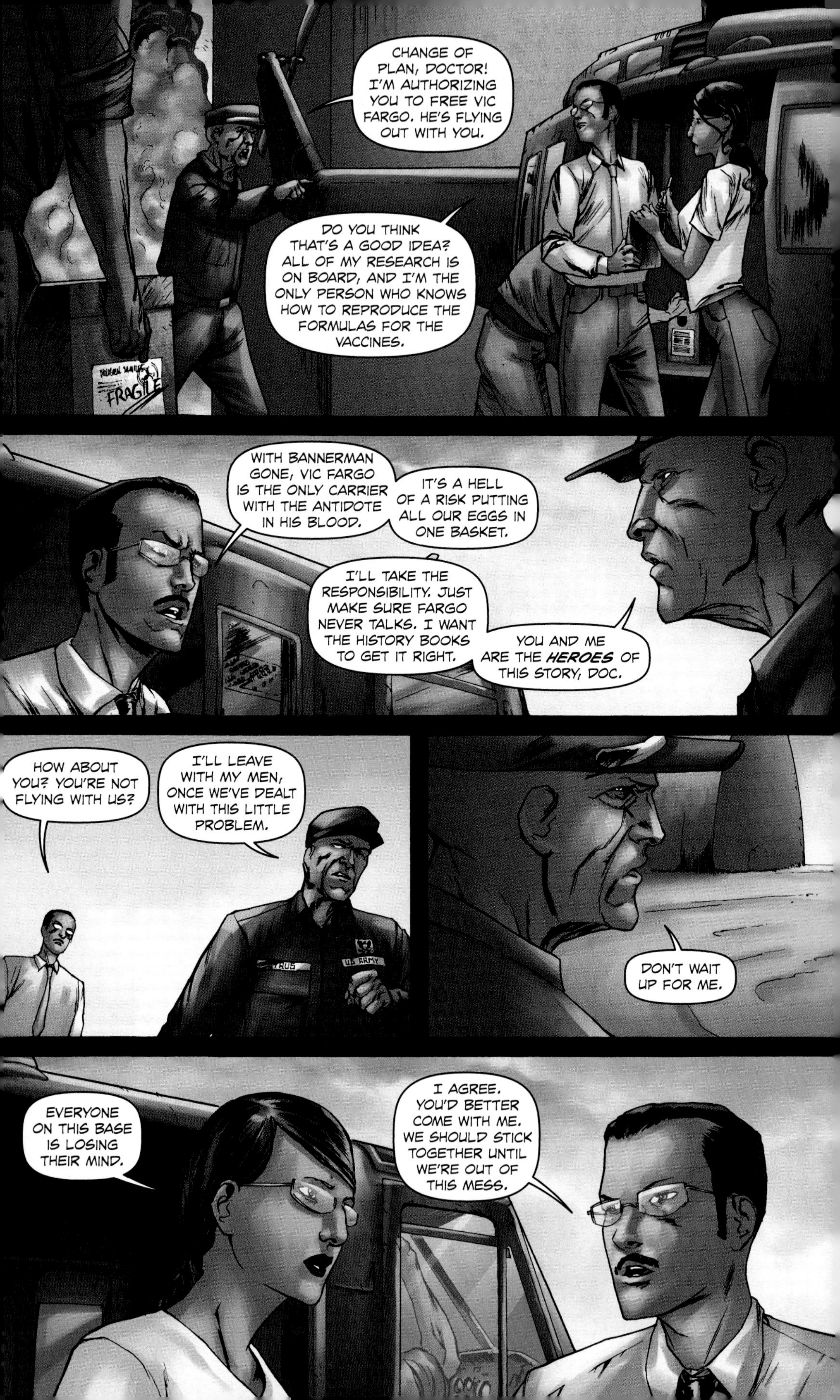
CHANGE OF PLAN, DOCTOR! I'M AUTHORIZING YOU TO FREE VIC FARGO. HE'S FLYING OUT WITH YOU.
DO YOU THINK THAT'S A GOOD IDEA? ALL OF MY RESEARCH IS ON BOARD, AND I'M THE ONLY PERSON WHO KNOWS HOW TO REPRODUCE THE FORMULAS FOR THE VACCINES.
FRAGILE
WITH BANNERMAN GONE, VIC FARGO IS THE ONLY CARRIER WITH THE ANTIDOTE IN HIS BLOOD.
IT'S A HELL OF A RISK PUTTING ALL OUR EGGS IN ONE BASKET.
I'LL TAKE THE RESPONSIBILITY. JUST MAKE SURE FARGO NEVER TALKS. I WANT THE HISTORY BOOKS TO GET IT RIGHT.
YOU AND ME ARE THE HEROES OF THIS STORY, DOC.
HOW ABOUT YOU? YOU'RE NOT FLYING WITH US?
I'LL LEAVE WITH MY MEN, ONCE WE'VE DEALT WITH THIS LITTLE PROBLEM.
U.S. ARMY
DON'T WAIT UP FOR ME.
EVERYONE ON THIS BASE IS LOSING THEIR MIND.
I AGREE. YOU'D BETTER COME WITH ME. WE SHOULD STICK TOGETHER UNTIL WE'RE OUT OF THIS MESS.

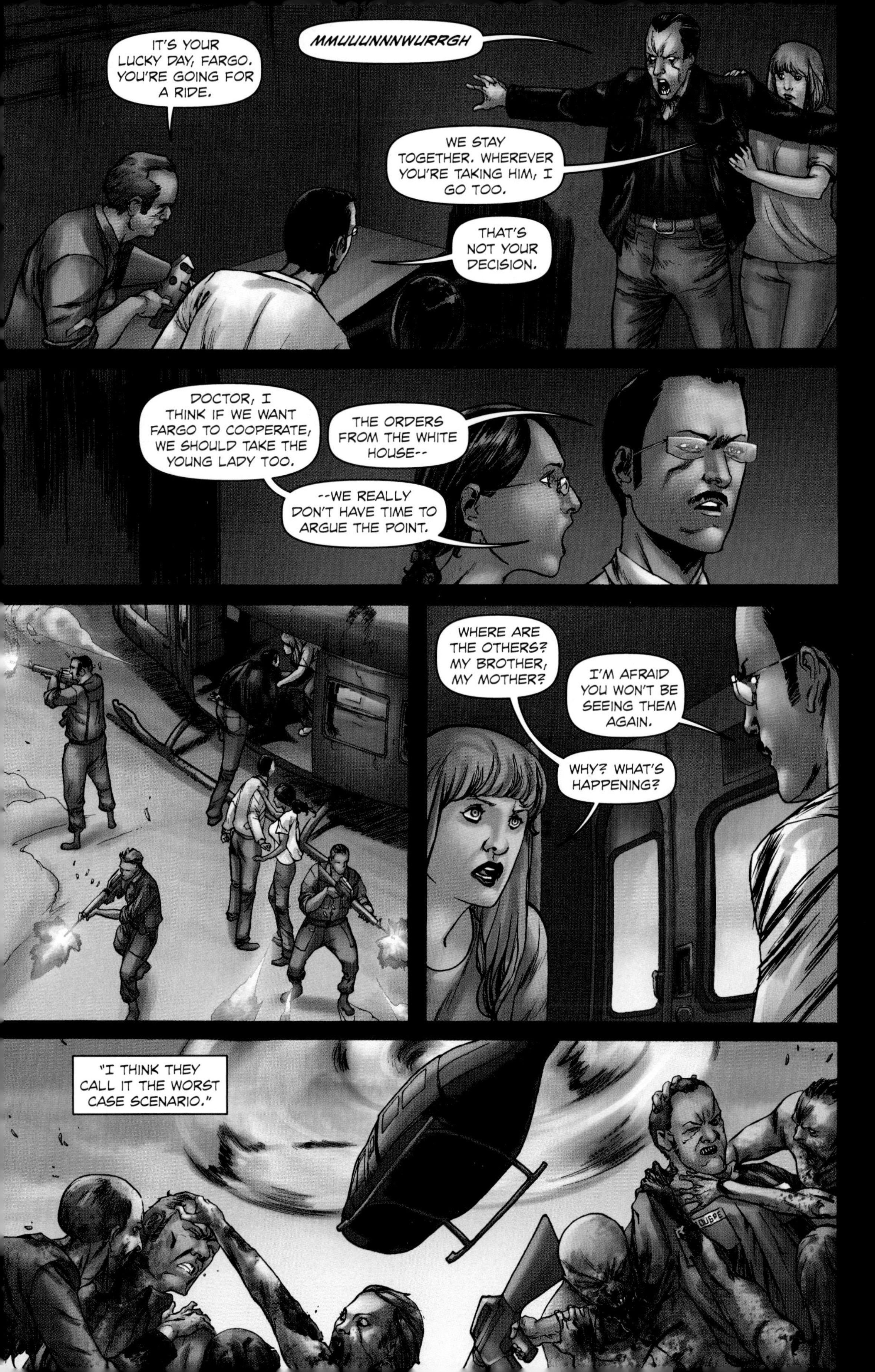
IT'S YOUR LUCKY DAY, FARGO. YOU'RE GOING FOR A RIDE.
MMUUUNNNWURRGH
WE STAY TOGETHER. WHEREVER YOU'RE TAKING HIM, I GO TOO.
THAT'S NOT YOUR DECISION.
DOCTOR, I THINK IF WE WANT FARGO TO COOPERATE, WE SHOULD TAKE THE YOUNG LADY TOO.
THE ORDERS FROM THE WHITE HOUSE--
--WE REALLY DON'T HAVE TIME TO ARGUE THE POINT.
WHERE ARE THE OTHERS? MY BROTHER, MY MOTHER?
I'M AFRAID YOU WON'T BE SEEING THEM AGAIN.
WHY? WHAT'S HAPPENING?
"I THINK THEY CALL IT THE WORST CASE SCENARIO."

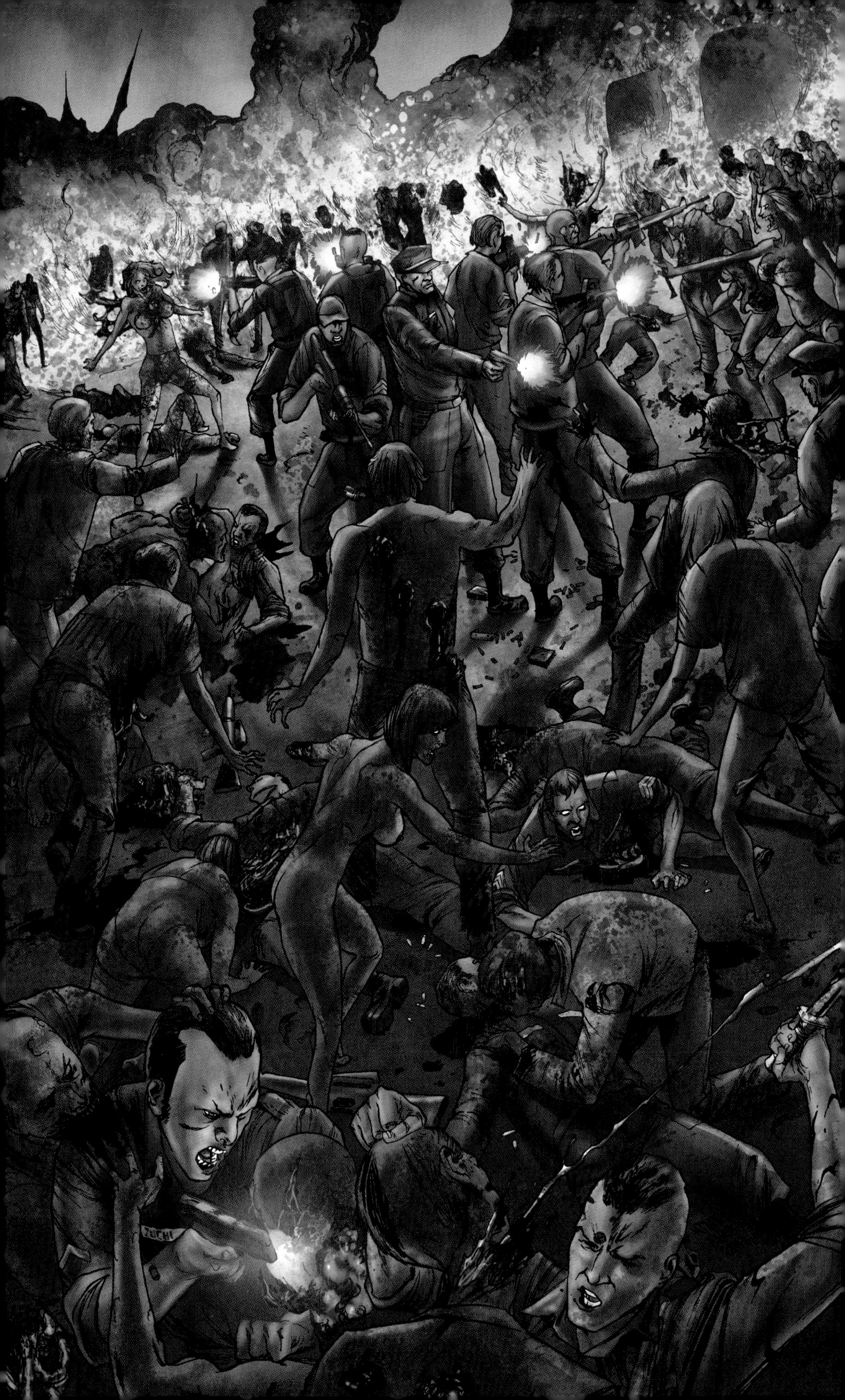

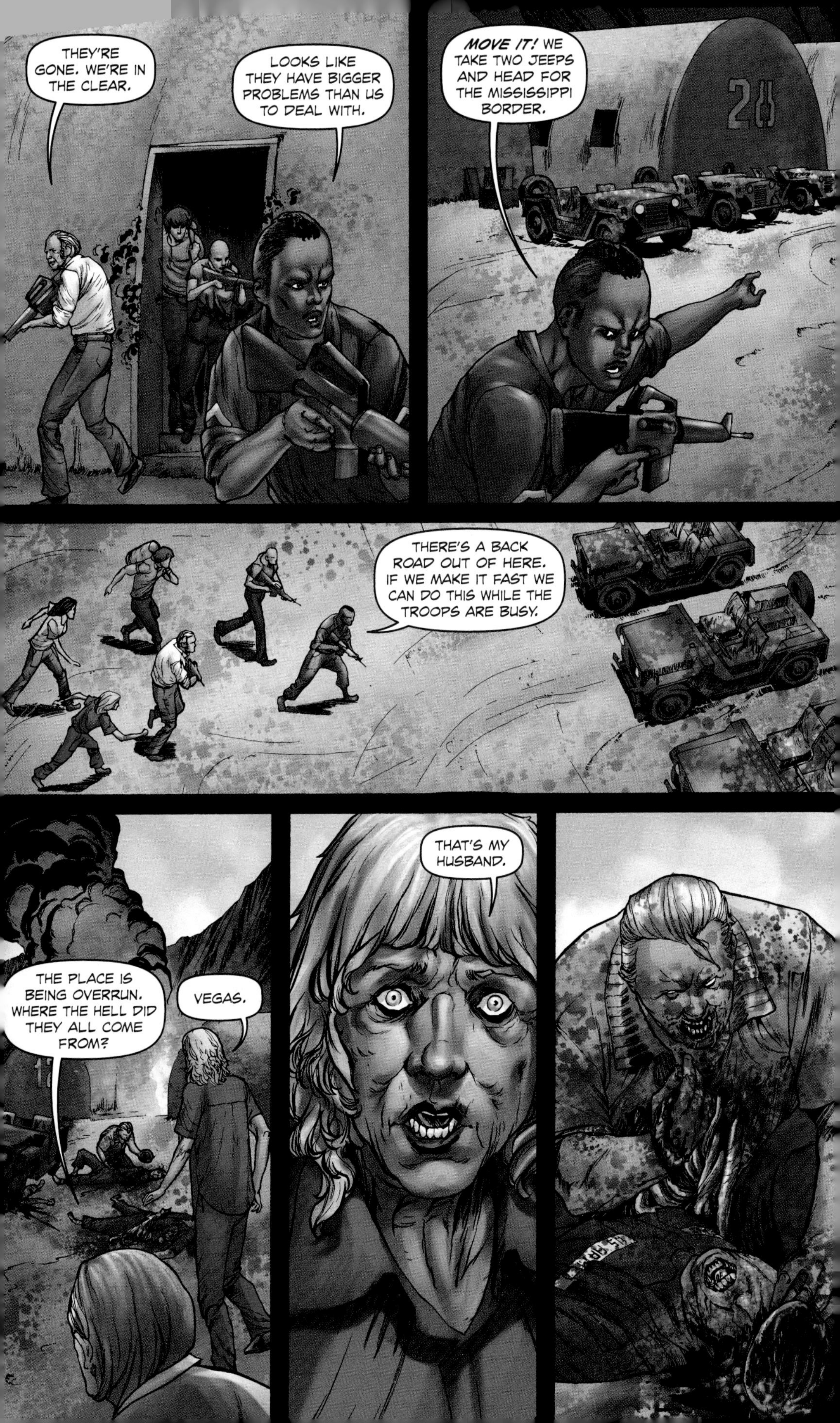
THEY'RE GONE. WE'RE IN THE CLEAR.
LOOKS LIKE THEY HAVE BIGGER PROBLEMS THAN US TO DEAL WITH.
MOVE IT! WE TAKE TWO JEEPS AND HEAD FOR THE MISSISSIPPI BORDER.
THERE'S A BACK ROAD OUT OF HERE. IF WE MAKE IT FAST WE CAN DO THIS WHILE THE TROOPS ARE BUSY.
THE PLACE IS BEING OVERRUN. WHERE THE HELL DID THEY ALL COME FROM?
VEGAS.
THAT'S MY HUSBAND.

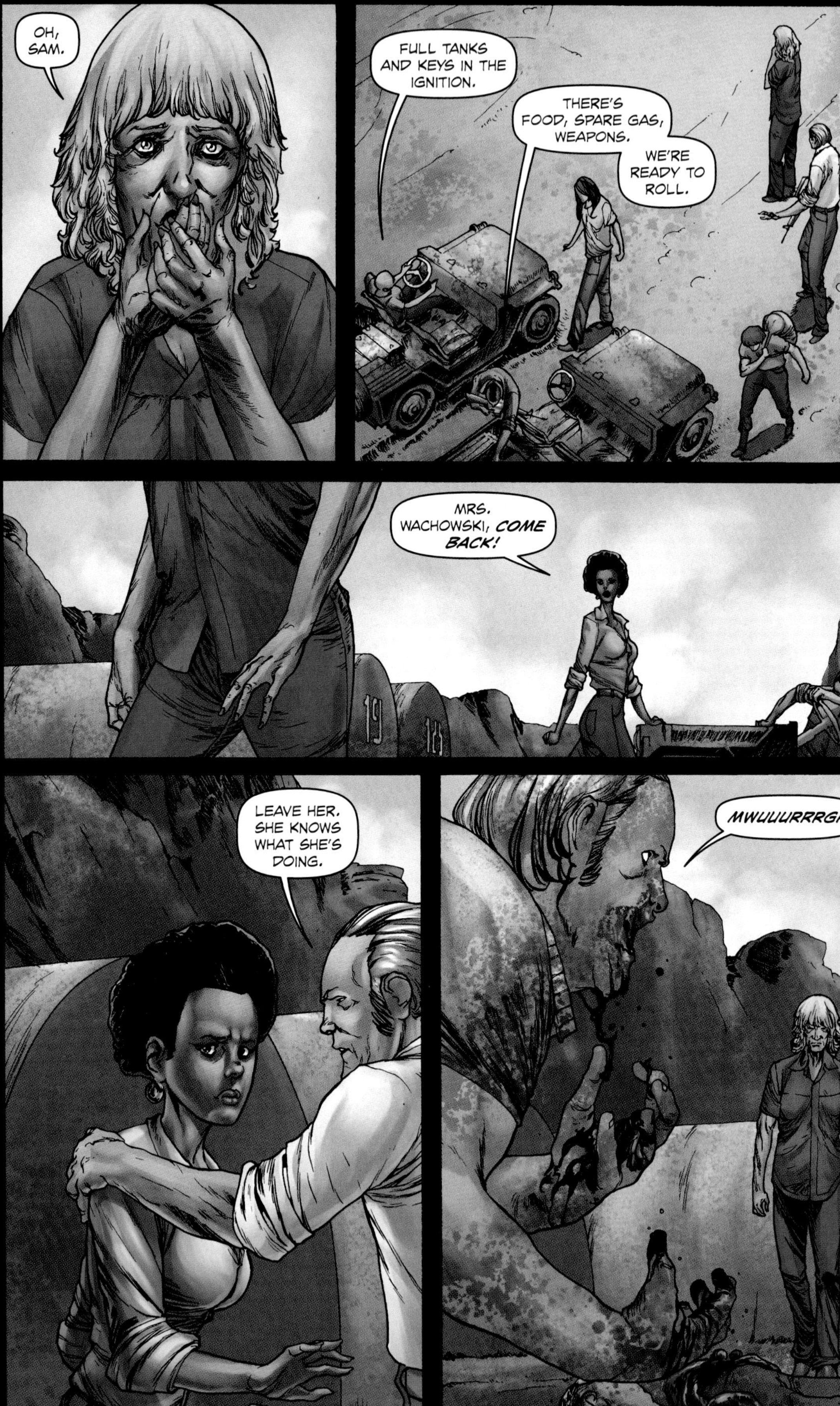
OH, SAM.
FULL TANKS AND KEYS IN THE IGNITION.
THERE'S FOOD, SPARE GAS, WEAPONS.
WE'RE READY TO ROLL.
MRS. WACHOWSKI, *COME BACK!*
LEAVE HER. SHE KNOWS WHAT SHE'S DOING.
MWUUURRRGH

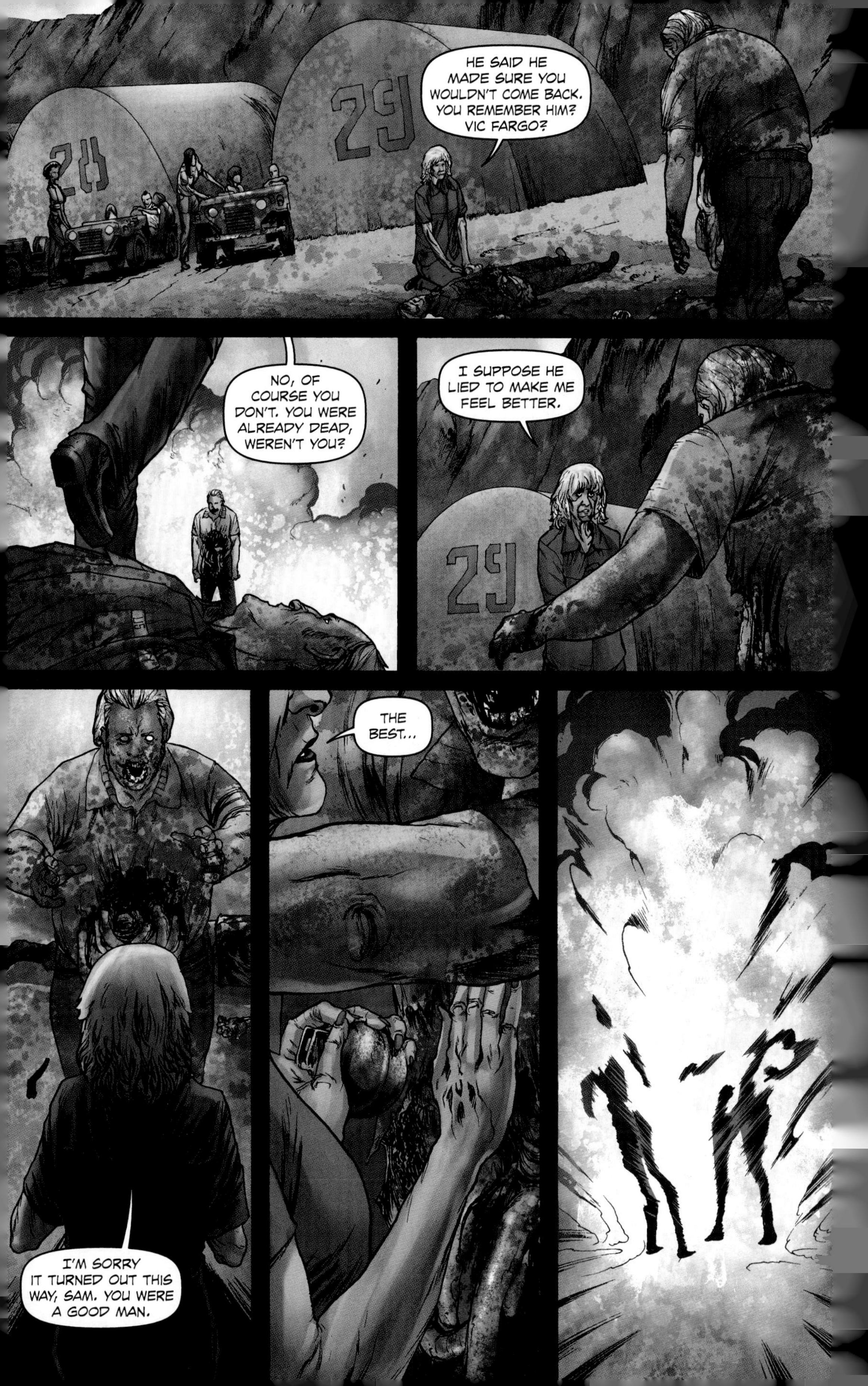
HE SAID HE MADE SURE YOU WOULDN'T COME BACK. YOU REMEMBER HIM? VIC FARGO?
NO, OF COURSE YOU DON'T. YOU WERE ALREADY DEAD, WEREN'T YOU?
I SUPPOSE HE LIED TO MAKE ME FEEL BETTER.
I'M SORRY IT TURNED OUT THIS WAY, SAM. YOU WERE A GOOD MAN.
THE BEST...

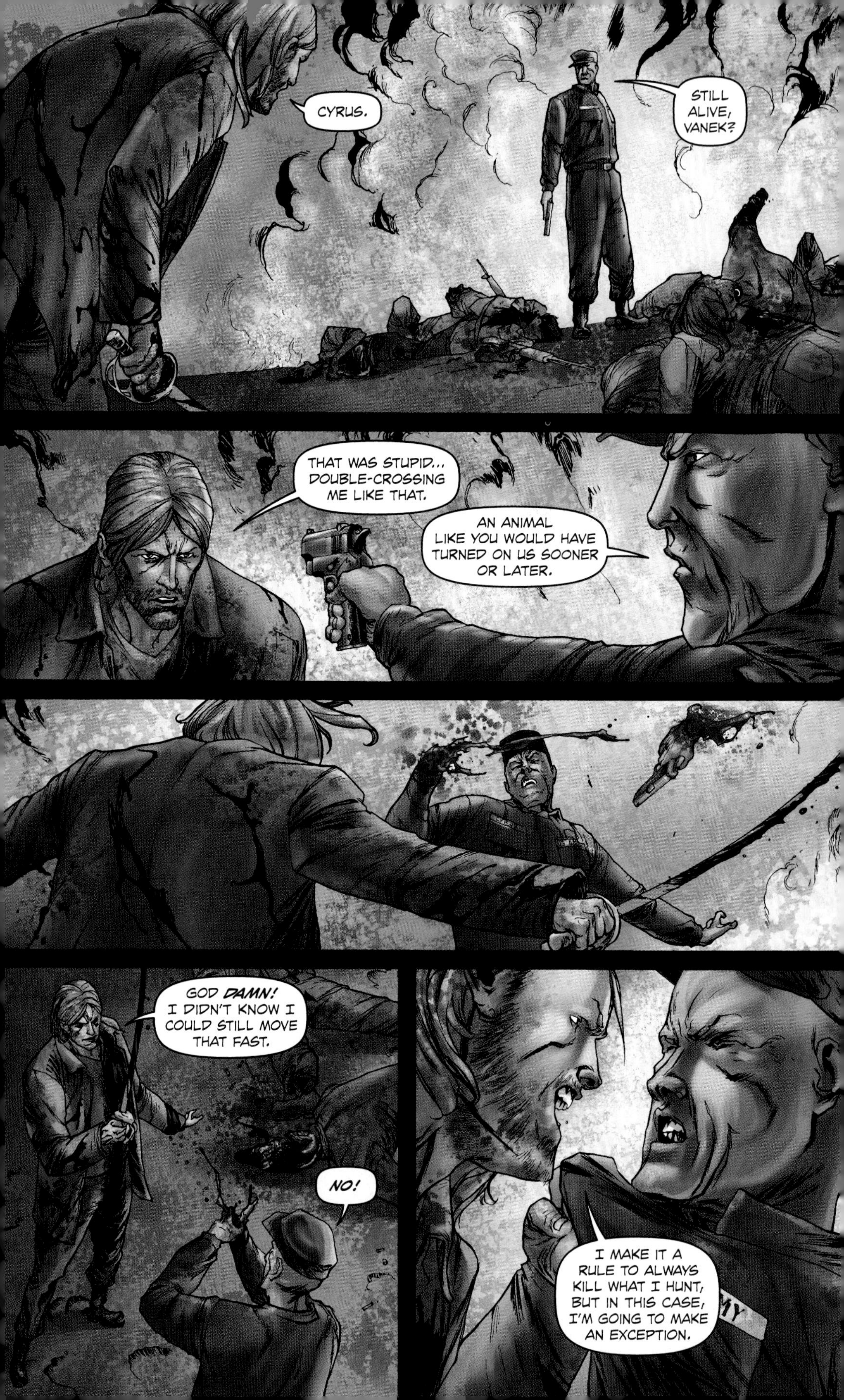
CYRUS.
STILL ALIVE, VANEK?
THAT WAS STUPID... DOUBLE-CROSSING ME LIKE THAT.
AN ANIMAL LIKE YOU WOULD HAVE TURNED ON US SOONER OR LATER.
GOD DAMN! I DIDN'T KNOW I COULD STILL MOVE THAT FAST.
NO!
I MAKE IT A RULE TO ALWAYS KILL WHAT I HUNT, BUT IN THIS CASE, I'M GOING TO MAKE AN EXCEPTION.

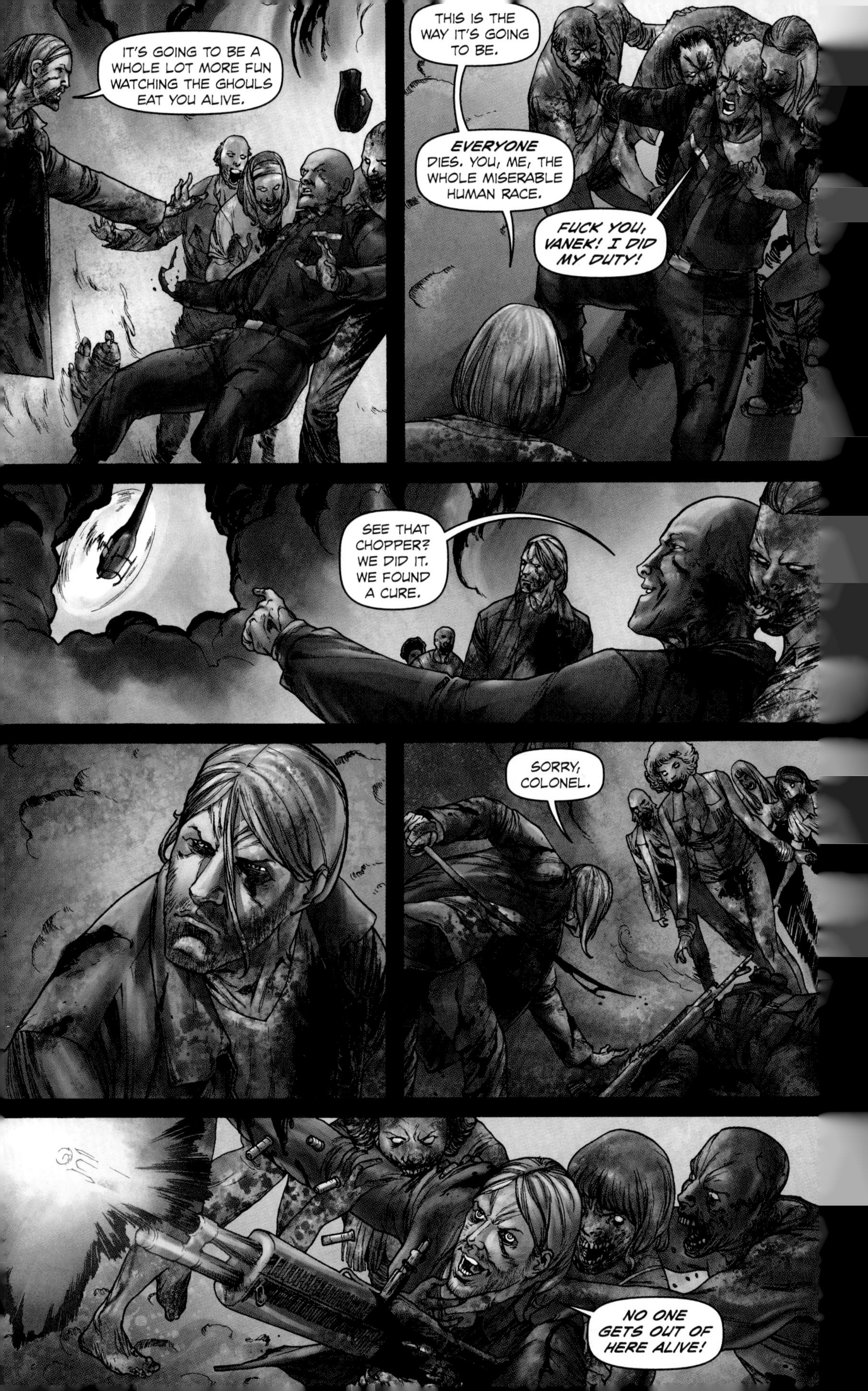
IT'S GOING TO BE A WHOLE LOT MORE FUN WATCHING THE GHOULS EAT YOU ALIVE.
THIS IS THE WAY IT'S GOING TO BE.
EVERYONE DIES. YOU, ME, THE WHOLE MISERABLE HUMAN RACE.
FUCK YOU, VANEK! I DID MY DUTY!
SEE THAT CHOPPER? WE DID IT. WE FOUND A CURE.
SORRY, COLONEL.
NO ONE GETS OUT OF HERE ALIVE!

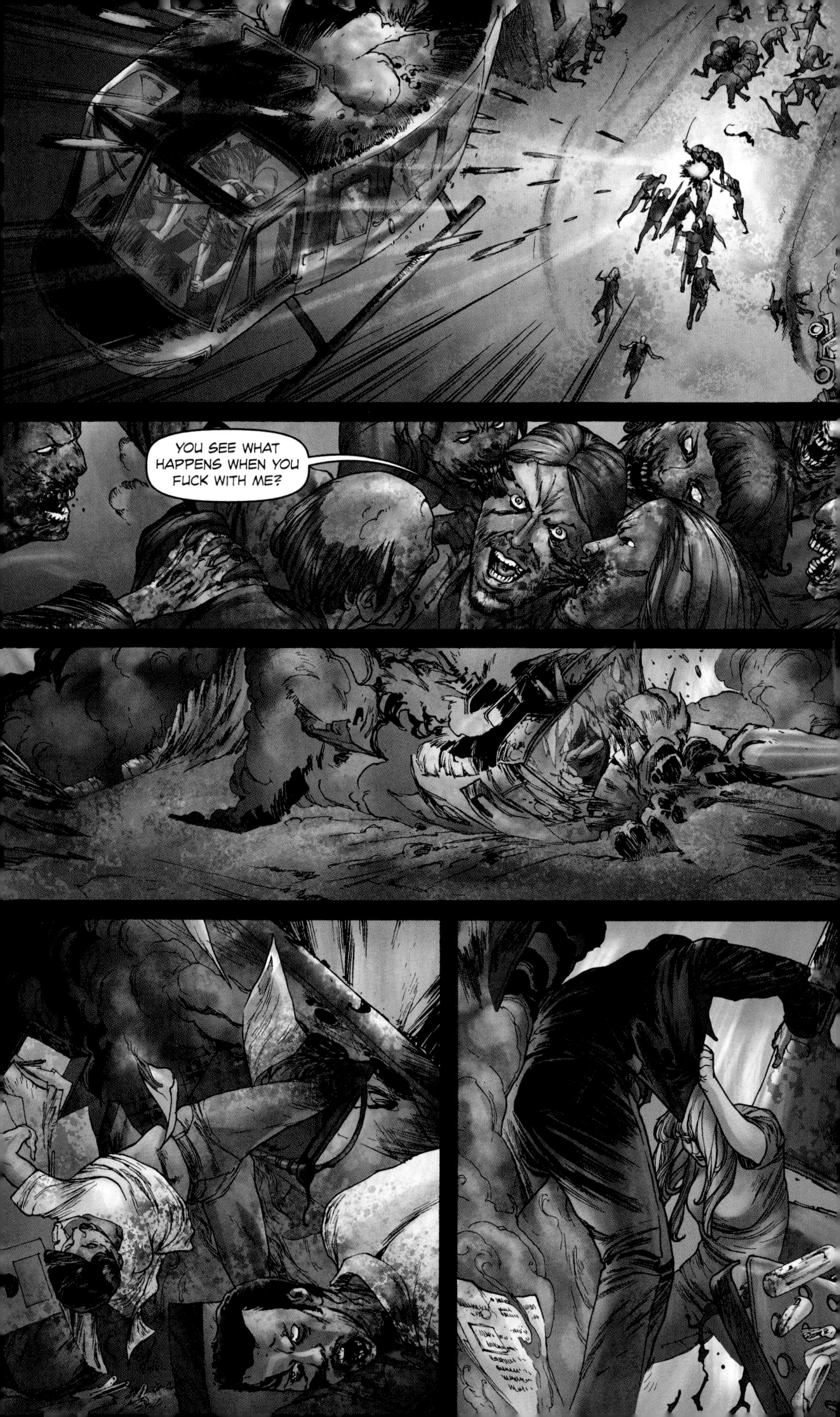
YOU SEE WHAT HAPPENS WHEN YOU FUCK WITH ME?

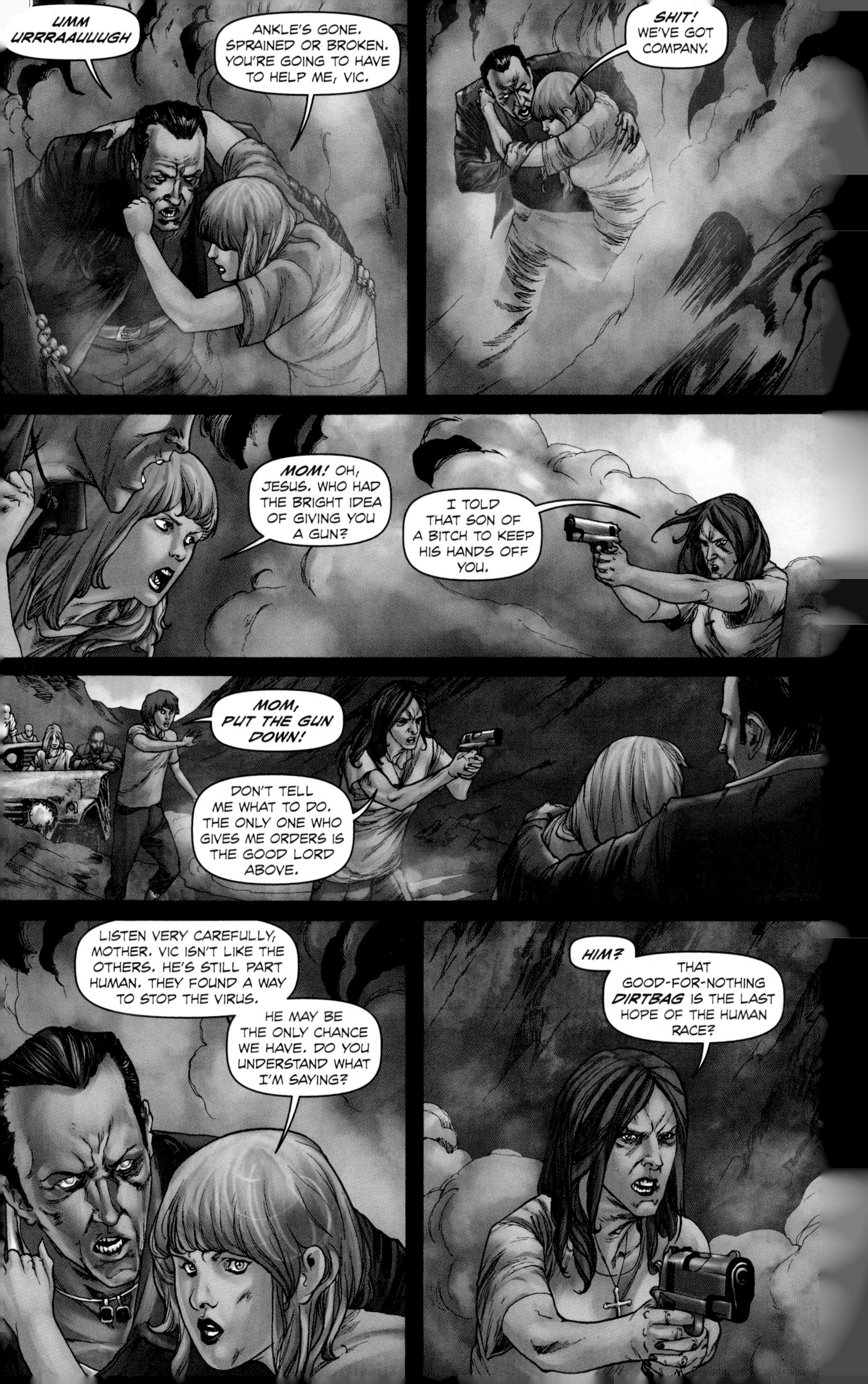
UMM URRRAAUUUGH
ANKLE'S GONE. SPRAINED OR BROKEN. YOU'RE GOING TO HAVE TO HELP ME, VIC.
SHIT! WE'VE GOT COMPANY.
MOM! OH, JESUS. WHO HAD THE BRIGHT IDEA OF GIVING YOU A GUN?
I TOLD THAT SON OF A BITCH TO KEEP HIS HANDS OFF YOU.
MOM, PUT THE GUN DOWN!
DON'T TELL ME WHAT TO DO. THE ONLY ONE WHO GIVES ME ORDERS IS THE GOOD LORD ABOVE.
LISTEN VERY CAREFULLY, MOTHER. VIC ISN'T LIKE THE OTHERS. HE'S STILL PART HUMAN. THEY FOUND A WAY TO STOP THE VIRUS.
HE MAY BE THE ONLY CHANCE WE HAVE. DO YOU UNDERSTAND WHAT I'M SAYING?
HIM?
THAT GOOD-FOR-NOTHING DIRTBAG IS THE LAST HOPE OF THE HUMAN RACE?

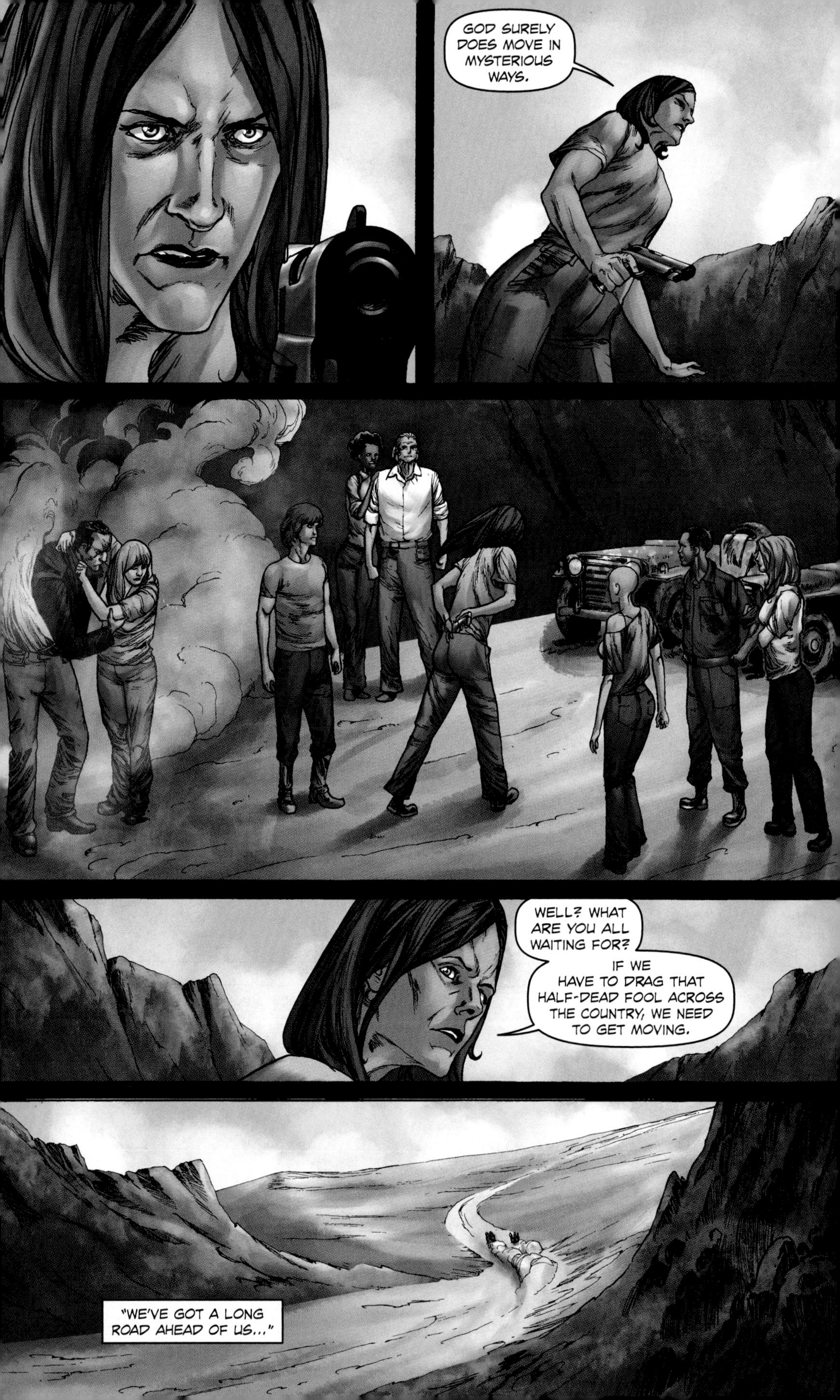
GOD SURELY DOES MOVE IN MYSTERIOUS WAYS.
WELL? WHAT ARE YOU ALL WAITING FOR?
IF WE HAVE TO DRAG THAT HALF-DEAD FOOL ACROSS THE COUNTRY, WE NEED TO GET MOVING.
"WE'VE GOT A LONG ROAD AHEAD OF US..."